A LETHAL INHERITANCE

A LETHAL INHERITANCE

A Mother Uncovers the Science behind
Three Generations of Mental Illness

VICTORIA COSTELLO
FOREWORD BY TERRIE E. MOFFITT, PhD

Prometheus Books

59 John Glenn Drive
Amherst, New York 14228–2119

Published 2012 by Prometheus Books

Cover image © 2012 Nordic Photos/Superstock
Cover design by Nicole Sommer-Lecht
Dedication photograph of Ellen Costello in 1911 courtesy of the author

Inquiries should be addressed to
Prometheus Books
59 John Glenn Drive
Amherst, New York 14228–2119
VOICE: 716–691–0133
FAX: 716–691–0137
WWW.PROMETHEUSBOOKS.COM

16 15 14 13 12   5 4 3 2 1

Library of Congress Cataloging-in-Publication Data

Costello, Victoria.
    A lethal inheritance : a mother uncovers the science behind three generations of mental illness / by Victoria Costello.
        p. cm.
    Includes bibliographical references and index.
    ISBN 978–1–61614–466–1 (pk. : alk. paper)
    ISBN 978–1–61614–467–8 (ebook)
    1. Schitzophrenia—Popular works. 2. Parents of mentally ill children. I. Title.

RC514.C645 2012
616.89'8—dc23

2011037539

Printed in the United States of America on acid-free paper

To my grandmother

ELLEN COSTELLO

Born 1885, Dunmore, Ireland
Died 1919, New York, New York

Who showed me that
I come from a long line of
mothers who never give up

CONTENTS

FOREWORD
  by Terrie E. Moffitt, PhD   11

INTRODUCTION   15

PART 1. THE FOURTH GENERATION: ALEX AND SAMMY

Chapter 1. Alex by the Dumpster   21
  Other Answers   31
  The Best Predictor   35
  Matters of Degree and Prevalence   37
  Fictions and Facts of Mental Illness   41

Chapter 2. Early Signs and Risk Factors   45
  The Science of Risk   47
  The Fine Print of Predisposition   53
  How Young?   56
  The Childhood Risk Factors for Schizophrenia   59

Chapter 3. "Boys Will Be Boys" and
  Other Lies We Tell Ourselves at 3:00 a.m.   65
  Chardonnay, Cannabis, and Other Drugs of Choice   66
  Bad Conduct   71
  Will He Grow Out of It?   73

Chapter 4. Before the Storm: Pre-Onset Psychosis   75
  Detecting Early Psychosis in Teenagers   77
  The False Positive   83

Anywhere but Here   85
Enough Is Enough   89

Chapter 5. Onset   91
The List of Early Warning Signs of Psychosis   95
The Plastic Brain in Action   96
Finding the Cliff's Edge   96
Alex on and off Meds   98

Chapter 6. My Little Prince Comes Undone   101
Adolescents and Antidepressants   104
The Antidepressant-Suicide Link Investigated   105
"Mom, I'm Joining the Marines"   108
A Leg Up or Down   110

PART 2. REVISITING THE FAMILY ILLNESS: GENERATIONS TWO AND THREE

Chapter 7. The Depressed Mother   115
Therapy Is Not a Career   118
Mothers, Children, and Depression   120
Your Brain at Risk for Depression   122
The Risk of Doing Nothing   123
My Little Yellow Pills   126

Chapter 8. My Sister Rita: Mental Illness and Self-Medication 129
A War on Drugs   130
Denial and Deceit   134
Which Comes First?   136
Collateral Damage   139

**Chapter 9. My Father Red: "The Heart-Ache and the
          Thousand Natural Shocks that Flesh Is Heir To"**   143
From Vice to Disease   145
Raised by Alcohol   150
Screening and Predicting Deadly Family Patterns   151

Chapter 10. The First Generation, My Grandfather 155
The Irish Factor 156
The First Lethal Gene Is Found 160
Desperately Seeking Answers 162
Artifacts in Search of Facts 164

Chapter 11. Grandpa's Psychological Autopsy 171
Unraveling an Unthinkable Act 172
Preventing Suicide 176
Suicide Prevention for Parents and Teachers 177
Death by Train 179
The New "Official Story" 181

PART 3. THE SCIENCE AND PRACTICE OF RECOVERY AND PREVENTION

Chapter 12. Thoughts of All Orders 187
Defining Recovery 188
Other Voices of Recovery 191
The Cost of Creativity 193

Chapter 13. From Inkblots to Alleles 197
Two Days as a Lab Rat 198
Comparable Disease Models: Alzheimer's and Parkinson's 204
The New, New Genetics in Action 207

Chapter 14. Preventing Mental Illness 213
First Line of Defense 214
Getting the Right Mental Health Care 215
Using Family History as a Guide for Treatment Choices 216
The Long Reach of Stigma 217
Learning Resiliency 218
The New, New Parenting 220
The Top Ten Things a Parent Can Do to Safeguard
    a Child's Mental Health 224

ACKNOWLEDGMENTS   231

READER RESOURCES   233

NOTES   235

INDEX   255

FOREWORD

As I read the gripping account of her son's hospitalization that begins Victoria Costello's fascinating and important book, I, too, experience the shock and grief she feels upon hearing a clinician pronounce the words *paranoid schizophrenia* for the first time. The fact that this scene unfolds at the UCLA Neuropsychiatric Institute where I completed my clinical hospital training and saw so many families go through a similar ordeal made it all the more real and poignant for me. There is no experience more wrenching for a psychologist than having to face a mother with such a difficult diagnosis.

For Victoria, we find there's more pain to come as her youngest son falls victim to a social anxiety disorder, and she is forced to confront her own life-long and untreated depression. Her account of how these events open up a window onto a tragic family past resonate powerfully to me again in light of the years I've spent studying family patterns in psychiatric disorders over multiple generations.

Today my perspective as a behavioral scientist investigating how genetic and environmental risks interact to shape psychiatric disorders gives me a "bird's-eye view" on the sort of human drama that Victoria so bravely shares in *A Lethal Inheritance*. Readers coming to this book with either a personal or a professional interest will find much richness here. From Victoria's struggle to find and understand the possible links between the mental suffering she and her sons face in the present and a trail of secrets and tragedies going back three generations, we can take away a vital message—the huge importance of knowing our family history.

At the first signs of a child's behavioral disturbance, parents and clinicians are faced with a difficult, sometimes terrible choice. Must we start treatment as soon as possible and risk doing harm? Or is "wait and see" the wiser option? At the end of this book, Victoria writes compellingly about the "new, new parenting." One of the most loving things parents can do is to find out about our children's psychiatric family history. As Victoria found, the quest takes bravery. Research is proving that for most psychiatric conditions, having a family history makes all the difference between treat now and wait and see.

As readers—and clinicians—expecting the worst from Victoria's story, we are in for a wonderful surprise. Over the course of fourteen riveting chapters, she masterfully interweaves self-revelation, family history, and cutting-edge science to share a story of hope and, ultimately, great joy as she and her sons find treatment and meaningful recovery. The factual information she shares about the disorders that trouble her family and the discoveries she makes about causes and new strategies for prevention are worth their weight in gold for readers, especially for parents.

In psychiatric research, we find ourselves at an exciting crossroads. Several intersecting avenues of investigation promise to reveal long-sought answers to mysteries concerning debilitating diseases such as schizophrenia, bipolar disorder, and severe depression. We see real progress being made to treat disorders that rob too many young people of what should be their best years of rewarding achievement and pure play.

For our research to yield the results we seek, we must communicate and cooperate at home and internationally to bring as many perspectives and experiences to light as might assist our common goals. And yet as a field, we haven't done very well in communicating with the public, whose understanding and voices of experience we need to solve some of the mysteries and challenges we still face. There is, for example, the potential to exploit geographic variation in disease prevalence to yield new information concerning its causes, which currently remain frustratingly unknown.

Bigger mysteries have been solved before when researchers have gone out into their communities and asked the right questions. In the first epidemiological study ever conducted, John Snow compared rates of cholera across areas of London during the 1854 cholera epidemic. Going against the then-prevalent "miasma" theory, which stipulated that diseases are carried by foul air, Snow surveyed residents about their source of drinking water and, using simple statistics, discovered that cholera cases were clustered around one particular water pump. This discovery led to the closing of the infected pump and prevented new cases. Moreover, although Snow was unable to identify the water-borne particles that cause cholera, his finding advanced the germ theory of disease.

Contemporary examples show that when populations vary on their exposure to risk factors, geographic comparisons of disorder rates can generate new hypotheses about etiology. High rates of asthma and allergy in developed Western countries, compared to developing countries, generated new hypotheses about the etiology of respiratory disorders, such as childhood exposure to antibiotics, exposure to dust mite allergens, and overly hygienic lifestyles.

In psychiatry, geographic comparisons reveal that the prevalence of schizophrenia in urban locations is more than double of that in rural locations. This observation generated new hypotheses now subject to intense research. Are city dwellers more likely to develop serious mental illness because of urban social isolation and fragile social-support networks? Or because of infectious exposure exacerbated by urban crowding and public transportation? The pressure to survive economically in high-cost urban areas? Exposure to violence? The stress of being on the poor end of the widening gap between urban rich and inner-city poor? Or is it because psychologically vulnerable young people tend to migrate from small towns to cities? Answers to these questions will lead to prevention strategies.

Victoria Costello applies her dual perspective as a science journalist and as a consumer to put the science of mental illness in the context of its immediate and potential long-term relevance to the people who most need it. She does so with sensitivity and attention to detail that is unusual and timely . . . and from the heart.

—Terrie E. Moffitt
April 4, 2011, St. Bathans, New Zealand

INTRODUCTION

Family Psychiatric History: Patient (Sammy) has a personal history of depressed mood and social anxiety. Older brother (Alex) with possible psychotic illness and substance abuse disorder; mother (me) with history of double depression; maternal aunt with depression, substance abuse disorders, died of drug overdose; maternal grandfather had depression, alcoholism; maternal great-grandfather with probable depression and suicide.

—From Sammy's psychiatric evaluation in 2005

Seven years later, and it's still painful to see my family reduced to these eight lines of clinical pathology. The psychiatrist's assessment of my youngest son, who I call "Sammy" on these pages, came in 2005 after Sammy's withdrawal from college on a medical leave. It took another three months to get an appointment with this in-demand Northern California psychiatrist, who I paid $750 (out-of-pocket) for a three-hour assessment.

Sammy sat quietly, looking hopeless and sad. I wasn't much better off. Once again, I feared that I'd waited too long to get one of my sons the help he needed. Sammy, my "little prince," had always been the easy, stable one of my two children. His older brother, known in this book as "Alex," already occupied the position of high-strung firstborn son. Alex's troubles had been the first to bring me face-to-face with a somber-faced psychiatrist—four years earlier.

When my second son became ensnared by the beastly thing I have since named "the family illness," I knew I'd run out of time to get to the bottom of this legacy that appeared to be coded into our DNA. My worst fear was that I'd lose one or both of my children the same way other family members had gone, one from each generation: my sister Rita, my father, Red, and my grandfather Michael—each of their deaths premature, tragic, and, I now believe, preventable.

Our genetic line and family culture made Sammy, Alex, and me vulnerable to what researchers now view as a cluster of related mental disorders and addictions, one that becomes more virulent and dangerous with each passing generation. As I detail in this book, with help from practitioners working in the recovery model of mental health care, we were able to stop and reverse its momentum.

I've learned three important lessons on my journey through mental illness. First, that I've done things in the wrong order. If we, as parents, get treatment for our own psychological or addiction issues, our children will suffer far fewer mental illnesses. If they're already struggling with a mental health challenge, we'll be of much greater help to them. That leads to my second discovery: intervening sooner for a mental health problem is better than picking up the pieces later—for everyone. Lastly, I've learned that although we're each born with inherited liabilities and assets, *throughout our lives*, our minds become largely what we make of them. Put simply, *nurture can trump nature*. In some cases, it can even turn an inherited liability into a possibility—yes, an asset. Once we get these three things, the game has changed, and we're living in the prevention model of mental wellness where healthy minds rule.

A deeper knowledge of our family histories—available to anyone willing to take a hard look—is a powerful guide for such a journey. It enables us to strengthen the nurture side of the equation, meaning everything from the amount of stress we allow into our households to *how* we express our emotions to loved ones. Although the science of mental health prevention is very new, sound insights have emerged that are actionable today. I invite you to join me on my passage from the swamp of personal pain I once lived in where my guilt as a "bad" mother filtered pretty much everything to a place of clarity, pride in my sons, and moments of great joy. Take to heart whatever resonates for you.

—⁂—

Author's Notes: In order to protect my sons' privacy as much as possible, their names, along with current details of their whereabouts, relationships and activities, are omitted from this book. Pseudonyms are also used for my brother, ex-husband (the boys' father), and an ex-significant other of mine. The same is true for some of our personal mental health providers, again to protect their privacy.

My medical records as well as those of my sons and deceased members of my family are authentic. Real names are used for any deceased family members that I've included. Although I have aimed for complete accuracy in my timelines and representations of what occurred, the memoir material in these chapters is by definition subjective.

To ensure accuracy in my representation of research findings, chapters have been reviewed by the individual scientists interviewed and by a pair of science writers. You'll find sources and citations for every study and interview in the notes at the back of the book.

Lastly, I offer this proviso. The information contained in this book is designed to educate and inform, but it is not intended as medical advice for any individual reader. This book is not intended to substitute for individual counseling and medical advice from a trained genetic counselor or physician. The reader should regularly consult physicians and other medical professionals about matters pertaining to his or her health, particularly regarding symptoms that may require medical attention.

PART 1

THE FOURTH GENERATION: ALEX AND SAMMY

Chapter 1

ALEX BY THE DUMPSTER

March 12, 1998

The psychiatrist on duty at the UCLA hospital adolescent ward, Dr. C., looked up from her desk where she'd been scrutinizing Alex's admission paperwork.

"How would you describe your son's recent behavior?"

I flashed on the afternoon when I found him hiding by the dumpster behind Fairfax High School. *I can't tell her that*, I quickly decided, searching for some less awful way to describe Alex's troubles.

"He's been withdrawn and has a lot of trouble sleeping," I finally said, well aware of the inadequacy of my response.

An entry in Alex's journal from the previous fall said it far better.

I sat down behind a dumpster, declared it my kingdom and began drawing soldiers. I drew an angel with eyes and tits. I drew knights to fight my holy war. I began to forget that I was back there 'cause I was scared of the world.

Alex's art teacher said she tried hard to keep him in her class on days like that one, telling him that he could draw or paint whatever he wished.

"I just can't," he told her on more than one occasion.

The afternoon I found him crouched between the dumpster and a low cement wall was one such day.

"Alex!" I yelled, when I spotted him sitting cross-legged on the cement, writing in one of his ubiquitous steno notebooks. He climbed into the car, throwing his filthy backpack on the floor between his long legs, as the nauseating stench of garbage filled the air. I opened my window to let in some fresh air and heard waves of multilingual chatter from hundreds of students spilling out the doors of the school and into the parking lot. I thought back to our meeting with the school principal the previous spring when we signed Alex up for this school, LA's public magnet for the visual arts. She explained there were no fewer than 113 languages spoken here. I recalled my instant unspoken reaction: Alex as one of 3,500 students in this mini–United Nations was a nonstarter; there was no way he could deal with the intensity of this human traffic. We went through the motions anyway because . . . well, just because we weren't ready to stop trying for "a fresh start."

I turned now to see Alex sitting expressionless with that vacant, haunted stare on his face; the one that said he was the last person alive on planet Earth, the words from a poem he'd recently left on my coffee table.

> *And I am the last human being*
> *And I am a bum.*
> *And the world looks only at me*
> *only they don't quite see me . . .*

The early rush hour traffic in West Hollywood made our drive home a slow, single-file trek from Melrose across Sunset and up into the hills above Beverly Hills.

"How was art class today?" I asked after several minutes of monotonous silence.

He moved his head another quarter turn away, barring any further conversation.

I took the coldness of his nonanswer as a final abandonment of any pretense of normalcy between us. It pushed my fear level up several notches until the pressure created a vice around my chest. I wanted more than anything to be reassured that he was still there and we were still connected. Instead, I took shallower breaths, surrendering to Alex's need for silence.

By this point, I realized I was losing my son to some malevolent internal force. A few weeks earlier, he'd been suspended from school for two days, with expulsion threatened. The vice principle on the phone complained that Alex insisted on walking around the halls and parking areas in his socks. This actually wasn't a surprise. He'd begun his shoeless habit at his last school, a tiny private institution where they'd also cited a big problem with Alex's shoeless state, claiming insurance concerns. Then as now, Alex explained that wearing shoes prevented him from feeling his feet on the ground. He'd promised to wear them again when he made the change to Fairfax, but, obviously, he couldn't pull it off.

During these months before his hospitalization, I could palpably see and feel Alex losing a little bit more of his core self every day. He was like a house in the marsh with a faulty foundation; each high tide pushing its structure another fraction off its piers—calamity quietly looming. I also suspected even then that Alex's impending "break" had begun a very long time before.

Here was Alex's rendering of what was going on in his life in a poem he titled "Revelation," again from the fall of 1997.

> *Looking down for the first time and realizing they've been reduced to a form, among other forms, thrown into a world where concise thought and language are obligatory, they can't talk or understand because where they come from, it was enough just to feel. . . . Taught the ways of man, they soon lose perspective and think it not all unusual to stand in lines and be told how to live. But they will never truly be happy, because somewhere in the bottom of their hearts and the back of their minds, they remember how it was.*

Knowing he wrote this when his emotions were so difficult to reach, I'm saddened. I recall his baptism, when he was eighteen months old. Living in a Maryland suburb of Washington, DC, Alex's father and I had recently joined a lively, racially integrated Episcopal parish that reflected our activist liberal politics. As a lapsed Catholic who missed the ritual of the Church, I'd been pining to have my firstborn son baptized. We chose a candlelight Easter Saturday Mass, unaware of the theatricality bestowed on this occasion by our new congregation, which took to heart the idea of children needing to be raised by a village.

First there was an intimate ceremony at the altar with Geoff and I standing next to Alex's godparents, two close friends. As our African American minister Joel splashed holy water on Alex's reclined forehead, I prayed silently, fearing that my shy toddler—the same child who eschewed touch or eye contact even from those of us who loved him—might break into a scream of horror. So far, so good, I thought, as Joel uprighted a still-calm Alex. As I extended my arms to retrieve him and sit down in our front pew, Joel surprised me by abruptly turning with Alex to face the congregation. He then strode triumphantly down the center aisle so that Alex could be petted, kissed, and effusively welcomed as the newest member of the church at each packed pew.

Amazingly, Alex, poised in Joel's arms, appeared radiant and content throughout the ceremony; soaking in love from all who greeted him and never once showing any sign of fear. My mother remarked how out of character Alex behaved that night. To our joy, this wide-eyed, sensitive, and trusting side of Alex continued to blossom, taking us through the next few years of what would become his quiet and uneventful early childhood.

Only now, fourteen years later, to find him cowered behind a trash dumpster, a shell of that younger self.

As we reached the crest of the hill separating LA from the San Fernando Valley, Alex closed his eyes and put his head on the back of the seat, ruling out any further contact between us. So I concentrated on staying in my lane as I navigated the hairpin curves of Mulholland Drive, maintaining my silence until we reached the curb in front of our Beverly Glen townhouse. As soon as the car stopped, Alex picked up his backpack with one hand and grabbed the door handle with the other, ready to jump to his freedom.

"I have to get back to work," I said. "Will you be okay?"

A look of pained tolerance sufficed for his answer.

After spending the rest of that week at home because, he explained, these were not "good days," Alex returned to school the following Monday and attended sporadically until January 28, his eighteenth birthday.

A birthday cake with eighteen candles sends terror through the heart of any parent of a disturbed teenager—when your options to influence his life radically shrink to few or none. This was exactly what happened on the morning of January 28 when Alex sat down with his bowl of Cheerios® and calmly announced his intention to quit high school. To silence my protests, before the week ended, he took the high school equivalency exam and passed with adequate scores to obtain his California GED. Fewer than three months later, he drove my car into the fence of the Fairfax High School parking lot.

—m—

At ten thirty the next morning, I was seated in a small, glass-enclosed office off the waiting room of the hospital adolescent unit. On the other side of a plain desk sat the psychiatrist who would do his evaluation. She was still focused on Alex's admission file. There were no diplomas or personal effects on the walls or desk, nothing to distract me. So I remained fixated on the letters of her name embroidered in navy-blue above the pocket of her white coat, its whiteness setting off her midnight-colored skin; the diamond stud on one nostril; and her long, black hair swept up in a bun. Lowered mini-blinds provided a modicum of privacy for this generic space where doctors came daily to deliver generally bad news to baffled parents like me.

"Alex has settled comfortably in the ward," said Dr. C. once she put down the file and raised her eyes to meet mine.

"We'll give him a complete physical exam along with urine and blood screens. He'll get neurological testing. And I'll be doing a three-hour interview with a medication assessment."

"When will all this be finished?" I asked, expecting her to say a couple of days.

"Except for the lab results, by the end of this afternoon."

"Oh." *By tonight we'll know what's wrong with him*, I thought, not sure whether to feel relieved or terrified by the prospect.

"He'll begin group therapy tomorrow," she explained.

As she filled me in on visiting hours and parent group meetings, my attention drifted. I was wondering how Alex was coping on the other side of the locked adolescent unit door. The intake nurse informed me earlier that he would be one of only two males in residence there. She described the other boy as having OCD (obsessive-compulsive disorder), and the remaining nineteen patients as anorexic girls. When I later saw some of these girls sitting in a group through a hallway window, I caught my breath. Their arms and legs were sticks; they looked like starvation could send them dropping to the floor at any moment.

At my first parent meeting on the adolescent unit, one mother told me that if I had a daughter instead of two sons, I wouldn't be so shocked at what I was seeing. *Well, then thank God I don't have a daughter*, I caught myself thinking. It was the opposite of what I'd felt since giving birth to Sammy six years after Alex, when I still held out hope of salvaging my marriage and adding a daughter to our family. But then the mind does strange things when your firstborn is locked up in a kiddie psych ward.

—⁓—

Alex's first day as a psychiatric inpatient also served as a line of demarcation for much more.

Before this day, I'd managed to deny or at least to work around my lifelong depression.

Before this day, I'd felt that Alex, Sammy, and I had weathered the divorce and our move to smaller quarters, new schools, and a new neighbor-hood pretty well.

Before this day, I would never have guessed that four years later, Sammy would fall from his station as the uncomplicated son and face his own diagnosis of an intractable mental disorder.

After this day, I would be forced to reexamine Alex's emotional, cognitive, and behavioral history since birth and see that it had contained many warning signs of his literal and figurative crash.

After this day, I would revisit the lives of several prematurely deceased family members from generations past, those who'd been described as "weak," like my sister and father, or as simply "no good," like my grandfather, and find the more likely reasons behind their individual tragedies.

After this day, I would begin a decade of searching for answers, time spent culling hundreds of studies and talking to researchers who would help me connect the dots between past and present until I finally understood how different mental illnesses come to traverse families such as ours.

Of course, none of this was clear to me at the time of these events. Nor did the realizations come all at once afterward. More in the manner of rising global temperatures, eroding ice caps, and flooded coastlines, the causes and results of this day wouldn't become clear until the evidence became irrefutable, meaning until all three of us had diagnoses and until my research helped me understand what they meant. I have absolutely no doubt that had we not intervened when we did, Alex would have followed the life paths of my sister and grandfather, and he would be dead or in jail right now.

And so I begin this book with the incidents that pushed me to finally see and act on what had been hiding in plain sight all along. In part 2, I work my way back through our family tree to find the roots of this difficult legacy. Then, in part 3, I complete our personal stories and offer a vision of how individuals and families like ours can navigate mental health care in decades hence in a new model emphasizing early intervention and prevention.

—⚏—

My trip to UCLA that Monday morning came after being awakened at three o'clock in the morning by a phone call from Alex, saying he'd just driven our 1985 Blazer® into the school's chain link fence, where it was presently stuck. He couldn't explain why he'd done it, but could I pick him up?

Agitated and pacing at home, he spoke incoherently about how he was really okay, and I was making too much of nothing. Once morning came, I called Alex's regular psychotherapist, Steve Hasenberg, who convinced me to take Alex to UCLA to have him evaluated. In his still-dazed state from the night before, Alex agreed. At the reception desk, I held my breath as he signed a temporary waiver of his rights. Given he was now legally an adult, informed consent was needed for the admission. With this document, he could be forced to stay for one week. After that, Alex could (and did) sign himself out.

I didn't know what to expect from Alex's treatment at UCLA. But I was hopeful—and desperate. We'd run out of options. Over the prior five years, Alex's father and I had tried everything we could think of to help our son survive adolescence. UCLA felt like our last chance to save him before Alex slipped completely out of reach.

Later that first day, Dr. C. asked me to return to her little glass office in order to complete a family medical history. In this interview, she explained, I would provide the causes of death for both sides of Alex's family going back three generations. I didn't quite realize it until we started that this was really about our family's *mental health history*. Once I knew what she was after, I told Dr. C. we wouldn't need to spend much time on my ex-husband's family. Geoff's relatives were amazingly normal. They were midwesterners, schoolteachers, accountants, or engineers, like Geoff. In twelve years, I couldn't recall seeing any of my in-laws take a drink, not even on holidays. His grandparents lived to their nineties and died of natural causes.

As she checked off places on her paperwork and flipped sheets, Dr. C. urged me to continue to my own family. I began with my mother's side, a robust line of Italian immigrants. Her father, Alessio LaMacchia, sailed with his parents and siblings from Naples to Ellis Island in 1898. After learning his craft in Lower Manhattan's garment district, Alessio became a master tailor and furrier at B. Altman's department store and married Carmela Cicchitti, another recent immigrant. To my brother, sister, and me, Grandma Carmela was Nana, queen of the kitchen, where she allowed us to crank fresh pasta out of an ancient-looking tool. We adored her huge lap and loving arms. Mom's sister, my aunt Lillian LaMacchia, stayed in Washington, DC, after the war to work in the state department at a time when career versus marriage was an either/or proposition for a woman. Mom, by marrying and having children, made the opposite choice and never made any bones about her regrets.

"And your father's family?" Dr. C. asked.

What had been an easy task, almost fun, became painful. "My father was an alcoholic," I began. "He smoked three packs of cigarettes a day and died of lung cancer at forty-six."

I didn't, couldn't look at her.

"Any other sib— " she started to ask.

"My younger sister Rita was a heroin addict, in and out of jail and rehab for most of her life."

"She is . . . ?"

"Dead."

"The cause?"

"Cardiac arrest was how her death certificate read."

I exhaled, thinking that at least now the worst was over.

"And your paternal grandparents?"

Straining under the weight of her gaze, I felt embarrassed, and ashamed. "Well, I remember hearing that my dad's mother, Ellen—that's my middle name—died of the flu. Very young; she must have been in her twenties."

"Your grandfather?"

"My grandfather's name was Michael, Dad's middle name . . ."

An odd echo had begun to follow each word I spoke, as if I was experiencing déjà vu in real time. "I'm almost sure that Grandpa Michael got hit by a train," I said, but it was as if someone else was speaking; I felt disconnected from the words and their possible meaning.

Dr. C. stopped scribbling and looked me in the eye. "Has it ever occurred to you that your grandfather's remaining on the railroad track may have been an intentional act?"

"No, never," I said, stunned by the question. "I mean, not until you just asked me."

All my senses suddenly kicked into high gear. I felt the hard plastic seat underneath my thighs again as the details of when and where I'd heard the story of my grandfather's death started rolling out in my mind like a home movie. I kept my eyes closed and offered each piece to Dr. C. as it came.

"I was eight years old; I know that because it was right after my father died. Dad's funeral was over, and everyone had finally left our house. I was sitting in Dad's big green chair watching a game show on TV when Mom came into the living room with a dish towel in her hands and said, 'At least now your father will finally get some peace. He never had any here.'

"Because they'd fought often during Dad's last months at home, I childishly took her comment to mean she was glad to have him gone."

Dr. C. cleared her throat, gently bringing me back. "And your grandfather?" she asked.

"That's when Mom started in on Grandpa. How he came to New York because there was nothing for him in Ireland, and he'd been lucky to get hired as an Erie Railroad fireman, stoking the engine with coal. I was still trying to imagine someone who looked like Dad covered with sweat and soot, tossing coal into an engine, when Mom said it—how one night Grandpa just lay down on the railroad tracks and didn't get up."

I didn't say that, even as a child, I suspected there was something wrong with her story. Every night, when we picked up Dad at the Pearl River train station, I could feel the platform shaking long before I saw the engine peek around the bend. *How come Grandpa didn't know a train was coming soon enough to get off the tracks?* But I didn't ask that question aloud, not then or at any other time.

"All right, then," Dr. C. said, seemingly uninterested in pursuing the issue of Grandpa any further. "I have completed my diagnosis of Alex." She spoke slowly, seemingly waiting for me to catch up with her. "He has paranoid schizophrenia."

She couldn't have just said that. My forehead began to throb, blurring my vision to the point where Dr. C. became a white coat with no face.

"His condition is complicated by his recent use of marijuana and methamphetamine, but the underlying symptoms of paranoia and delusion are clearly present. I'd like to keep him here for a month to stabilize him with an antipsychotic medication."

After a long silence, my wits returned enough for me to ask Dr. C. if she wouldn't mind explaining how she'd come to her diagnosis.

"He has hallucinations," she said. "He believes he is being watched by aliens."

Oh, God. I knew this was not good news, but I was still not sure what she was saying.

"I'm sorry?"

Reading from her notes, the doctor related Alex's belief that we're being observed by beings from other planets who mingle among us in human form. He calls them "walk-ins," she explained.

Oh, so that's a hallucination, I remember thinking, still confused.

I'd heard him talk about aliens before. It was, after all, 1998, the peak year of popularity for the television series *The X-Files*, in which only the clueless didn't believe in aliens. In the series, the FBI has a special unit charged with investigating their alien antics.

When I asked Dr. C. about the television show, she told me she'd never seen it. *No doubt she worked long hours. She had no wedding ring, probably no kids.* I moved on.

"What else?" I asked.

She reached into her file and held up a picture, a self-portrait by Alex. In it, behind a painfully intense set of eyes that I recognized as his, Alex sketched a mass of jangled cables and broken circuits. I'd seen that image countless times, imagining it to be a reflection of teenage moodiness. Sitting there with Dr. C., I had to acknowledge that it could mean that something much more serious than teen angst was affecting my son.

Schizophrenia. Although I didn't yet know details, what I thought I knew boiled down to its being the worst possible disease a young person could have, akin to a death sentence. I didn't think to question the doctor's conclusion or her explanation that schizophrenia was a "chronic, lifelong illness."

Nor did I think to resist when she explained that Alex would need ongoing psychiatric care, which, depending on how well he complied with taking medications, would likely include several more stays in mental facilities like this one.

Without using the words, she was telling me that Alex's mental illness was *chronic and incurable*; the best we should hope for was for him to learn to manage his worst symptoms. Oh, and we'd better give up our expectations of what our son might still accomplish in his life. The message was clear: it would be counterproductive for us as parents to think of the patient as the same son or daughter we had known and loved. That person was gone. It was far more constructive, we were to understand, to get on with the business of symptom management.

As I gathered my things to leave her office, Dr. C. suggested I attend a support group for parents of the mentally ill. I said nothing; the idea of doing something to make me feel better about the tragedy that had struck my son sounded ludicrous.

I remember nothing of the rest of the day until I put a piece of pizza on a plate for Sammy's dinner, then robotically sat down across from him with one of my own. Normally, I would have asked Sammy about his day. I simply couldn't manage it, not that night.

"Where's Alex?" he finally asked.

"He's in the hospital. It's not serious; he's just getting checked out."

Sammy, who had a telepathic ability to read my every mood—the result of being the child of a depressed mother and the younger sibling of a mentally disturbed brother—took a bite and stood up with his plate in his hand. "Can I go watch TV?" he asked diplomatically, leaving me to fret in private.

"Sure, go ahead," I replied.

OTHER ANSWERS

Well-meaning family and friends were sympathetic but clearly pessimistic about Alex's chances of recovery. One recommended Alex "learn a trade," so he might remain independent. Others spoke as if my son was already dead, suggesting I allow myself to "mourn his loss."

As it turned out, my most important asset at this time—beyond the false sense of control I'd acquired as the adult child of a long line of alcoholics—was my professional training as a science journalist. Although I was more comfortable dealing with environmental subject matter than psychiatry or neuroscience, I at least knew how to read a scientific report. I quickly moved my search for answers to the national mental health databases and professional journals. Since I was also a working single mother, these research efforts had to be squeezed into early mornings and late nights while I spent the better part of each day working as a freelancer writing television scripts for Hollywood production companies, assigned to cooking and gardening shows for cable channels, and the occasional nature special for Disney. Many days, I felt like I was leaving a disaster movie unfolding in slow motion at home to escape for a few hours of fun at Disneyland®, famously pegged as "the happiest place on earth."

It was only after I began meeting other *consumers*, most of them mothers of sons in the same state as Alex or worse, that I realized the complexity of what I was suddenly dealing with. From talking with other parents in clinic waiting rooms and at local National Alliance on Mental Illness (NAMI) meetings, I quickly saw the importance of this peer-to-peer information sharing—with all of us learning from those who'd gotten there before us. I regained some hope for Alex's future.

A bit here on terminology: *Consumer* is the imperfect but preferred term in the United States (*client* is used in Europe) to describe someone getting mental health care services or a family member of that person. It is intended to replace *patient*, *case*, or *subject*. The point is to view the provider and consumer as equal participants in an exchange of information and, given the still-lacking parity for insurance coverage of mental health care, often cash for a professional service. I've tried to use *consumer* consistently on these pages, but you'll find me occasionally lapsing back to older terms where it otherwise feels forced.

One of the "treasures" of the mental health advocacy movement, author and professor of psychiatry at Johns Hopkins School of Medicine, Kay Redfield Jamison, confessed in one of her wonderful memoirs that she disliked the term *bipolar*, saying she didn't like thinking of herself as one of two "poles." She preferred the old-fashioned term *manic depressive* to describe her own illness.[1]

Whatever we choose to call these disorders or ourselves, anyone dealing with a mental illness is much more than her diagnosis. For that matter, no two cases of mental illness are alike. Take schizophrenia. In many ways, this disease functions as a catch-all for "brains acting strangely." In the past decade, brain imaging studies have uncovered concrete evidence of just how much damage can be done to the brain by a major mental illness like schizophrenia, bipolar disorder, or major depression. It's still not entirely clear how the discovery of these "biomarkers" in far-off laboratories will help people who may have just found themselves with strange new symptoms of a possible mental illness. But the fact of their arrival onto the scientific scene remains important for two reasons: as proof and promise—more on both next.

On a 2009 trip I made to Western Ireland to visit my grandfather's ancestral home, I met neuroscientist Dara Cannon. Cannon has family roots in Galway and now codirects the Clinical Neuroimaging Laboratory there. We met in a café overlooking Galway Bay to talk about the work that took her to Bethesda, Maryland, before she returned home to have her first child and take on research and teaching duties at Ireland's National University lab. Over coffee and muffins, Cannon patiently walked me through the nooks and crannies of the brain from a neuroimagist's perspective. I gave up taking notes and marveled as she described the new state-of-the-art MRI scanning technology she uses to investigate the white matter of the brain and how it can reveal the reduced integrity of these structures that facilitate communication between different brain regions in individuals with schizophrenia.[2] Her passion for her task moved me.

Prior to coming back to Galway, Cannon trained at the National Institutes of Health in Bethesda, Maryland, where she carried out her contribution to a recently published American study lead by Dr. Wayne C. Drevets (senior investigator at the National Institute of Mental Health, Mood and Anxiety Disorders Program) that produced some stunning new evidence of brain changes caused by bipolar disorder. Using the even higher-resolution MRI technology available to Cannon and her fellow researchers at their US lab, they found that bipolar patients who were not medicated had a significantly smaller amygdala—a structure in the brain's emotion and sensory processing system that goes awry in a variety of mental disorders, including bipolar disorder. The shrunken amygdalae of these patients was evident when compared to the same brain structure in age-matched "controls"—a separate group of study participants who did not have bipolar disorder whose brains were also imaged.

In a subsequent phase of the study, Cannon described how investigator Dr. Jonathan Savitz and Prof. Drevets saw something novel: when they scanned the brains of bipolar patients who were taking the medication lithium, they found that their amygdalae had returned to their larger size, nearly matching those in the control group of healthy brains.[3] These results, showing a clear biological difference of people with and without a mental disorder and a return to brain health in those being treated with a psychiatric medication, constitutes "proof"—otherwise known as a biomarker—and it should speak volumes to any remaining mental illness deniers out there.

Cannon capped our impromptu brain science lesson with an optimistic prediction—the "promise" I noted previously. "In the near future I hope the field of psychiatry will be in a position to make the dramatic leap to incorporating our latest biological evidence into practice." When I asked how it would make a difference to a teenager cowering in his bedroom or hearing voices for the first time, she explained, "Clients and clinicians alike can look forward to help from biological tests, be they brain scans to diagnose or predict treatment response, genetic tests to predict risk, or other blood-based tests to identify trait markers or facilitate early diagnosis."[4]

What Cannon means here when she refers to "treatment response" as a variable is the increasingly clear evidence that every person with a mental illness, even those with the same diagnosis, has a different disease and route to recovery—since both are the combination of his or her unique genetic and environmental liabilities and assets. This is not a one-size-fits-all science. It never was, but the realization is fairly new among researchers, whose jobs—to find cures and better treatments—became harder as a result.

Of course, to make a big difference in treatment outcomes, diagnostic tests using biomarkers would have to be made available to mental health providers on the front line of treatment, but that's another issue. With biological tests for mental illness within our reach, we can reasonably imagine a day when the diagnosis of schizophrenia or depression will at least be in the same realm as cancer—a tough verdict, but at least one without the fictions that currently cloud the treatment of mental illnesses.

SOME ESSENTIAL BRAIN STUFF

In neuroscience, the same brain structures and systems tend to come up when we discuss different mental disorders. I begin in the middle, (evolutionarily) older part of the brain where three structures comprise the *limbic* system, responsible for regulating our emotions and other autonomic functions—everything from sleeping and eating, to startling at a surprise stimulus, to telling us when to feel fear and joy.

The **amygdala** is a one-inch-long bean-like structure responsible for regulating the emotions. The amygdala controls responses associated with fear, arousal, emotional responses, and hormonal secretions. It's where your "fight-or-flight" impulses come alive.

The **hippocampus** is responsible for encoding long-term memories and for consolidating short-term episodic memories.

The **thalamus** is believed to process sensory information as well as relay it and receive messages back from the cerebral cortex. It plays a major role in regulating sleep and wakefulness, arousal, our level of awareness, and motor activity.

Nearer to the front and top of the brain is the cerebral cortex, a (cortical) layer referred to as *gray matter*. It is divided into right and left hemispheres and encompasses about two-thirds of the brain mass. It is the most highly developed part of the human brain and is responsible for thinking, perceiving, producing, and understanding language—sometimes referred to as our "executive functions."[5]

Other neuroimaging studies in the last decade have shown that the thalamus (that central processor of information between parts of the brain) in people with schizophrenia is smaller than that of controls, and, surprisingly, this reduction was present in the same proportion no matter at which stage of schizophrenia the person was—one year or ten years post-onset.[6] This particular finding unnerved me as the parent of a teenager diagnosed with this disorder at eighteen. I couldn't help but wonder if Alex's brain was irreparably "broken" after having once reached this state of diminishment. I now marvel that the brain is capable of recovering from what sounds like such a radical alteration.

More correlations and replications of studies tying together specific biomarkers and mechanisms of brain diseases will be needed to boost such findings from the realm of basic science to new clinical protocols. In the meantime, the use of structured interviews and behavioral scrutiny by a clinician sitting face-to-face with a consumer is still the primary means available for detecting the presence of mental disorders in adults and children. Another term for a psychologist who conducts research is *behavioral scientist*.

All told, my research into the science of mental illness took more than a decade, and, for many reasons, this length of time turned out to be a good thing. The boys and I made meaningful progress in our recoveries, providing many more therapeutic insights for me to share. So, too, did the science and practice of psychiatry evolve; with today's focus on the complex interactions of genes and environmental factors promising better answers than those I struggled with at the beginning of the decade. My questions also evolved.

Instead of viewing DNA as a fixed and passively inherited legacy, I now see risk and responsibility for the health of one's brain as a larger, shared undertaking. It begins with the individual and then moves outward to include anyone with whom we come into significant contact. Still, in the end, all my questions boiled down to one: *What makes one person in a family (or community) more vulnerable to a mental disorder than another?*

THE BEST PREDICTOR

Knowing your family history is now and will remain absolutely critical to ascertaining your risk for mental illness and getting proper mental health treatment. In science speak they say it's the "best predictor" of risk.[7] Even then, don't labor under the mistaken impression that your family history puts everything you need to know in a neat, black-and-white profile of measured vulnerability. Risk is best seen as a moving picture, not a snapshot. Even after you've filled in all the blanks about relatives long gone, your risk profile will remain filled with grays, or I should say "factors," since we are now talking about a "multifactorial disease model" for most mental (and physical) disorders. This is not necessarily bad news. Put simply, it means you have the opportunity to make up for anything "lethal" that nature heaped on you with some conscious self- and child-directed nurture to counteract its effects.

As offspring of a parent or grandparent with schizophrenia or bipolar disorder, we can inherit a strong predisposition to that disorder. But we now have many more nuances to add to this simplistic view of heredity. The inheritance may come in the guise of a lesser form of the same mental disorder—for example, attention deficit hyperactivity disorder (ADHD), which appears much more often in the children of bipolar parents and grandparents. Through three-generation family studies, we know that the density of mental disorders—including alcoholism and other addictions—going back a few generations is another important determinant of a person's individual mental health risk.[8]

—⁓—

Long after Dr. C. explained her diagnosis of Alex by pointing to his symptoms of *psychosis*, I learned that a vulnerability to that distorted state of mind was as heritable as the full-blown psychotic diseases known as schizophrenia and bipolar disorder.[9] Their symptoms overlap: paranoia, strange thoughts, hallucinations, heightened sensory perceptions, cognitive decline, loss of motivation, and social withdrawal—all the things I started seeing in Alex during his mid-adolescence.[10]

In the general population, the incidence of psychosis is 3 percent,[11] which makes it more common than diabetes. But everyone (even those of us with a family history of one of these diseases) doesn't share the same level of vulnerability to psychosis. Young people between the ages of sixteen and thirty are at higher risk than most people over thirty. More boys fall victim to psychosis at younger ages than do girls. Another predictive risk factor is smoking cannabis (pot). According to robust science (as good as it gets), cannabis use moderately increases the risk of psychotic symptoms in *all young people*, but it has what's called a "dose response" relationship—meaning it delivers the highest firepower—in those with an inherited predisposition to psychosis.[12]

Researchers think they've located one of the likely mechanisms for how cannabis can interact with a predisposition to psychosis to change the brains of these young people after they smoke a great deal of it. In studies, a genetic risk can be conferred to a young person who carries a specific allele (an alternative version of the more commonly held gene; for example, a gene that is shorter, longer, missing a part), in this case of the COMT (catechol-o-methyl transferase) gene. COMT is an enzyme that regulates the neurotransmitter dopamine. Individuals who have this allele were found to be more susceptible to psychosis by their intake of cannabis compared to those who carried another version of the COMT gene—and didn't have a family history.[13]

A young person who sees fleeting hallucinations or hears occasional voices doesn't always progress to a more severe mental disorder.[14] Many factors come into play to determine whether someone at high risk for a psychotic disease—also called "ultra-high risk," meaning he carries a genetic liability *and* shows early symptoms—will go all the way to manifesting a psychotic disorder. Next, I take a closer look at some of these factors. But first, a few more unfamiliar terms need to be made familiar.

MATTERS OF DEGREE AND PREVALENCE

Central to the genetics of mental illness is a set of terms describing the "degree" or extent of genes you share with other members of your family. First-degree relatives are anyone to whom you are linked to by 50 percent of your genes, so this refers to parents, offspring, and siblings. With your second-degree relatives you share 25 percent of your genes, putting grandparents, uncles and aunts, nieces and nephews, and half-siblings in this category.[15] Most family studies—the fundamental human-powered research that can track the diseases for which our children carry the greatest risks—focus on first- and second-degree relatives. Because of their proximity to us, these family members' stories (and secrets) have the most to tell us about our own lives and possible mental health futures.

Some studies go broader and include third-degree relatives who share 12.5 percent of genetic material, meaning one's great-grandparents, great-uncles and great-aunts, and (first) cousins. Their lives and mental illnesses become significant for family studies investigating the presence of a disease in multiple generations, where its density in a family tree is considered a significant factor when assessing current and future disease risks. For example, if your child of seven to ten is acting out with consistently bad behavior—and in most cases, that child is a boy—his behavior is much more likely to predict a bad outcome—worse anti-sociality or even psychosis—if your family tree is full of alcoholics or "rage-aholics" with attention problems. If your family history is without these disorders, a completely different outcome may be expected.[16]

—m—

The statistical *prevalence*, defined as the presence of a disease in a given population over a specific period of time (e.g., for the previous twelve months or for a lifetime), for two of the most serious mental disorders in the general population—schizophrenia and bipolar disorder—sounds very low: in the 1 to 3 percent range. These percentages apply to you if no one in your immediate family has the disease in question. Schizophrenia in the general population is put at 1.1 percent,[17] making it seem nearly insignificant. On the other hand, 1 percent is twenty-four million people worldwide.

In a city the size of my current hometown, San Francisco, with our estimated population of 815,000, there are approximately 9,000 men and women living among us with schizophrenia. It's a small enough place that there's a very good chance I interact with many of "them" as I travel on the BART (Bay Area Rapid Transit), go to the opera, picnic in Golden Gate Park, and do my grocery shopping. However, now that my son Alex is one of "them," I find it changes everything. Now I readily recognize their struggles when I see them. But the fact is *they* can no longer be *them* at all. Suddenly they are *me* and *mine*. Stigma against the mentally ill, which we all carry to varying degrees, becomes much more difficult to maintain.

The prevalence of bipolar disorder in the general population is a little higher, at 2.6 percent,[18] giving my city around 21,200 individuals who are challenged by this other severe psychotic disorder. Before the decade I describe in this book came to an end, the adult daughter of someone close to me began to show bipolar symptoms. As her father, my friend, watched in near-constant worry, his daughter's manic spells would fly out of control. Unable to sleep, she would spend large amounts of money on luxuries and talk at lightning speed about the grand things she was going to do. That is, if she wasn't spiraling down into a weeks-long depression. Meanwhile, she would often miss work and disappear for days at a time, abruptly severing ties with any family member or friend who dared to confront her erratic behaviors. She rejected the idea of getting evaluated or treated since she saw any problems in her life strictly as a spiritual challenge, not as a set of symptoms deserving medical attention. Suddenly bipolar disorder had become all too real to me, too.

—〰—

Secrecy and denial in a family become habitual. If you and your relatives speak openly of mental illness, let alone of a suicide in the family, yours is a rare and fortunate family. Most of us don't know our real risks for mental illnesses because so many family members in past generations were not diagnosed or treated—and with treatment rates still at only about 60 percent for serious mental disorders in the United States, the same pattern unfortunately persists.[19] Often, those who have been treated for a mental illness have kept it a secret from even their close relatives. A social worker at an agency I currently consult for recently told me that it was only after her mother's recent funeral that an aunt confided a long-held family secret: the diagnosis of schizophrenia her mother received in her twenties. Now in her fifties, my colleague suddenly had an explanation for a lifetime of her mother's odd behaviors and unexplained absences. I argue in this book that this stance of silence and secrecy is no longer a viable option, least of all for parents of young children in a family with a pattern of mental illness and addiction. Secrets can cause harm and even kill.

You may be surprised to learn, for example, that if a prepubescent child's family has a high aggregation of mood disorders, meaning a lot of depression or bipolar disorder along with alcoholism, that child is far more likely to develop a mood disorder *before puberty*,[20] considerably earlier than the common age of onset for depression in mid-adolescence. Just knowing this information alerts parents to the need to monitor such a child's moods closely—as well as their own.

THE COMMON CHILDHOOD AND ADOLESCENT MENTAL DISORDERS

This list is not intended to be complete. Rather, it serves as an introduction to some of the mental health disorders affecting children and adolescents mentioned in this book.

Attention deficit hyperactivity disorder (ADHD) is the most common mental disorder in children, affecting up to 12 percent of the population under the age of eighteen. Symptoms of ADHD include chronic abnormal levels of inattention, hyperactivity, or a combination of the two.

Depression is a mood disorder, meaning the individual has a neurobiological problem that causes changes in behavior and related emotional states. The most salient is an inability to enjoy life due to an overwhelming sense of sadness. There are two types of depression: A mild to moderate level of depression that is more or less constant is called dysthymic disorder or dysthymia. A more severe type that occurs in episodes of two or more weeks is called clinical or major depression. Children and adolescents can have both types of depression at once.

Anxiety disorders. Everyone, including teenagers and younger children, experiences passing bouts of anxiety. But those whose day-to-day routines are disrupted by long periods of anxiety lasting for days and even weeks probably suffer from an anxiety disorder. Examples of fears that can escalate and become disabling include fear of leaving the house, fear of interacting with other people, fear of contamination, an inability to concentrate on a task, an unreasonable fear of becoming overweight, and a generalized feeling of anxiety that makes one's life basically dysfunctional. The most common anxiety disorders affecting children and teenagers are separation anxiety disorder, social anxiety, obsessive-compulsive disorder (OCD), phobias, and the eating disorders anorexia nervosa and bulimia.

Pervasive developmental disorders (PDD), a category that includes autism and Asperger's syndrome, cause mild to severe limitations in a person's sense-dependent interpersonal abilities. As a result of their disorders, children with PDD often manifest an inability to respond to touch and other forms of interpersonal contact.[21]

Before the arrival of Alex's schizophrenia, the undiagnosed psychological problems in my family included several cases of mild and major depression, certainly alcoholism, a host of other addictions, and at least one, possibly two, unacknowledged suicides. I now also have good reason to think that my sister, Rita, and my grandfather, Michael, would today be diagnosed with bipolar disorder. Both displayed Jekyll and Hyde flip-flops between catatonic depression and reckless, grandiose behaviors; both drank heavily; and both died in "accidents"—Michael at twenty-eight; Rita at thirty-eight. Many more pieces of the puzzle of my "family illness" have now fallen into place. But I wasn't conscious of any of them until my son landed in the UCLA psych ward more than a decade ago.

—〰—

Psychiatric epidemiologist Myrna Weissman told me that she sees mental health consumers in the United States facing two big problems. "Beyond the fragmented state of our service delivery system," Weissman began, "there is an unacceptable gap between research and training."[22] Translated into everyday consumer reality, this means that even if you get past your primary care gatekeeper to see a mental health specialist, you may not get evidence-based treatment, as there is a gap between research findings and their entry into practice. As Weissman points out, that's just not good enough.

The researchers and clinicians I've talked to for this book are making discoveries that have immediate implications for all of us—although much of their work remains buried in professional journals most people never see. In upcoming chapters, I'll share highlights from this exciting work with an emphasis on research that is actionable today to protect and preserve your family's mental health.

FICTIONS AND FACTS OF MENTAL ILLNESS

I close this chapter with two brief lists. The first offers my view of the three most damaging and persistent fictions about mental illness that we encounter today. These are the persistent misunderstandings that produce stigma and cause people to avoid treatment. Then, I give you three reasons for optimism, based on solid new science that offers great promise for recovery and prevention from even the most severe mental illnesses.

First the fictions that can cause us all harm:

Fiction 1: Mental disorders, because they must be diagnosed through the observation of behavior and not with blood tests, biopsies, or thermometers are *less real* than other (physical) diseases.[23]

Fiction 2: Great numbers of people are being misdiagnosed and over-medicated for mental disorders they don't really have.[24]

Fiction 3: A mental illness is a life sentence; once someone is given a diagnosis, he will remain that way.[25]

The facts tell a different story. Mental disorders are just as real as any other illness, but because of stigma and other barriers to treatment, far too many who have them still suffer in silence.[26] I'll present much more evidence of who is and isn't being treated and why in chapters to come. But next, I give you three evidence-based scientific facts that give us all reasons for hope.

Fact 1: Taking into account family history and known risks, it is possible to determine a child's basic risks for a mental disorder even before her first overt symptoms become apparent.[27] Secondary prevention—meaning averting illness in someone who's at risk—is then possible by taking concerted *neuroprotective actions* to support healthy minds—and I don't necessarily mean medications.[28]

Fact 2: If someone has manifested the first signs of psychosis or a full-blown disease like schizophrenia or bipolar disorder, early intervention—meaning treatment within the first six months of the appearance of symptoms—yields better treatment outcomes, including remission and complete recovery.[29] As I argue, the risk of doing it the old way, of waiting until schizophrenia has been fully present for six months or longer, is that the young person ends up with more severe and permanent impairments.[30]

Fact 3: For an individual whose major mental disorder is chronic, treatment based on strength-based rehabilitation and family psychosocial groups enables significant recovery and a return to a meaningful life in the community.[31]

One immediate implication of this new model of early intervention, recovery, and prevention: a seventeen- or eighteen-year-old with psychotic symptoms like those Alex had in 1998 would never hear a doctor say, "You have a severe and chronic psychiatric disorder that will worsen over time, and for which there is no cure."

In 1998, I was forty-three years old and had two teenage sons: one newly diagnosed with paranoid schizophrenia; the second, just two years away from the emergence of serious symptoms of another mental disorder. Still, through the fog of my own untreated depression, I was determined that though I'd missed the obvious in Alex until it was nearly too late, I would not let that happen with Sammy. Little did I know how much more complex my journey would become.

Chapter 2

EARLY SIGNS AND RISK FACTORS

Did you have any infectious diseases while pregnant with Alex?
None that I recall.

Here's what I wasn't asked about and didn't volunteer to Dr. C. about Alex during our interview at UCLA.

From the moment he was handed to me in the delivery room, Alex seemed not happy to be here. His eyes were bottomless, his expression grave. He spent his first three months writhing and screaming inconsolably, the word *colic* wholly insufficient to describe our collective suffering. It wasn't until his brother Sammy arrived that I realized just how different Alex was compared to other babies. Sammy cried only when he was hungry or wet. He made easy eye contact and loved to be stroked, hugged, and kissed—all the things Alex recoiled from as an infant.

Later, when I took Alex to play groups, he crawled away from the other toddlers to do his own thing, so we quit going. It wasn't that Alex appeared unhappy. He would sometimes sit and smile with satisfaction for no apparent reason. At ages two and three, while we were living in Washington, DC, Alex attended a Montessori preschool. Although he enjoyed the hands-on activities, his teachers often commented that he usually ignored them as well as the other children. There's no denying that his disinterest in other people was a set pattern by the time he was three.

After moving to Los Angeles, we enrolled Alex in a private elementary school that espoused the philosophy that reading and writing couldn't happen soon enough—if parents wanted to get their child on the academic fast track. Geoff and I jumped right onboard; that is, until Alex abruptly jumped off. He was only a month into the first grade when his teacher called to say that she thought he must be hard-of-hearing, since he routinely ignored her directions, especially the daily reading and writing drills she assigned her class of six-year-olds.

Although I knew this teacher was wrong about Alex's "deafness," we had him tested just in case. As expected, Alex wasn't deaf, although the tester told us he saw a visual learning disability. He suggested a form of remedial therapy we could do at home—for an hour every night. At the time, this sounded overwhelming and impossible to pull off given our schedules and my already depleted energy level from managing a full-time job and two kids under six—with my untreated depression. That's when we took Alex off the fast track and moved him (and us) to the far northern end of the San Fernando Valley where, at Highland Hall, a Waldorf school, Alex found his place anew in a gentle, old-world style education.

The Waldorf pedagogy, created by philosopher-reformer Rudolf Steiner in mid-nineteenth-century Vienna (and still going strong with independent schools operating throughout the United States and Europe), delays reading in favor of the integration of math and language learning into movement, music, drama, and drawing—in an effort to support the growth of the "whole child." In the third grade, reading is introduced with children's classics, such as Hans Christian Andersen's fairy tales. These stories are read aloud in a song and response style, with reading and writing coming last.[1] At Highland Hall, Alex was able to fully engage his imagination and learn in a more self-paced fashion while receiving gentle support for staying on track within a group.

After learning about the kinds of events and experiences that increase or decrease a child's risk for schizophrenia, I realized that we had lightened Alex's stress load by changing schools when we did. Based on both his inherited risk and early childhood behaviors, Alex was already facing intense internal pressures from a disease process that probably began before he was born and showed signs by his third year. Once he started elementary school, the learning difficulties he encountered also fit the profile now identified as belonging to the at-risk child.[2]

At the beginning of my learning process, I was deeply affected by the words used by Scottish parents to describe the infancies of children who went on to develop schizophrenia in the Edinburgh High Risk Study, one of the first ever done with families of schizophrenics. The most common phrase from the mothers, "[I]t was as if their child was in a world of his own," was the exact way I'd so often thought of Alex.[3]

Knowledge of schizophrenia as a long-term disease process has existed since the early twentieth century. These first Edinburgh High Risk Study results were published in the mental health literature as early as 1996, two years before Dr. C. took our family mental health history and diagnosed Alex. And yet, beyond her question about infections I might have had during my pregnancy, at no point in our interview did Dr. C. ask me whether Alex had had any developmental delays as a younger child, nor did she go beyond the "official" causes of death of family members already deceased. There was nothing unprofessional about Dr. C.'s conduct of this interview; the protocols for a psychiatric intake didn't then and *still don't* include such probing questions.[4] As a result, as Alex's intake psychiatrist, she made no attempt to find out about his life in between his birth and the period immediately before he entered the UCLA adolescent unit. It was as if this disease had manifested suddenly like the flu or measles. This couldn't have been further from the truth.

As the German researcher Joachim Klosterkötter wrote in a 2001 essay, the initial signs of the neurodevelopmental process that can lead to schizophrenia, the impaired body sensations, reduced tolerance to stress, increased emotional reactivity, and, especially, social deficits, "can make their first appearance anywhere from *two months to thirty-five years before the onset of the disorder* [italics mine]."[5]

THE SCIENCE OF RISK

Current research findings on risk factors and the early signs of schizophrenia are rapidly breaking new ground, but most clinicians view the disorder as it was viewed by their counterparts a century ago.[6] In an 1896 treatise, German physician Emil Kraepelin, who is credited with naming both schizophrenia and manic depression as diseases that are both genetic and biological in nature, observed that many of the children of his schizophrenic patients, especially those who would go on to develop the disease themselves, were "a little different in character and behavior from their peers—beginning in early childhood." Among the words he used to describe their behaviors was "peculiar." When I read this, I knew exactly what Kraepelin meant.

Kraepelin's definitions of schizophrenia and bipolar disorder as diseases— not character defects or evidence of the devil's handiwork—represented progress for 1900. The problem today is that much of the profession still holds a Kraepelinian view of these psychiatric disorders in one unhelpful respect: they assume that the worst patient outcomes documented over the past century are still the only possible outcomes for these disease processes. Stuck in "asylum era thinking,"[7] they focus their attention on the debilitating, full-blown end stage of the illness rather than on its beginning, when diagnosis and interventions might stand a chance of altering what they're treating as an inevitable course.[8]

Rachel Loewy, a University of California–San Francisco professor of psychology who serves as clinical director for PREP (Prevention and Recovery in Early Psychosis), a university-affiliated early psychosis clinic, points to the experience of some UCSF residents who staff the hospital's psychiatric ER as a legacy of this old way of thinking about schizophrenia. She notes that these about-to-be psychiatrists tend to regularly see the same chronically ill homeless men and women with severe and often untreated schizophrenia. Of course, Loewy says, interns still occasionally see a young person experiencing hallucinations or extreme paranoia for the first time. But now in San Francisco that patient is more often than not referred to the PREP clinic for treatment of his early psychosis—where he will usually recover or at least stabilize, rarely or never to return to the ER.[9]

Only 10 percent of thirty clients in the PREP clinic were hospitalized during their first year in the program, a rate that is much lower than what would be expected of this population, according to Robert W. Bennett, president of Family Service Agency, a partner with UCSF and the Mental Health Association of San Francisco in PREP.[10] This good news may be yielding another, inadvertent result; by keeping these patients out of the ER, the UCSF medical school's newest psychiatrists are not getting as full and detailed a picture of schizophrenia in its initial stages as they otherwise would.

Meanwhile, the body of observational data on those small differences that Kraepelin first noticed in the children of his schizophrenic patients has grown by leaps and bounds, with the first three-dimensional models of how psychiatric risk shows up in real lives over the first two decades of the lifespan now emerging. Intense international research efforts have focused in two directions: first, on those things that lead vulnerable people closer *to* a mental disorder, then, and more recently, on environmental factors that may steer them away *from* these same disorders.[11]

THE MAJOR HERITABLE MENTAL DISORDERS

Schizophrenia is characterized by disturbances in logical thinking, emotional expression, and interpersonal behavior. The cardinal "positive" symptoms are illogical thinking, hearing or seeing someone or something that isn't there, and rigidly held, false, illogical beliefs. "Negative" symptoms include social withdrawal, lack of motivation, and declining self-care. Schizophrenia is rare in children under the age of twelve, but as I discuss in later chapters, early signs of each of these symptoms are present in many children who go on to develop schizophrenia in adolescence and young adulthood.[12]

When **pediatric bipolar disorder** is present, the child's mood undergoes large swings, shifting from one extreme to the other. Such children are said to be "cycling" between a high mood, also called "mania," and a low state of depression. Bipolar disorder usually shows up in late adolescence or early adulthood, but it also can appear in younger children. It may begin in childhood as depression with or without periods of extreme irritation or as attention deficit hyperactivity disorder (ADHD).[13]

Although I focus first on the negative factors in a child's life that can increase risk, later I share some of the newest research on resiliency and prevention. For example, a higher IQ and a sociable temperament are two examples of mitigating factors that can diminish other risks.[14] Growing up in a stable home with loving, supportive parents is the most powerful "neuroprotector" a vulnerable child can have on her side.[15]

Environmental (nongenetic) negative risk factors for schizophrenia come in different forms. Having an older father is one surprising risk; the child of a man older than fifty is three times more likely to develop schizophrenia than children born to younger men; this is thought to be due to the DNA in the older father's sperm having mutated from environmental toxins.[16] Being bullied can significantly raise the same risk.[17] Living in an urban environment is another big negative, even if epidemiologists are not sure why. The bottom line is that a vulnerable young person can only take so many of these additional environmental insults before he reaches the point of no return.[18]

Alex, with his own particular mix of inherited vulnerabilities and stress factors, reached such a tipping point in puberty, when he first began to manifest the
so-called negative symptoms of schizophrenia, including a loss of motivation,
social and emotional withdrawal, a disinterest in hygiene and dress, and trouble
sleeping. The term *positive symptoms* refers to the more obvious behaviors we
think of as "crazy"—and they would unfortunately come too, a little later, as
they are known to right before the first *psychotic break*.[19]

Although subtle signs in Alex manifested slowly in the course of his
early and middle childhood, after he reached his fourteenth year, to say that
"all hell broke loose" would be an understatement. I was, then, not surprised
to later read national epidemiological data identifying fourteen as the year by
which half of all adult mental disorders begin, including anxiety disorders,
bipolar disorder, depression, eating disorders, conduct and oppositional disorders, psychosis, and schizophrenia.[20]

Scientists looking into this phenomenon attribute it to the tremendous
growth spurt that begins in puberty when an adolescent's brain, body, and
emotions are transformed as never before, or ever again. They cutely
describe it as a time when "moving parts get broken."[21] It has also been
noted that this is the age when the mental disorders affecting boys and girls
sharply diverge, with girls suddenly more vulnerable to depression, while
boys begin to populate clinics specializing in early psychosis. We don't
know why some pubescent children get derailed by this normal maturational
process, while others sail through, showing only the usual "growing pains"
of adolescence to worry their parents. Researchers are getting closer, but
we're not there yet. In the meantime, there are known warning signs.

Knowing risk factors and warning signs can save many children from
being diagnosed too late for the most effective treatment. This is already evident with autism, with parents alerted to possible behavioral signs such as a
baby avoiding eye contact, being slow to babble, or experiencing sudden
developmental regressions that might spell trouble. Largely as a result of lob-
bying efforts by parent advocacy organizations such as the Autism Society of
America and Autism Speaks, the American Academy of Pediatrics has offered
guidelines for physicians to begin screening babies for autism symptoms
beginning by the age of nine months in the course of well-baby visits.[22]

To help parents begin to think similarly about other childhood mental disorders, I provide information (see the textbox on page 51) reflecting the consensus of researchers looking into the ways that schizophrenia and bipolar
disorder can travel through families and show up in children and adolescents.

THE LOWDOWN ON PARENT-CHILD TRANSMISSION OF MENTAL DISORDERS

The *prevalence of bipolar disorder* (BP) in the general population is 2.2 percent. But if one parent has BP, the child has an 8 to 13 percent increased risk of developing a BP spectrum disorder, including attention deficit hyperactivity disorder symptoms and oppositional behavior, defined as a pattern of frequent disobedient, hostile, and defiant behavior that lasts for six months or more. This suggests that these symptoms of less severe disorders may reflect different ways BP manifests early in a person's life. The symptoms of second-generation BP children usually start earlier, before the age of 12. The child of a BP parent also has a 26.5 percent risk for any mood disorder, such as depression, with a 20.9 percent chance by age 12 and 40.8 percent by age 18 (versus 8.3 percent chance in offspring of healthy parents).[23]

The *prevalence of schizophrenia* (SZ) in the general population is 1.1 percent, but if a parent has schizophrenia, the child has a 10 to 12 percent increased risk of developing SZ. She also has a 17.1 percent chance of developing a personality disorder in the same spectrum (paranoid, schizoid, schizotypal), along with a 16 percent higher chance for any anxiety disorder and a 13 percent increased risk for a conduct disorder.[24]

So why don't consumers get evaluated for a mental health disorder even when they know a mental illness runs in the family and they may already be experiencing symptoms? Epidemiological research reveals a handful of common reasons. Many people fear the stigma if they admit that either they or a family member have a mental illness; they have no mental health insurance coverage; they have the same symptoms and so don't recognize them as anything out of the ordinary in a child; they believe people should "fix" signs of emotional or mental problems in themselves without professional help and psychiatric medications; or they say they don't believe mental health treatment works. Men are less likely to go for a mental health evaluation than women. Younger people, from eighteen to twenty-five, are the least likely to seek help or to get treated.[25] Of course, this age group is also the most susceptible to an onset of the two major psychotic illnesses, schizophrenia and bipolar disorder.

It isn't only consumers who are often tentative about getting treatment for clear and present symptoms. University of California–San Francisco professor of psychiatry Demian Rose, who serves as medical director at the PREP early psychosis clinic, complains that he still hears clinicians making comments such as "I'm going to wait until he's suicidal, because then I'll know for sure that he's depressed" or "If it isn't a full-fledged hallucination, I'm not going to do anything."[26]

Skeptics may wonder or worry that my intent here is simply to encourage parents to medicate their children at the first sign of emotional or mental distress. It is not. The good news is that there are often other good therapeutic options worth trying before psychiatric medications are indicated for a younger child. The bad news is that these better options are not always available to us.

Child psychiatrist Kiki Chang is an associate professor and director of Stanford University's Pediatric Bipolar Disorders Program. Because of his specialty and (acknowledged) research alliances with pharmaceutical companies, Chang has been the target of critics concerned about the substantial spike in diagnoses of pediatric bipolar disorder (and its common precursor ADHD) in children and their subsequent medication.[27] In an interview with the PBS series *Frontline*, Chang conceded that diagnoses and prescriptions had increased substantially for pediatric bipolar disorder over the previous decade—and he agreed with the criticism that not all of them were warranted. He then offered his own analysis of the reasons behind this spike.

"Overall, I'd have to say it is probably folks who don't have access to good psychosocial interventions or good family-based programs in their communities. There's not enough money in poorer areas, so they have to rely on medications more. . . . In a lot of places general psychiatrists who have no child psychiatry training are forced to treat kids because there's no one else to do it. Pediatricians, too."[28]

Stanford's Bipolar Disorders Program, which includes an adult and pediatric clinic, is one of the nation's best. In addition to medication therapies, it has offered adjunct therapies including psychosocial family groups and mindfulness for bipolar patients. It also created the first summer camp for bipolar kids, Camp Opehay. Because it is a research-based and teaching-based program, access to Stanford's treatment for bipolar adults and children is generally limited to participants in its clinical trials.

Elsewhere in the world, where state-of-the-art services are not generally available, the much-discussed rush to medicate[29] and general lack of access to psychosocial interventions can be traced to financial incentives that make it more profitable for insurance companies or HMOs to authorize a general practitioner or pediatrician to prescribe medications for childhood mental disorders rather than to offer the services of a trained psychotherapist. Here's why. A therapist might spend anywhere from six to twenty-six sessions of fifty-minute "person hours" with a client, whereas a prescription generally involves one psychiatric evaluation and a few three-month follow-ups. The math comparing the immediate cost savings between these two options is pretty easy to do. Although there are exceptions, notably the nonprofit health provider Kaiser Permanente® and a handful of others, most insurance companies have not demonstrated interest in the longer-term savings available with preventive mental health care.[30]

If the wills of the psychiatric profession and our political system were to align and make a fundamental shift to a system inclined toward preventive mental health care, there is robust science available to help make it happen. At the end of this chapter, I include a laundry list of the known childhood risk factors for schizophrenia that have emerged from the research of the past three decades. This list should be made known to all new parents—particularly those with a family history of mental disorders and addictions.

THE FINE PRINT OF PREDISPOSITION

Most parents—especially those who don't have a first-degree relative with schizophrenia or bipolar disorder—view themselves and their children as having a 0 to 2 percent risk for these diseases. In other words, they consider themselves the winners in the genetic crapshoot that separates the lucky from the unlucky among us.

Not so fast, researchers say.

This is where we get to the fine print of "predisposition." As parents, we pass on more than our "good" or "bad" genes. Actually, with the exception of a handful of diseases in which one gene is destiny—like Huntington's—there really isn't such a thing as "good" or "bad" genes. Most of the time, our genetic expressions give us varying degrees of vulnerability to physical and mental illnesses—subject to specific environmental triggers. As noted previously, when a grandparent or parent has schizophrenia, it's also possible for offspring to carry a vulnerability to a disease in the same "spectrum" as schizophrenia, such as schizoid personality disorder.[31] This same inherited liability for schizophrenia can alternately manifest as a learning disorder. Recent studies with "unaffected" children of schizophrenics have established their higher risk for a retinal eye defect that can produce a visual learning disorder.[32]

But it gets even more complicated. There is another, almost silent type of transmission that occurs when a well parent functions as a carrier for a psychiatric disorder. This occurs when he or she passes on a risk for the disease to offspring without manifesting its symptoms, or not manifesting them to a noticeable or bothersome degree. A carrier may have symptoms that are below the clinical threshold for a disorder; for example, a mother who displays what psychologists call "an idiosyncratic use of language," a low-level version of the same higher-level "thought-disorder" symptom (some simplify it further and call it a "thinking problem") that can occur in her adult child with psychosis.[33] This example is vivid to me because I discovered such a low-high symptom linkage between me and Alex.

I'd never given a name to this odd thought-speech dynamic I'd long wondered about in myself. It arose when I'd go "blank" mid-sentence, being briefly embarrassed by the words coming out of my mouth and scrambling to compensate with another clarifying sentence. When the thought-disorder concept was first introduced to me by research psychologist Deborah Levy, I readily recognized it. Levy, who directs a study of traits that commonly appear in family members of schizophrenics at Harvard's McLean Hospital, offered a useful example of a low-level version of this symptom with the phrase "Rectangularly speaking, the response to our study has been very positive from the local population."[34] This sentence suggests that something good happened as a result of Levy's recruiting process for her study but that the core logic of it is lost somewhere between the speaker's intention and the words she spoke. However, as soon as I heard it, I knew the speaker in question could easily have been me.

I trust you're getting the picture that everything about your family's medical and mental health history—from a relative's weird habits, addictions, and "moodiness" to any diagnosed medical or neurological condition (such as Alzheimer's or multiple sclerosis) and unexplained accidents—can be relevant to your or your child's mental health care today. When Stanford psychiatrist Kiki Chang was asked about the kinds of things he looks for in family history, here is some of what he said in another recent interview: "With family histories, we will go very closely and try to diagnose by proxy, asking the parents questions about their direct relatives (e.g., "Did your brother have this? Did he have a manic episode? Did he have a depressive episode?"). Often, if the patient had a family history of drug abuse or alcoholism, we find either depression or sometimes even bipolar disorder."[35]

As Chang's answer suggests, mood (depressive) and addictive disorders are now increasingly recognized as different faces of the same or related psychological disease processes. This is due, in part, to their high "comorbidity," meaning the co-occurrence of more than one disease in a person. Comorbidity among certain disorders is more common than others, for example, OCD and autism or depression with alcoholism. This latter comorbidity of a mood disorder with an addiction to alcohol or drugs is thought to also come as a result of the afflicted person self-medicating for prior symptoms—a significant factor in my own family history.[36]

Because so many of us don't know our family mental health histories, we're often thrust into the role of sleuths, connecting the dots between pieces of evidence drawn from at least three different realms—a child's behaviors, family history, and the relevant new science—to identify a vulnerability that may be lying in wait. Researchers, too—particularly those doing multigenerational family studies—do a more technical version of this same sleuthing.

In one extraordinary 1990 family study led by Elaine Walker of Emory University, researchers collected early home movies from fifteen families with a schizophrenic adult. As they suspected, early motor differences were vividly depicted in the home movies taken of these children (filmed with their siblings) decades before they went on to develop schizophrenia; in fact, these differences were evident by the age of eight. Researchers watched the home movies blind to the identity of which children were which. They easily identified the pre-schizophrenic children from their siblings because of their flatter emotional states (they showed less joy or distress) and less coordinated movements.[37]

So it seems we can add home movies to our checklist of potential sources of family history—and risk factors. The list grows larger.

HOW YOUNG?

Even knowing that schizophrenia manifests in strange and subtle behaviors long before its formal onset, I was still as amazed as anyone reading recent studies that document early psychotic symptoms in children as young as twelve and even five years of age. You may wonder as I did, *don't all five-year-olds play pretend and have imaginary friends*? The answer is yes, they do. However, researchers say, trained mental health workers using reliable diagnostic interview tools can tell the difference between ordinary childhood fantasies and any deeper signs of psychological trouble.[38] None of the children participating in these studies were identified at the beginning as mentally disturbed, making the documentation of their lives and vulnerabilities a process of discovery for these researchers.

One such study, the British Environmental Risk (E-Risk) Longitudinal Twin Study drew from a "base sample" formed in 1999–2000, during which 1,116 mothers with five-year-old twins participated in home-visit assessments. Participants represented the full range of socioeconomic status in the general population of England. The 2,232 children in the study were evaluated first at the age of five and then followed to age twelve with 96 percent retention—a high retention rate and an indication of the study's reliability.[39] As the word *environment* in the study title suggests, in addition to measurements of the children's mental health, interviewers assessed a wide range of factors in the child's family, school, and home that might contribute to a higher risk for psychosis.

First, in order to detect possible psychosis in the E-Risk Study children, interviewers explored garden-variety symptoms of psychosis with basic interview questions that were not unlike those posed to Alex. One such question was "Do you ever hear or see things that other people can't hear or see?" As it turns out, the vast majority (95 to 98 percent) of normal five-year-olds answer these questions as would the same proportion of normal sixteen- and thirty-year-olds from a general population, with a simple "no."[40]

In the E-Risk Study results, 169, or 7.9 percent (of 2,232 total children), answered "yes" to this question, putting them in the category of having a "probable" symptom of psychosis. But when researchers probed deeper, it was determined that only 90, or 4.2 percent, had a "definite" symptom of an auditory hallucination. To find out whether any of these children may have experienced a delusion, researchers asked, "Have you ever thought you were being followed or spied on?" Here, 54, or 2.5 percent, had the probable symptom, but in the end only fifteen or 0.7 percent were found to have the definite symptom of delusionary thinking.[41]

Once psychotic symptoms were identified and confirmed in these 125 children (out of the 2,232 screened), researchers then looked for common risk factors present in their lives. The most telling commonality to emerge about these seventy-one boys and fifty-four girls concerned the data showing that all the twelve-year-olds with current psychotic symptoms had had significantly more emotional, behavioral, and educational problems at age five than did their asymptomatic peers.

By following the same children from age five to twelve, researchers were able to track the worsening of their symptoms. It also mattered what sorts of psychological problems they had at age five. The most predictive, thus serious, symptoms present in their initial assessments were antisociality and hyperactivity, but symptoms also included childhood depression and anxiety. The researchers acknowledged that these symptoms, even the psychotic ones, were not specific to schizophrenia and can occur in the context of other disorders including ADHD, antisocial conduct, and depression and anxiety, and so pointed out that these symptoms may also be "developmental precursors" to other adult disorders.[42]

One particular cause for alarm: these children with early psychotic symptoms were also more likely to have engaged in self-harm, which, according to their mothers, included cutting themselves with razors and beating their heads against the wall; one child even attempted a hanging.[43] "Strikingly," the researchers wrote, "like young people with clinical psychosis, and adults with schizophrenia, children with psychotic symptoms were more likely to engage in self harm or suicidal behavior . . . and given the fact that children can conceal self harm from parents, the association between psychotic symptoms and self-harm may be underestimated here."[44]

Other important findings from the E-Risk Study about the *families* of these children included these facts:

- Approximately twice as many of the affected twelve-year-olds' relatives had been admitted to psychiatric units (forty-seven relatives).
- Twenty-nine relatives of the twins in the study had made suicide attempts.[45]

In addition to evidence of family psychiatric problems, researchers also looked at social and child-rearing factors in the affected children's lives, finding the strongest correlations with educational problems (70 percent), urban residence (64.8 percent), paternal age (31.8 percent), tobacco use (25 percent), and physical maltreatment (16 percent).

When commenting on what if anything should be done for children like those identified as prepsychotic in this study, the study authors recommended that such children be "actively assessed" but not necessarily rushed into treatment. Researchers also observed that the children's "psychotic symptoms generally occurred in the context of other childhood psychiatric problems,"[46] referring to disorders of lesser severity for which remedies such as parent psychosocial education and family or child psychotherapy were available.

It is one of the leitmotifs arising out of a number of the studies I've seen; a warning cry from researchers (albeit couched in careful clinical language) that, while the vast majority of kids grow out of their early childhood emotional and behavioral challenges, an important minority do not get better "on their own." Those at highest risk are living in households where there are other serious mental health problems present.

Results similar to the E-Risk Study on childhood mental disorders came from a longer-term study in a population known as the Dunedin Cohort (after the southeastern New Zealand city where the participants lived). These infants were all born in Dunedin between April 1972 and March 1973, totaling 1,037 children who were assessed at ten intervals between three and twenty-six years of age.

When 605 children from this cohort (who were not initially thought to be at high risk) were evaluated in prepuberty and again at ages twenty-six and thirty-two, investigators found that when psychotic symptoms were present in a child at age eleven, their presence was strongly predictive of later schizophrenia or of related personality disorders for that child in young adulthood. Specifically, 42 percent of those who later developed either schizophrenia or a related personality disorder had reported experiencing a psychotic symptom, such as a hallucination, when they were diagnostically interviewed at age eleven.[47] An important aspect of both the E-Risk and the Dunedin studies was that they were prospective, meaning they followed the children going forward and evaluated them using standard assessment tools. They did not depend on parental or patient recollections of symptoms. The specific age of the older children in these studies was also helpful to researchers. According to Terrie Moffitt, "On the one hand, preadolescents are cognitively mature enough to understand what the questions are about. They can provide valid self-reports of hallucinations and delusions. On the other hand, they have not yet learned by sad experience that they must conceal their psychotic symptoms to avoid stigma, ridicule, and rejection by others. Thus, preadolescents are willing to share frank self-reports with a sensitive interviewer."[48]

The summary that follows reflects a large body of longitudinal studies, including the E-Risk and Dunedin studies, as well as others, like the Edinburgh High Risk Study, that were retrospective, meaning they asked parents and the individuals themselves to look back at their lives as they grew up.

Another nuance of terminology needs elucidation. Sometimes the word *risk* describes an individual's exposure to a disease agent, such as a mother's flu during pregnancy. But a risk factor can also describe a simple fact of life; for example, your urban home or a traumatic life event, such as war or a natural disaster. If, as a parent, you recognize any of these psychotic or otherwise troubled behaviors in your child, you may choose simply to monitor her more closely and defer treatment decisions. But you may alternately decide that the symptoms are plentiful and worrisome enough to bring her for an immediate evaluation. I certainly wish I'd known the implications of Alex's behaviors and symptoms—and my own, for that matter—much sooner than I did.

THE CHILDHOOD RISK FACTORS FOR SCHIZOPHRENIA

Here's what the research tells us about the risk factors and early indicators about someone, including a child or an adolescent, who has an above-average risk of developing schizophrenia.

1. Presence in family history of any of these:[49]
   Schizophrenia
   Any other psychotic disorder (schizophrenia, bipolar disorder, severe
     depression with psychosis)
   Suicide
   Repeated hospitalizations for psychiatric disorders

2. Prenatal and parenting risk factors:[50]
    Older father[51]
    Maternal emotional stress during the first trimester; especially the
       loss of a spouse
    Obstetrical complications; any loss of oxygen
    Winter birth
    Maternal malnutrition or famine
    Disease agents: influenza, rubella, especially during the middle
       trimester[52]
    Chaotic household[53]
    Maternal depression[54]
    Physical maltreatment[55]
3. Social-economic risk factors:[56]
    Being a migrant or the offspring of migrants[57]
    Living in an urban environment
    Lower socioeconomic status
    Bullying by peers[58]
4. Behavioral Risk Factors in a Younger Child:[59]
    Sitting, walking, and talking later
    Lack of physical coordination in later childhood
    Fewer expressions of joy and flatter affect (emotional expression)
    A preference for solitary play at age four
5. Behavioral Risk Factors in an Older Child/Adolescent:[60]
    Lack of physical coordination; being viewed as clumsy at age sixteen
    Having two or fewer friends at seventeen
    Lower IQ, especially immediately before onset, and learning
       problems in school[61]
    Social anxiety and withdrawal
    Depression[62]
    Problems with working memory (the type that takes you from one
       end of a math problem to the other)
    Antisocial behavior and conduct disorders; problems with peers,
       teachers, authorities
    Acts of self-harm, including head banging and cutting; suicidal
       ideation
    Early tobacco smoking
    Cannabis use, especially three or more times per week and before
       age fifteen

With the exception of smoking cannabis and experiencing maltreatment between the ages of three and eight—two factors thought to have a significant "dose response" correlation with psychosis—each of the factors on this list bestows only a slight effect in adding to a vulnerable child's total risk. Scientists say it is in the aggregate and in combination with a family history of psychiatric problems that these factors take on significance.

This presents a challenge for researchers and consumers alike seeking to draw neat lines between cause and effect, risk and disease. For example, scientists calculate that 30 percent of the risk for schizophrenia can be traced to maternal prenatal infections, lending urgency to research into this category of preventable risk.[63] One Finnish study—drawing on the enormous bank of statistical data available in the national birth registry as well as hospital discharge records—began with the hypothesis that a specific upper–urinary tract infection during pregnancy might be such a schizophrenia risk factor. After following 9,596 women who were treated for this infection while pregnant, researchers found that the two factors—schizophrenia and the infection—did not connect, except when *one other variable* was present: a family history of schizophrenia. If the mother had a parent or sibling with schizophrenia, the effect of the prenatal urinary tract infection in raising her child's risk was five times greater than those mothers who had the infection but did not have a family history.

Further statistical analysis by the Finnish researchers narrowed their finding down to this: an estimated 38 to 46 percent of offspring born between 1947 and 1990 who developed schizophrenia had both a prenatal exposure to this infection and a positive family history of psychotic disorders. From this they concluded that a higher risk for schizophrenia resulted from the synergistic action of both factors. By implication, neither factor alone would have been sufficient, making it what scientists call a gene × environment, or G × E, effect.

When used to study and describe the causes of mental illness, a G × E effect usually comes under the banner of the "vulnerability hypothesis." This theory and the research that supports it identify factors in a person's environment (for example, a urinary tract infection) that can "turn on" a person's genetic "switch"—the gene or genes that confer greater vulnerability to a disease such as schizophrenia). One of the questions the Finnish results raised was whether a woman's family mental health history should be integrated into her primary care and maternal care records as a matter of course.[64]

In later chapters, I discuss G × E interactions that have been identified as most likely to cause depression in predisposed children and adults—as compared to those who do not carry a genetic vulnerability for depression—when both groups experience the same environmental stressors. By applying the scientific method—creating control groups that don't have the disorder or carry the genetic risk, and by keeping researchers "blind" to these variables as they compile results—such studies are now obtaining quantifiable, replicable results that show who's at highest risk and why.

Other G × E research is going in another tantalizing direction, showing that when certain environmental interventions are made, a child with a "bad" gene, one conferring genetic vulnerability to a mental illness such as ADHD or bipolar disorder, can actually have an advantage over his genetically protected peers. In 2009, journalist David Dobbs amassed an impressive cross-section of this sort of surprising positive G × E research in an article in the *Atlantic* titled "The Science of Success."

Among the most interesting studies Dobbs cited was one by Marian Bakermans-Kranenburg at Leiden University. This professor of child and family studies tracked the behaviors of toddlers who were at high risk of developing a serious disorder for two reasons: by ages two or three, they already displayed troubling behaviors associated with ADHD and conduct disorders, and they had an alternative version of a gene associated with ADHD known as DRD4 (which processes the neurotransmitter dopamine). Interestingly, the study involved two groups of toddlers, with both displaying the same symptoms of hyperactivity and hitting, kicking, screaming behaviors—but with only one group carrying the at-risk gene for ADHD.[65]

The mothers of both groups of children were given special training, using videotape of themselves interacting with their children to identify how they responded to them. The mothers were then taught new, more sensitive and effective ways to respond to a child's cue—for example, recognizing when he wanted some soothing from Mom—such as having him sit on her lap and being read a story—before problem behavior escalated.

Over eighteen months, both groups of children benefited from their mothers' newly learned responses, but the final results defied researchers' expectations. Instead of those children with the "good" gene benefiting the most from this enhanced parenting environment—as would be expected, using the vulnerability hypothesis as a guide—it was the genetically vulnerable ones (with the "bad" alternative DRD4 ADHD susceptibility gene) who outperformed their peers. Their problem behaviors were reduced by a whopping 27 percent, compared to 11 percent in the genetically protected group. Somehow, the vulnerability of these at-risk children had translated into a greater receptivity to a positive intervention.

Given such results, it's easy to picture a future time when parents will have genetic information about themselves and their children in hand and will be able to use it to take advantage of other new non-pharmacological mental health treatments and prevention strategies. This area of research may also finally help answer some tantalizing questions, such as why, after so much evolutionary adaptation, mental illness remains at such stubbornly high rates in the human population—by pointing to the possibility that, when appropriately nurtured, these "bad" genes can turn "super-good" and bestow learning and adapting advantages.

Perhaps this research will also eventually shed some light on the porous boundary between "madness" and creative genius. I can only imagine if and how this type of knowledge might have helped me better parent my artistically gifted but increasingly withdrawn and tormented son Alex in the period between his fifth and fifteenth years. Short of such breakthroughs, we are left with the imperative to know our family histories of mental illness and to learn the language of basic neuroscience: the signs and environmental risk factors that can increase a child's vulnerability. With this information, we will do what we can with the resources currently available to us.

One cautionary note: as we become more informed and adept at spotting signs of possible trouble in our children, it's important to keep in mind that the majority of late walking and talking toddlers and withdrawn or antisocial kids *do not* go on to develop mental disorders. Still, the evidence makes increasingly clear that the observation first made by Emil Kraepelin more than one hundred years ago—that a significant number of individuals later diagnosed with schizophrenia have a number of common and often peculiar traits and experiences during childhood and adolescence—has only gained significance with the benefit of substantial research. In the realm of preventive mental health, this data has already proven to be an essential tool.

Chapter 3

"BOYS WILL BE BOYS" AND OTHER LIES WE TELL OURSELVES AT 3:00 A.M.

Alex did well during his six years in the Waldorf setting of Highland Hall. He was well liked by his teachers and made some friends. Then, between the ages of nine and thirteen, several big changes took place in his life. I separated from his father. My sister Rita, by then a heroin addict to whom Alex was exceptionally close and who, I learned later, he emulated, took another nosedive. And my mother, who thought of Alex, her first grandson, as the sun, moon, and stars, died suddenly of a heart attack—for Alex it represented many losses in a short time.

I spent much of those years alternating between grief, panic, and depression, so I was not of much help to him. Alex's tipping point appeared to come when we moved from Northridge to Santa Monica, forcing him to leave the safety of his Waldorf cocoon and enter the wild west of a big, public junior high school.

The negative effects of all these changes manifested quickly in him. Instead of quiet and introverted, he became sullen, angry, and withdrawn. In the course of three months, he transformed from a thirteen-year-old who liked to come right home after school to play video games and eat cookies to one who surreptitiously got his kicks from smoking pot, tagging (*tagging* refers to painting graffiti on buildings, houses, and street signs—and I had no idea what it was when I first heard Alex's therapist use the word), stealing, and many other awful things I wouldn't hear about until later.

Admittedly, while all this was happening, I had my own reasons for not wanting to connect Alex's problems with the divorce, since ending the marriage had been my idea. I now understand that this choice to break up our family when Alex was nine contributed to his deterioration. It was probably not nearly as significant as his family history of mental disorders and the pot he smoked in junior high school, but it added yet another ill-timed, high-stress event nonetheless.

A landmark longitudinal study that became the best-selling book *The Unexpected Legacy of Divorce* surprised many professionals and divorced parents who, like me, were confident of our children's ability to weather family breakups without long-lasting negative emotional consequences. The stunner from this study was the finding that the majority of the 131 participants interviewed after twenty-five years told how the major negative impact of their parents' divorce didn't hit them until early adulthood. In their mid-to-late twenties, they felt strong apprehensions about marrying for fear of experiencing divorce again as adults. And they stayed single much longer than their peers. They experienced high levels of anxiety in their intimate relationships and felt a loss of closeness with their parents following the divorce, especially with their fathers.[1]

The science of mental illness tells us that however a child's family becomes destabilized—whether though divorce, unemployment, homeless-ness, natural disaster, or acts of violence between parents—any sustained period of family instability in consort with heavy genetic loading can con-spire to convert a child's vulnerability into an adolescent's nightmare.[2]

CHARDONNAY, CANNABIS, AND OTHER DRUGS OF CHOICE

Another undeniable risk factor for Alex at this time was my untreated depression[3] and the excess alcohol consumption that went with it. I regularly depended on anywhere from a half to a whole bottle of wine to get through a night—just enough to allow me to stop paying attention to my feelings, or his. It was what I thought I needed to keep things together and get through the divorce. To Alex and Sammy, my "checking out" was a form of aban-donment, as real as packing a bag and driving away. It was all too painful to take in at the time, but it was nonetheless true.

One harder-to-miss signpost of my son's rapid demise was the straight Fs he received at the end of eighth grade at Santa Monica Junior High School. Alex had never before failed a class, let alone a whole grade. A sharp drop in an adolescent's cognitive abilities, which can manifest as suddenly poor grades, is another potential sign of an early phase of psychosis.[4] And it makes sense; when you see MRI images of the brains of individuals scanned at the onset of the schizophrenia disease process, the parts of their brains that control such critical faculties as communication between thought and perception and memory are literally shrinking.[5]

It was around then that I found the marijuana stuffed in a shoebox in his bedroom. Confronted about the pot, he confessed—being new at this, Alex's ability to lie was still crude. He admitted to smoking marijuana and to selling bags of it to younger kids to support his new habit, something he'd been apparently trained to do by the local gangbangers who recruited junior high kids for this purpose. Here I thought I'd moved us into a nice neighborhood in Santa Monica—only to discover that it had been adopted as a training ground for the notorious street gang, the Crips.

I became a whirling dervish. Research into rehab options for a fourteen-year-old neo-criminal and pothead yielded dozens of programs, from camps patterned on basic training (most of these located in Idaho or Utah with a frightening militaristic tone to their descriptions), to cushy therapeutic retreats in Malibu or the Berkshires. Neither extreme seemed right to me. So I kept looking.

In those pre-Internet days, the personal recommendations I got from friends and acquaintances who were involved in Alcoholics Anonymous and other twelve-step programs proved the most valuable. That's how I found the Catherine Freer Wilderness Therapy Program based in Bend, Oregon, which still operates a highly regarded summer program like the one Alex attended, and which has since founded a boarding school for troubled teens.[6] Reading their brochure and talking to them by phone, I became convinced that Freer offered the right balance of boot camp and therapy. There would be a psychologist supervising the trek counselors, with pre- and post-trek parent meetings held with the trekkers and counselors present.

To get Alex on a plane, I described the trip as a backpacking adventure with other boys and girls his age; proposing it as a change of scenery after a dreadful year. In other words, I lied. Alex rolled his eyes and protested loudly but quickly gave in. He knew he was in big trouble—especially after I found and removed cigarettes and a bag of pot from his backpack the night before his departure.

Things went poorly from the start. After two weeks, the trek psychologist called to strongly suggest Alex stay with them for another three-week session. "He's dealing with a lot of anger," he explained. No doubt about that. The following journal entry was written while Alex was on a "Solo," a three-day trek on his own with a tarp and some meager rations. His assignment was to find his emotions.

They told my mom and she bought it that I had to stay here another three weeks because I wasn't putting any effort into my treatment. Shit, I've been trying to get in touch with my feelings. What if I can't find any? Most of the time I'm just kind of vague. Like okay or not okay. It didn't really sink in that this wasn't normal until my Solo. Then I was kind of surprised and hopeless, which, get this, my counselor Rick says is a good thing.

The state Alex described in this entry has a name: flat affect. It's a primary symptom of depression, but it's also a warning sign and negative symptom of schizophrenia.[7] In my memory of the years leading up to this time, Alex had been progressively shutting down his feelings since before the divorce. His next entry confirmed that.

I'm trying to get in touch with my feelings. I'm having a hard time 'cause I haven't had feelings in a long time for some reason. My counselors say it's the drugs but I don't know. It seems to me I didn't have any feelings before I started using either.

Studies have shown that an adolescent's risk for psychosis from cannabis—after smoking the amount of marijuana Alex confessed to—is raised fivefold. And that's even after they stop.[8] How much was he using? In another part of his trek journal Alex wrote that he smoked "bud" two to six times a week, usually during afternoons or evenings with his friends. His second choice of substance was alcohol, which he admitted to drinking (until he became drunk) two to five times per week. He added that he'd blacked out twice. Lastly, he mentioned acid, which he said he'd tried twice—and "liked a lot."

When asked by his counselor (and recorded in his journal) how many times he'd tried to quit using drugs, he said never. About how he might be different after beginning to use these drugs, he admitted having a shorter attention span. He also admitted to having trouble reading.

Once it was decided to have Alex do a second trek, the Freer coordinator called from Bend to suggest that Geoff and I attend the family meeting that would occur at the end of the third week. Since Alex would be repeating the program, trekking for a total of six weeks, this meeting would be happening between his two sessions, and they thought it might help Alex's therapeutic process if he had a chance to see us. I knew that meant I would go by myself, since, at that time, well in advance of Alex's hospitalization, Geoff thought his troubles were more about disobedience than any psychological issue. Geoff stayed home with Sammy, and I flew alone to Portland, feeling vulnerable and nauseous most of the trip—and that was before I heard Alex confess his litany of crimes.

—⁓—

We parents met in a group of ten—all mothers except for two fathers present. Leading the group was the Freer consulting psychologist who came to Bend from Portland to administer this session. Two trek counselors who'd been with the kids, hiking by day and leading therapy around the campfire at sundown, also joined our circle. And then the kids filed in, seven in all.

Alex was the tallest, having reached six feet by the age of fourteen. When he approached me, he kept his eyes locked on the ground, avoiding my gaze even after he sat down. My spirits sank. He looked several pounds lighter, with a scratched, tanned face and arms. There was an air of quiet fury about him, like a wild horse resisting being broken.

After thanking us for coming, the psychologist got right down to business. "Parents, your children have some things to tell you about behaviors they've carried on at home."

And then the real theater started.

Josh, a slight boy standing barely five feet two and looking more like a twelve-year-old than his reported sixteen years, got up to speak first. But first he walked to other side of the circle to face his petite, meticulously groomed mother, who sat with her legs pulled back against a log. I watched all the color drain from her face.

"I've been skipping school a couple times a week and signing your name to the parent slip." Josh said in a soft voice. "Then I slashed a bunch of car tires and tagged our entire neighborhood."

Josh's mother appeared to shrink in size as she listened to each of her son's disclosures. I couldn't help but identify with her dismay.

Jimmy, of Asian descent with a tattoo of a hammer on his forearm, went next.

"I've been smoking pot and robbing houses for a year and a half. Never got caught until now."

Jimmy's father, a short man with graying hair and a confused expression, cleared his throat. He apologized for interrupting and then asked Dr. Walker the question of the hour. "I don't understand why he does these things. My son doesn't need any money."

The doctor assured Jimmy's father that his was a good question and then went on to explain how teenagers steal as a "substitute" for a drug high. Whether shoplifting, tagging, or destroying private property in an upscale suburban neighborhood, the behavior produces adrenalin rushes much like those they might get by ingesting drugs. The purpose of these behaviors, the doctor explained, was to avoid underlying psychological issues.

Next, a chunky thirteen-year-old girl with a cropped haircut rose slowly to her feet, her stomach and rear-end barely contained by tight, low-slung jeans that were filthy from three weeks of trekking. She told us her name, Amy, and wiped tears on the sleeve of her sweatshirt before sharing.

"I slept with anyone who'd help me feed my coke habit," Amy began.

I don't think I heard much of what Amy said after that. As sympathetic as I felt for Amy's mother, whose face was already red and wet from crying, I concluded it would be even worse to be there as the parent of a teenage girl instead of a boy. Then I'd have to add pregnancy to the list of things to worry about.

When Amy sat down, it was seventeen-year-old Chloe's turn to speak. With her long blonde hair still neatly combed and plump lips parted seductively, Chloe looked like a soap opera vixen. Perhaps because she was the oldest trekker, or, as I learned later, because it was her second consecutive summer in the program, Chloe demonstrated the most petulant attitude of the group. As she stood staring at the ground, I wondered if she would speak at all. After some stern prodding from the psychologist, Chloe turned to her parents and offered her confession, still maintaining her disinterested, put-upon pose—a confession that involved my son.

"I snuck some joints in my underwear and got Alex and me in trouble. Now, I have to carry all the food for the rest of the trek." Changing her tone, Chloe seemed to end on a repentant note. "And that's what I deserve for not being sincere about coming here."

I was furious, ready to blame this girl for getting Alex in even more trouble than he'd managed on his own. But then it was my son's turn to speak, and all such thoughts fell away.

For the first time since I'd arrived, Alex looked at me. His discomfort with the situation couldn't have been clearer. Soon I knew why.

"I smoked pot with my friends every day before and after school. I stole stuff from stores and broke into some apartments. I've been tagging since Christmas vacation. I stole about seven bikes and gave 'em to my guys for pot. Oh, and one time I threw a little kid off his bike and took it from him. Then we all laughed at him crying on the ground."

I covered my face, deeply ashamed for having created such a monster. Finally, I asked, "How could you have been so cruel to that little boy?"

Alex looked sheepish and clueless. "I didn't really think about it."

At the end of the family meeting, I got one awkward hug from my son. He dropped his hands quickly. As he stepped back and away from me, he mumbled, "Thanks for coming, Mom."

I was at a complete loss for words; I was, I suppose, still in shock. My tears made it hard to see as I watched him pick up his enormous backpack and return to the trail behind the other trekkers. I felt completely drained of energy as I got back in the rental car and found my way down the mountain to the Bend airport. The flight back home to Los Angeles was also a blur. I was stuck in my feelings of shame and horror at the transformation of my sweet, sensitive son into a thief, bully, and drug dealer. In the days and weeks that followed, I remember feeling only an aching, unending fear that I'd already lost him.

BAD CONDUCT

Having a "conduct disorder" during early childhood or puberty puts a boy at high risk for becoming an antisocial young man and/or a psychotic adolescent.[9] I find there's an enormous amount of ignorance of and resistance to this diagnosis—or even the fact that frequent aggressive behavior in children can constitute a mental disorder. Put simply, a conduct disorder is when "boys being boys" crosses the line and becomes delinquency. Delinquency means breaking the law or the rules if it's a younger child—not just once or twice, but often. Romanticized in the film *West Side Story* and glorified in Gangsta Rap, delinquency means hurting people and stealing their property.

Certainly I missed the signs of a conduct disorder in Alex at age fourteen. In addition to the distractions created by my own declining state of mind, another reason I believe I didn't see it was that I was *so* prepared by the omnipresent cultural messages predicting every teenager's slide into extreme moodiness and disobedience that I didn't see the reality slouching in front of me. I expected the worst, and got it. With this filter, I didn't recognize actions that went well beyond an adolescent's "normal" attempts to establish his independence. In retrospect, it was wishful thinking on my part. Another word for it is *denial*.

At the time, Alex's father, Geoff, was seeing our son's bad behavior with a clearer eye than I was. But his response—to punish Alex by taking away privileges, adding chores, and grounding him—proved unsuccessful. He was right that Alex should have been punished. The problem was that by this time our son's psychological problems were running so deep—greater discipline was just not enough of a response.

With hindsight, it's far easier to see the worrisome larger picture evident in Alex's flunking classes, taking and dealing drugs, and committing petty acts of vandalism like "tagging"—even carrying out the act of cruelty against a younger child that he'd admitted to on the trek. Of course, I didn't know he had done all those things until that parent meeting. Before that, I knew only that that he appeared glum and angry around me, and, in his mannerisms and dress, he had begun emulating rappers whose lyrics turned my stomach. Still, I'd seen these as signs of a passing phase, not as aspects of a worrisome deeper problem.

WHEN ACTING OUT CROSSES THE LINE

Three different diagnoses may apply to these problem behaviors.

Oppositional defiant disorder (ODD) consists of more than six months of rule breaking, temper tantrums, hostility toward authority, and school and home disruptions committed by a child.

Conduct disorder (CD) applies when a youngster violates the rights or physical person of others. CD includes bullying, harming animals, destroying property, theft, assault, and other serious harmful behaviors.

Antisocial personality disorder (ASPD) is defined as a pervasive pattern of disregard for, and violation of, the rights of others that begins in childhood or early adolescence and continues into adulthood.

Some professionals use the term *antisocial* to refer to behaviors that could fit into any of these three named disorders.[10]

A small but alarming number of children and teens—believed to be up to 10 percent of all children[11]—engage in frequent, serious forms of antisocial behavior. It's the frequency and severity of the behaviors that make them pathological.[12] That's when professional treatment involving the whole family is indicated. Alex's wilderness therapy trek represents one such treatment option, something he eventually acknowledged had been important in getting him off the "wrong track." It certainly woke me up.

WILL HE GROW OUT OF IT?

One question that bedevils parents dealing with a child's or teenager's chronically bad conduct is how to know whether he'll simply "grow out of it." I remember voicing concern about Alex during this period to family and friends, and several responded by saying I shouldn't worry; it was normal "acting out." It would pass.

Some chilling findings have emerged from the Dunedin Cohort to demonstrate that when antisocial behaviors begin early in younger boys—psychologists call this "childhood-onset conduct disorder"—the boys do much worse as they age compared to those who begin showing antisocial behaviors later in adolescence. When followed to age twenty-six, the young men who had childhood-onset conduct disorders were found to have worse mental health problems. They had more psychopathic personality traits, substance dependence, financial problems, work problems, and drug-related and violent crime, including violence against women and children.[13]

But not all of them went this route. So, again, how can you predict which ones will do this badly? Researchers looked into this issue retrospectively and found that the risk factors in their childhoods that best predicted the children who would make this negative slide from misbehaving boy to delinquent young man had little to do with the child himself, and everything to do with what was going on in his family.

According to Terrie Moffitt: "A family history of mental health problems; alcoholism, drug addiction, ADHD, or antisocial personality, is a very accurate way to predict which youngsters who have conduct problems will grow out of them, versus which will go on to develop a more serious prognosis as young adults. Of those kids with [such a] family history, over 75 percent had persistent conduct problems that lasted into adulthood."[14]

Moffitt and her colleagues acknowledged that parents with these sorts of problems are often resistant to entering family therapy or a parent training program. However, they point out that the predictive value of this data can help social workers and mental health providers when they encounter such children—or when an agency is forced to intervene after a report of mal-treatment surfaces in such a family.[15]

As if that's not bad enough, the news from researchers looking at child-hood conduct disorders gets even worse. The bad behaviors of these young boys doesn't just put them at risk for anti-sociality, criminality, and jail time in their young adulthood. It can also spell psychosis. "The Antecedents of Schizophrenia," a meta-study done in 2008 of eleven birth cohorts from seven countries, provided a composite picture of the qualities of the pubescent male who was at the most elevated risk of developing schizophrenia. I was struck by the number of studies showing that boys who went on to develop schizo-phrenia had had conduct problems when they were young. The word *exter-nalizing* is often used to describe their early problem behaviors, such as those tracked in the previously noted Leiden study of unruly toddlers.[16]

Results from many places and studies all point in the same direction. One Baltimore survey followed boys who had been referred to a child guid-ance clinic, and who later developed schizophrenia. Researchers found anti-social behavior to be a consistent presence in their childhoods and adoles-cences. Meanwhile, the girls who later developed schizophrenia from the same cohort had more "internalizing" behavior; for example, mood disorders (like depression) during early adolescence. In school records from a Massa-chusetts study, boys who would develop schizophrenia were often described as "disagreeable" in grades seven through twelve.[17] When adolescents in Great Britain who had displayed antisocial behavior and would later develop schizophrenia were asked to look back at early puberty and rate their own behaviors, those who proved to be at the highest risk for later schizophrenia saw themselves at age thirteen as having been shyer and more socially awk-ward than their peers. Interestingly, they did not see their younger selves as antisocial.[18]

Having been the mother of a shy, withdrawn twelve-year-old who became an antisocial fourteen-year-old and then, a few years later, developed schizophrenia, these two qualities—social awkwardness and anti-sociality—don't seem mutually exclusive, quite the contrary. It's not hard to see and feel the anger brewing under the awkwardness of many twelve-year-old boys, mine included. I'm convinced my son was desperate to be stopped.

Chapter 4

BEFORE THE STORM: PRE-ONSET PSYCHOSIS

September 1995

After Alex's summer in wilderness therapy, we knew we had to put as much distance as possible between him and the buddies who'd taught him everything he now knew about LA gang life. We decided on a small boarding school ninety minutes to the north called Happy Valley, recommended by a friend whose low-achieving son had found new direction there. Money for the steep tuition came from my Aunt Lillian, to whom I'd appealed, saying I didn't want what happened to my sister Rita to happen to Alex. Though baffled, she quickly agreed.

Alex was anything but happy about being shipped off to Happy Valley School, but he could do little about it. At fourteen, he didn't drive, had no money of his own, and was still feeling sheepish after his summertime confessions of disobedience and mayhem. As bad as it is for any parent to stand by as a son or daughter implodes at age fourteen or fifteen, you can at least be grateful about the timing. It's far more difficult to face the same problems in a legally "of age" adolescent of eighteen or nineteen. Of course, it's hard to make any teenager do something he doesn't want to do. But at fourteen and fifteen, a parent can usually convince him to give something a try—at least until he finds his own reasons for being there.

Because Happy Valley School was known for its close community of dedicated teachers and eclectic group of students, we hoped it would give Alex the same sort of nurturing environment in high school that Highland Hall had provided during his elementary years. Set on a chaparral laced with vineyards, ranches, and vacation spas in the town of Ojai, the school was far enough away from his old scene to keep him out of trouble but close enough so that we could reach him in a hurry if things went wrong—and, of course, they eventually did.

But for the next two years, with some rough patches, Happy Valley worked well for Alex. His cultural heroes went from Snoop Dog to Jack Kerouac and the Beat poets. He also began painting again, encouraged by another wonderful art teacher. The biggest lifesaver for Alex at Happy Valley was its resident student counselor, Zackery Terry, who quickly gained Alex's trust. With Zack's input, Alex, who had never acted before, was given the lead role in *Suicide in B Flat*, a dark, edgy play by Sam Shepard. In a brilliant counterintuitive bit of casting, Alex played the part of the character whose job it was to talk his best friend out of killing himself. I drove up to Ojai on the night of the premiere fearing he would blank out onstage or simply bow out at the last minute; I was instead stunned by my son's flawless, believable performance. I hoped the worst might be behind us.

As good as Happy Valley was for Alex, it proved to be another temporary respite rather than a long-term solution. His decline now took on an inevitable quality: confusing, terrifying to watch. I later learned that schizophrenia usually begins with losing the ability to organize things or your thoughts, isolating yourself from other people, bouts of paranoia, and having hygiene going by the wayside. At this stage, symptoms come and go, with the person's grip on reality still stronger than the disease. Looking back, I see that staving off Alex's worst symptoms for a year or two longer was important since it gave him some basic confidence and life skills that would reemerge and become important later. I feel the same way about the private schools that had eaten up so much of our savings—I can see their value in his thinking and abilities today.

In contrast, by the end of Alex's freshman year, the decline in his academic performance, after initially stabilizing, became a major worry. He had much less ability to sustain attention, with the notable exception of his art work, which still earned him As and accolades. Otherwise, he crashed and burned, with an insufficient GPA to pass either the ninth or tenth grade. Alex's emotional state got progressively unsteady, too, with regular alarming incidents necessitating my attention: days when he wouldn't leave his room, the night he broke into a storage area to get a book he wanted (rather than simply asking a teacher for it), and several times when he got caught with banned substances: cigarettes, pot, and, once, LSD. And yet, because the students and faculty were so tightly knit, Alex gained a sense of community and some close friendships from his time at Happy Valley; two with male friends that he holds dear to this day. It was another buffer to help Alex make a softer landing when his "crash" finally came.

I feared that that day was already upon us when one morning, near the end of Alex's sophomore year, Zack called me to say he thought Alex could no longer handle the pressure of being there. He had fallen into a depression and had talked to Zack about suicide. I called in sick and drove there immediately to bring him home. Alex made it through two school years at Happy Valley. It was April 1996.

DETECTING EARLY PSYCHOSIS IN TEENAGERS

During this same time period when Alex was in Ojai slowly losing his ability to think, speak, and sleep normally, a quiet revolution began in the mental health field concerning how and when to treat the disease process that was responsible for Alex's accumulating losses. In the mid-to-late 1990s, several groups of behavioral scientists set out to tackle schizophrenia with an eye toward someday being able to stop and reverse the progression of this disorder in its youngest victims.[1] Their initial goal was the more modest one to document the pre-schizophrenic markers of disintegration. Many of their colleagues considered these efforts futile, and, as these early psychosis researchers got closer to their main objective of treatment, some even used the word *dangerous*.[2]

This more strident criticism wouldn't gain traction until several years later; for the time being, the researchers were only seeking data. To obtain it, a consortium of research centers was formed to run a thirty-month observational study known as the North American Prodrome Longitudinal Study (NAPLS).[3] It involved eight research sites in the United States and Canada. Among the study's total 888 participants, 372 were young people deemed at high risk of psychosis, with the remainder serving as unaffected controls. Among the participants who had begun the study "at risk," 82.1 percent had received psychosocial and/or pharmacological treatment prior to entry.[4]

The same research objective to study the prepsychotic disease process was being tackled simultaneously in other parts of the world. In Israel,[5] researchers gave population-wide mental health evaluations to draft-age youth at conscription, and then reevaluated these individuals after multi-year intervals. A similar broad study was performed in Finland. In these and several subsequent undertakings, the same low-level psychotic symptoms and precursor mental disorders were identified in a significant minority of young people. So were certain common high-risk behaviors, such as substance abuse, found to be present in these youths in the years leading up to their first episode of psychosis.

From observing the at-risk participants in the NAPLS study over two and one-half years, researchers pinned down a typical time frame between the beginning of psychotic symptoms and the onset of a full-blown psychotic disease (including schizophrenia, bipolar disorder, major depression with psychotic features, and other schizophrenia spectrum personality disorders). They referred to this in-between time as the "prodrome" period, meaning predisease, more popularly called "early psychosis," and they found that it could last anywhere from one to five years.

They found that young people in a prepsychotic state typically became extremely depressed, to the point where neuroscientists now think depression must be part of the disease process of schizophrenia, rather than simply a response to the anxiety brought about by fleeting psychotic symptoms. In a more recent study, depression occurred in 80 percent of young people at one or more phases of their first episode of psychosis. A combination of depression and suicidal thinking was present in 63 percent of this same group. Depression in this early phase has been found to be the most significant predictor of future depression and acts of self-harm.[6]

The NAPLS research team found that 35 percent of the at-risk young people in their study who had been initially diagnosed with psychotic symptoms progressed to a full-blown psychotic illness within two and a half years of symptom recognition. Of course, that meant that 65 percent did not. This should not be construed to mean that these (not psychotic) young people went home healthy and happy. The majority of the so-called false positives were diagnosed with other serious psychological disorders.[7]

THE BEST PREDICTORS OF SCHIZOPHRENIA IN HIGH RISK YOUTH

- A genetic risk of schizophrenia combined with a recent sharp deterioration in cognitive or social functioning
- Higher levels of suspicion/paranoia
- Greater social impairment
- High levels of unusual thought content
- A history of substance abuse

If a young person showed any *two or three of these variables*, their likelihood of conversion to a full-blown psychotic illness rose from 35 percent to anywhere from 68 to 80 percent.

—From the North American Prodrome Longitudinal Study (NAPLS)[8]

Several of the clinicians who carried out this initial observational research immediately went on to work in clinical trials so they could apply and test two specific treatments: a form of talk therapy adapted for psychotic patients called cognitive behavioral therapy (CBT)[9] and two new so-called second-generation atypical antipsychotic medications. The researchers' goal was to see if anything they offered could delay, lessen the severity of, or prevent schizophrenia—if and when it came. Once again, even the use of the word *prevention* in connection with schizophrenia generated alarm bells within their profession.[10]

—⚬—

Patrick McGorry is the Irish-born Australian psychiatrist who, by the late 1990s, had become the lightning rod in this debate. He earned this distinction by being one of the first to make the leap from simply observing to intervening with prepsychotic young people, and then by being vocal about it. Controversy continues to follow McGorry. In 2010, the year he was named "Australian of the Year" for his advances in preventive public mental health, McGorry was simultaneously labeled George Orwell's worst nightmare by a chorus of more extreme anti-psychiatry critics and derided in nearly as shrill terms by some professional peers.[11]

McGorry operated then, as he does now, out of an adolescent mental health treatment and research center affiliated with the University of Melbourne. That's where, in 1999, he recruited fifty-nine people between the ages of fourteen and thirty who had been experiencing low-level positive and negative symptoms of psychosis. His clinical trial treating these young people lasted for one year. McGorry's research objective in this trial was to see how many of the randomly selected experimental group of thirty-one participants given a low dose of antipsychotic medication (risperidone) with weekly cognitive behavioral therapy sessions would convert to psychosis. He then compared these results at six-month intervals to those of another twenty-eight young people with the same prepsychotic symptoms in a control group. This second group received therapy and social support, but only as their need for either form of treatment was indicated and to what extent they sought help.

At the conclusion of the study in 2002, McGorry came up with inconclusive results. After the first six months, things had looked promising when only three of the thirty-one young people in the experimental group who received both medication and targeted psychotherapy made the jump to full-blown psychosis. This was compared to ten of the twenty-eight participants in the control group, who, after receiving only support services, had progressed to "first-episode psychosis."

However, after six more months of treatment, three additional youths from the experimental group who had been taking the antipsychotic drug progressed to a first episode of psychosis. This made the difference between the two groups statistically insignificant. In his published analysis, McGorry concluded that his experimental use of medication and targeted CBT had at least delayed the onset of psychosis and may have prevented it in a few cases.[12]

A few years later, Yale psychiatrist Thomas McGlashan, who had directed one of the eight partner sites in the NAPLS observational study, ran the next significant controlled double-blind clinical trial. With funding from the National Institute of Mental Health (NIMH) and Eli Lilly, the maker of the second-generation atypical antipsychotic medication olanzapine (which Alex had taken under the brand name Zyprexa®), McGlashan's study produced mixed results similar to McGorry's. After one year of treatment, 16.1 percent of the Yale study participants taking the antipsychotic drug olanzapine converted to psychosis. This compared to a conversion rate of 37.9 percent for those taking a placebo, making the hazard for conversion about 2.5 times greater for the placebo group than for the olanzapine group.[13]

Then, during the second phase of the clinical trial, when neither group in McGlashan's study was given any further treatment, symptoms worsened for nearly as many who had taken the antipsychotic drug as for those in the placebo-taking group. Once again, the rate of conversion did not significantly differ between the experimental and control groups.[14] Unlike his Australian counterpart, McGlashan took a glass-half-empty perspective on these results. McGlashan's conclusion: the significant weight gain caused by olanzapine (an average nineteen pounds) was more significant than any improvements gained by the medication. He cited weight gain as the main reason for the sharp drop-off rate in his study from sixty participants to seventeen at its conclusion. Based on these results, he felt the benefits received did not outweigh the negative side effects and declared the trial a disappointment.[15]

But there were two other interesting results from McGlashan's first clinical trial. Those who were helped the most showed improvements immediately—very similar to what occurred for Alex after beginning his antipsychotic medication. For the small number of study participants in the olanzapine-taking group who converted to psychosis during the first year of treatment, their conversion to more serious symptoms happened right away; within the first four to six weeks of taking the drug. To explain, McGlashan suggested that these young people may have been misdiagnosed at the start of the study; meaning they may have already crossed the threshold to full-blown schizophrenia.

The heterogeneity of young people seeking help for early psychosis—some whose symptoms put them close to full-blown psychosis, some already taking antipsychotic medication after a first episode, some only in psychosocial therapy but not getting better—appears to be one of the obstacles preventing these clinical trials from producing nice, neat results of the sort that might silence the critics—and satisfy researchers like McGlashan himself.[16]

This long-running debate within psychiatry can be baffling to outsiders. It's not as if anyone in the mental health field wasn't aware by 2000 that the "off-label" (prescribing a drug without FDA approval) dispensing of antipsychotic and mood-stabilizing medications to young people with symptoms of psychosis, bipolar disorder, and other diagnoses had become commonplace. By 2010, the class of so-called second-generation antipsychotic medications—which differed from earlier drugs used to treat psychosis in their better track record of effectiveness and fewer (but still onerous) side effects—were also being used to treat severe depression, as well as the tantrums and outbursts that accompany severe autism.[17] The issue for psychiatrists is whether to recognize formal diagnoses specifically addressing children and adolescents who are deemed to be at risk for certain disorders such as bipolar disorder and schizophrenia and, by so doing (some fear), open the floodgates to more widespread medicating of young people.

—〰—

Consumers' voices are rarely heard in this debate. From the perspective of a parent who was forced to make a difficult decision about treating a possibly psychotic adolescent son, several aspects of our ordeal speak directly to these issues being hotly contested. Alex first received a prescription for the second-generation antipsychotic drug olanzapine at age seventeen after receiving a diagnosis of schizoid personality disorder from a psychiatrist he was referred to by his psychotherapist, Steve Hasenberg. But, at that time, while he was still in high school, Alex refused to take it. Nine months later, when Alex was given his new diagnosis of paranoid schizophrenia from Dr. C., the psychiatrist at UCLA, he received another prescription for this same antipsychotic medication, and this time he began to take it.

Had Alex's symptoms by then reached the diagnosis of full-blown schizophrenia as laid out in the *DSM-IV* (*Diagnostic and Statistical Manual of Mental Disorders, Fourth Edition*), the so-called Bible of psychiatry, by the time he entered the adolescent unit? Dr. C. said they had. But Steve, who'd been treating Alex on a weekly basis for almost a year, insisted they had not. Steve's view was that the drugs Alex had been using, namely pot and speed, had created the (temporary) psychotic symptoms that Dr. C. found in him.[18] I remember this discussion well; wanting very much to believe Steve, but fearing I would be slipping back into denial about Alex's deeper problem if I didn't go along with Dr. C.

Certainly street drugs such as speed and marijuana can, as Steve said, trigger the onset of psychotic symptoms, and that's a possibility in Alex's case.[19] However, it appears that psychosis is an elusive condition no matter how it gets started. In 20 percent of cases, a person has one episode of hallucinations, and they never come back. More often, however, the farther the person crosses the threshold into full-blown schizophrenia, the worse in severity and frequency the symptoms become.

It may have simply been a matter of when, not if, Alex would have needed this medication to stop the forward march of his psychotic symptoms. Still, the timing issue—when these drugs should be prescribed for young people experiencing the disease process that *may* lead to schizophrenia—is a huge one, not just for my son, but for the entire field.

Steve's worst fear for Alex was not about him taking the antipsychotic medication. He considered the Zyprexa a necessary response to Alex's symptoms, but he still worried a lot about the diagnosis he'd been given. "If we tell him he's schizophrenic, that's what he'll become," Steve said of Alex at eighteen.[20] Steve's comment reflects a legitimate concern that is another major theme you'll hear again and again in this debate about whether and when to treat a young person for psychotic symptoms—and what to call the problem or the "patient" when you do treat him.

Looking back, I'm thankful about the timing of Dr. C.'s diagnosis in one respect: I don't believe Alex would have gone on an antipsychotic medication if he hadn't been hospitalized and been given the attention-getting diagnosis of paranoid schizophrenia. Then, I suspect it would have taken him much longer to treat the symptoms that were clearly getting progressively worse. In the sequence of the mental health care Alex received, including the cognitive behavioral therapy he did with Steve and the medication he stayed on for eighteen months, Alex received the benefits of an early intervention for psychosis without his treatment ever being called that. When I related Alex's psychiatric history to Demian Rose, who as PREP San Francisco's medical director makes the medication decisions for all patients at the clinic, Rose said my description of Alex's symptoms at age seventeen closely fit the profile of the adolescents who now arrive on a near-daily basis seeking treatment at PREP. Rose also pointed out that for any of his incoming clients already experiencing hallucinations, he usually prescribes an antipsychotic medication to stabilize them.[21]

THE FALSE POSITIVE

The possibility of a young person receiving a false-positive diagnosis for schizophrenia or bipolar disorder has worried researchers like McGlashan and plenty of people outside the psychiatric profession. The central facts of the debate are not in question: based on the available studies, only one-third of young people with early symptoms of psychosis actually progress to a full-blown, more serious disorder—*without treatment*. At issue is the cost-benefit analysis of the early intervention option. This debate gets increasingly contentious in advance of the release of the fifth edition of the *DSM*, now set for 2013.

If a particular disorder receives the status of an official diagnosis in this book, this guarantees its public recognition and increases the likelihood that people who have the cited symptoms will seek and receive treatment. A first draft of the new *DSM-5*, released in 2010, suggested a formalization of an "at-risk" stage for bipolar disorder and schizophrenia, reigniting a storm of protest. Much of the controversy surrounding both of these new "not quite the full-blown disease" diagnoses stems from the fact that they are geared primarily at underage youth.[22]

Patrick McGorry pinned the vehemence of the current controversy on residue from other recent disputes within the American psychiatric profession. In 2006, he complained to *Time* magazine that while research and funding to support early psychosis treatment is blossoming in other countries, "it has ground to a halt" in the United States. "They've clouded the issue with the whole business of overmedication of younger children for ADHD," he said. Defending his work and the concept of prevention, McGorry explained, "It's unacceptable to wait for patients to slide into madness, though it's impossible to predict with any certainty which ones will. You've got to do something."[23] By this, he seemed to mean adding an antipsychotic medication to the treatment mix.

I appreciated McGorry's clear understanding of just how miserable his patients typically are while they struggle with the onset of psychotic symptoms. In the *Time* article, I found his description picture-perfect: "They've got no friends. They're sitting alone in their bedroom, their lives passing them by. You've got to actively research what's going to help them. The critics have been right to raise issues, but you can't neglect people when they clearly have a disorder, just because you can't technically fit them into our arbitrary system of classification."[24]

Since his original clinical trial, McGorry and his Australian colleagues have gone on to treat many more young people who are at ultra-high risk for psychosis. Some guardedly good news has emerged from these recent trials. The six-month transition rate to psychosis, which was a 34 percent rate in McGorry's earlier trials, had, by 2010, dropped to 9.2 percent. What does it mean? McGorry speculates that this drop in conversions correlates with many of his patients being identified earlier in their disease processes. As a result, he thinks they respond better and quicker to the interventions they're getting. McGorry does not think, as some of his critics assert, that most of these young people were "false positives" when they first entered treatment.[25]

These days, McGorry is very careful to describe his treatment approach as strictly "needs-based." He outlines a clinical staging model, in which an individual's treatment moves from one stage to the next only after his symptoms escalate. After determining that the individual meets the criteria of ultra-high risk—someone between the ages of sixteen and thirty who is experiencing attenuated symptoms of psychosis, or is within one year of a first psychotic episode—the first stage of care he receives at McGorry's clinic is cognitive behavioral therapy and the daily intake of omega-3 fish oil, a readily available nutritional supplement that has been shown to be effective in treating early psychosis, likely by enhancing the ability of the brain's synapses to communicate. Antidepressants will also be considered if the young person's depression is present and severe, and she doesn't respond to CBT. And then, if indicated, McGorry recommends a very low dose of antipsychotic medication, ideally for a limited period of time of six weeks.[26]

This same model for treating early psychosis has now been replicated and studied in a growing number of national health systems and university-affiliated clinics in the United States, United Kingdom, Europe, Scandinavia, and around the world. From the outside, it looks to be a constant balancing act between risk and benefit; the codifying of each symptom and step of treatment into a fixed clinical protocol an ongoing process—with a high level of cooperation by clinicians working and communicating with each from early intervention clinics around the world.

—ⱳ—

ANYWHERE BUT HERE

"Anywhere but here" is the refrain heard from the majority of teenagers who, if given a choice, would give serious thought to cutting off a finger before agreeing to see a "shrink." Demian Rose in his role as medical director for PREP San Francisco offers an insight into how and why young people initially arrive at his clinic for care, explaining that most don't come because they're failing at school, or even because they're hearing voices. These fleeting psychotic symptoms no doubt fuel their anxiety and depression, but most come for an evaluation, Rose says, "when they become socially isolated and emotionally distant from their peers." Research confirms that mood fluctuations and stress trigger and exacerbate the recurrence of psychotic symptoms in those at risk.[27]

The good news may be that since friendships and budding romantic feelings are such a priority to adolescents, when this area of their lives gets messed up, they have a greater motivation to get evaluated and treated. In the process, they may stave off the psychosis that could be laying in wait.

The therapeutic goal at PREP is to help the psychologically distressed individual (around ten to one are male) retrain and reframe his thoughts and behaviors toward more socially acceptable habits.[28] This is also the essence of the cognitive behavioral therapy (CBT) used with young people who are treated at PREP. This form of psychotherapy has been around for decades, but it has only recently been adapted by psychologists in the United Kingdom for the treatment of psychosis. (CBT in its original form is a widely used form of talk therapy to treat most other common mental disorders, including depression). As adapted for psychosis, CBT teaches an individual who becomes suspicious or paranoid to become consciously aware of a negative thought pattern that is about to escalate and then to learn how to "catch it, check it, change it."

Imagine that a young man who is experiencing fleeting psychotic symptoms is sitting on a packed bus at rush hour. In his discomfort at the crowd pushing up against his knees, he might acquire the distinct feeling that the middle-aged woman standing a few feet away is staring at him, angry that he has a seat and she doesn't. He may also fear that she's scrunching up her nose because she believes he smells badly. He could go off even further on this paranoid tangent, becoming suspicious she will report him to the bus driver, who will request he get off at the next stop.

Before saying something inappropriate to the woman or getting up to leave the bus preemptively to avoid the feared outcome, CBT teaches this young man to stop and *catch* his wayward thought process. *Checking* to see if there's any other viable explanation for the woman's behaviors then reveals to him the more likely possibility that the woman simply has nowhere else to look but in his direction. Further, he realizes that there's no concrete evidence to support the belief that she blames him for her situation or judges his appearance negatively—nor that she has any intention to speak to the bus driver about him. This reframing allows the young man to *change* his thoughts and to then relax his mind and body for the duration of the bus ride. It's the CBT mantra in action: "Catch it, check it, change it."

In the figure on the following page, Demian Rose, Rachel Loewy, and their colleagues writing in *Current Psychiatry* use a continuum model to demonstrate how the human spectrum of thought and perception ranges from ordinary to heightened and then on to varying degrees of psychosis. They demonstrate how a clinician can respond to a young person's unusual comments or behaviors without "pathologizing" his behavior and risk alienating him. This approach offers the client perspective and a choice. On one hand, he can continue expressing his unusual thoughts openly and risk alienating others. Or he can choose to keep these thoughts to himself and gain social acceptance. Rose points out that in the prepsychotic stage, this interactive discussion and decision-making process is much more viable.

This same advice can be useful to parents of an adolescent or a younger child whose altered behavior or speech might suggest that he is close to this outer edge of the continuum. Putting science aside, I remember as a parent

Taken from "Re-envisioning Psychosis: A New Language for Clinical Practice,"

in *Current Psychiatry* (Oct 2010) with language modifications made with permission for the benefit of clarity to lay readers.

SYMPTOM	CONTINUUM	ATTENUATED EXPERIENCE	PATHOLOGICAL EXPERIENCE (DISORDER STAGE)	PSYCHO-THERAPEUTIC INTERVENTION
Suspicious feelings/ paranoia/ Delusions	What we make of people and things in our environment and our relationships with them.	Confusion about the accuracy of thoughts • Increased paranoia about the negative attitudes of others • Feelings of special purpose or meaning • Loss of control over own thoughts	• Increased frequency • Preoccupying • Leads to maladaptive, unsafe behaviors	• Encourage evidence gathering to test suspicions • Design new safety behaviors • Encourage individual thinking or formulation about experiences
Hallucinations	Higher order sensory processing; people take in and evaluate sensory input differently; some see, hear or feel more than others; e.g. a painter or a composer.	• Perceptual changes • Increased sensitivity to light and sound • Senses "playing tricks"	• Frequent • Intrusive • Distressing • Conviction about influence from an external source leads to maladaptive behaviors	• Discuss phenomenon as an exaggeration of normal brain function • Focus on socially appropriate coping skills
Thinking problems/ disorganized speech	The use of narrow vs. broad conceptual thinking and meanings; tangential thinking and speaking; e.g. a poet.	• Difficulty getting point across. • Use of incongruent ideas and mismatched words	• Little insight • Inability to control attention	• Emphasize social appropriateness of linear thought and speech • Encourage tangential thinking as a creative outlet.

Figure 4.1. Reproduced with permission from Demian Rose, MD, PhD et al., "Re-envisioning Psychosis: A New Language for Clinical Practice," *Current Psychiatry* 9, no. 10 (Oct 2010): 20–28. Quadrant HealthCom Inc.

watching Alex in this state, and it was terrifying. As he left "reality" behind, I felt him slipping away from me, too. But the alternative to *pathologizing* this behavior, Demian Rose points out, is *normalizing* it, which allows you to open up an honest conversation with your child (or another adult) about thoughts and feelings that may not fit our definition of normal but may in fact be very human. I didn't have this insight to guide me at the time, but it made perfect sense when I heard Rose explain that this sort of conversation is the best way to find out what someone in this state is feeling and thinking, and what he really needs from you.

In addition to training their clients to use this thought-reframing drill, the PREP program also includes family members and caregivers in ongoing treatment. The model calls for bringing the clients' parents and other family members together in a regularly meeting "multi-family group." There they receive psychoeducational treatment, meaning they learn about psychosis and how they can help the affected person stay on track. Getting together with other families provides much-needed emotional support to parents faced with the often daunting task of providing care to a troubled adolescent.

The man credited with developing this model is William McFarlane, a pioneer in early intervention for psychosis whose PIER Clinic (Portland Identification and Early Referral) was established in Maine in 2000. McFarlane's studies show that ongoing support groups made up of several families meeting together significantly reduces relapse rates for the schizophrenic family member—when compared to not involving families in care or offering psychoeducational support to one family at a time.[29] The PIER program was also the first to demonstrate that teachers, social workers, pediatricians, and therapists in a community could be trained to successfully identify psychotic symptoms in distressed young people and then intervene by referring them to PIER for an evaluation.[30]

When an adolescent is diagnosed properly as "ultra-high risk," he may be as little as one month or as long as one to two years away from developing full-blown schizophrenia—*if he is going to convert at all.* Demian Rose put the clinician's dilemma succinctly: "The problem with the current diagnostic standard is that it 'waits' until it's absolutely sure that dysfunction has been present for six months before confirming schizophrenia; so the message to parents and patients is all too often: 'Let's wait this out. You're either going off a cliff. Or you'll be okay. We're not sure which.' The real question should be how can clinicians reduce the risk of conversion while minimizing the risk and burden of any treatments."[31]

One guiding principle at PREP is to use as small a dose of antipsychotic medication as possible to keep the individual stable, and to err on the side of less is more. Convincing clinical data is accumulating on the positive outcomes coming from clinics using the approach practiced at PREP. Those who get treatment within the first six months to one year of the appearance of symptoms of psychosis show a much higher rate of remission and long-term recovery. If their symptoms convert to a diagnosis of full-blown schizophrenia (the usual diagnosis if they do) or bipolar disorder, their treatment is usually more effective, meaning their impairments are fewer, and their recovery is greater over the long term. But if they receive the same treatment from one to three years after psychosis has firmly taken hold, the rate of remission is lower, and the risk of side effects from long-term use of the medication goes up.[32]

Now in its second year of operation, the PREP program has treated thirty young people, ages sixteen to thirty, with a mean age of twenty-two years. Twenty-one of these patients had already progressed to full-blown schizophrenia before coming to PREP, but they were recent-onset patients. Nine hadn't yet reached that threshold and so were considered ultra-high risk.[33] In the future, if the PREP-PIER model is permitted to become the standard for mental health care, we could reasonably expect this ratio to reverse; more young people could receive help *before* going "over the cliff" into a full psychotic episode, not after. Then their care could begin with CBT and be far less likely to progress to medication, at least not for a long period. The important thing is that they would learn the necessary self-regulating skills to stay safe.

—∿—

ENOUGH IS ENOUGH

Meanwhile, the "battle to define mental illness," as a cover story in *Wired* characterizing the ongoing debates over how or whether to treat at-risk syndromes in young people, rages on.[34] In opposition, none other than lead editor of the outgoing version of the handbook in dispute, the *DSM-IV*, Allen Frances, wrote that early intervention would cause "a wholesale medical imperialization of normality," and create a "bonanza for the pharmaceutical industry," for which "patients would pay a high price [of] adverse effects, dollars, and stigma." Quoted again in the *Wired* story, Frances said he regrets the role played by the *DSM-IV*, as he saw it, in creating "the bipolar fad" of the last decade by opening up that diagnosis to children and adolescents.

In a professional journal, Thomas McGlashan, who led the Yale Study and came out with what he saw then as disappointing results, laid out the evidence for the opposite argument as follows: (1) the patients are currently ill, (2) the patients are at high risk for getting worse, (3) no *DSM-IV* diagnosis accurately captures their current illness or future risk, (4) the diagnosis has been made with reliability and validity in the research setting, and (5) placement in *DSM-5* would help promote the needed treatment and prevention research to enable articulation of a standard of care to benefit these patients and their families. He closed by pointing out that any potential harms can be minimized by patient, family, and provider education.[35]

To my ears, this debate comes down to the question of who has the right to decide when an individual and a family have suffered enough. By continuing this now very public, fever-pitch argument over the difficult choice of whether to give a child or teenager a psychiatric medication, I think we've lost sight of what's really at stake here. As Doctors McGlashan, McGorry, and Rose make clear, these young people are already very ill when they come seeking help. My sense of urgency comes from having watched Alex's two painful years of decline until he became a shadow of his former self. No young person should have to stay in that state any longer than necessary.

Chapter 5

ONSET

1996–1998

Alex in his sixteenth year was somewhere in the middle of the messy, imprecise disease process that divides early psychosis from full-blown schizophrenia. When he could no longer deal with the added pressures of being at boarding school, I struggled to find another school he could attend as a day student while living at home. After an exhausting search, I found a courageous principal at Concord Academy, a prep school of some 150 students in Santa Monica, who was willing to take him.

It was probably already too late for Alex to be in such a setting, as he never really settled comfortably at Concord. Over the course of another semester, he became even more withdrawn. Alex would come home after school and lock himself in his room. When I'd get him to open the door, I'd often find him scribbling in a notebook filled with page after page of nonsensical sentences and drawings of distorted faces. He still painted, but now he used scrap lumber he found on the street instead of canvas.

One day, I walked into Alex's room to see him frowning at an acrylic painting of a silver dolphin leaping out of a deep blue ocean. At the edges of the dolphin I could see a chipped veneer tabletop, his scavenged canvas. The painting was remarkable for its sense of joy and hopefulness. I asked Alex if I could hang it on the living room wall. He didn't give away any emotion, grunting something I took as a yes, and so I left the room, much cheered.

When I entered his bedroom the next day and asked where he thought we should hang the dolphin, the painting was gone. "Where is it?" I asked.

"I sold it," he said, without looking up from his drawing pad.

"But . . . for how much?"

"Five dollars."

"Why?"

"I needed money for cigarettes."

Just a few days before I'd refused to give him the extra allowance to buy cigarettes, hoping I could get him to quit smoking.

In the weeks that followed, Alex papered his bedroom walls with a more familiar motif: brains gone haywire in colored chalk. Then he took to cutting his own hair, asymmetrically, giving his face a permanently haunted look. That's also the period when Alex's thinking became noticeably strange; he would start one sentence and finish another. Or he'd lose his train of thought entirely.

Alex would say things like "*The Idiot* is the best book ever written . . . I like to play it atonally." Alex had read everything by Dostoyevsky; he called him the greatest writer of all time. But he never played an instrument, so I had no idea what atonal music he might be referring to and why the two belonged in the same sentence. He didn't seem to care much that he was not being understood, so rapidly was he retreating into a world of his own.

In my ignorance of what might be happening to Alex during this period, I searched for things that would get him out of his room and give the three of us another chance to be, or to at least act like, a family. I bought tickets for us to go to the new Getty Museum, a big, exciting deal for Alex, I thought, since there seemed to be nothing in his world but art. When I mentioned getting the tickets, he seemed happy. I reminded him of this outing at least once a day and twice that Sunday morning.

"Our parking voucher is good for three o'clock, one hour, that's it," I said, half to myself as I opened his bedroom door. "Use it or lose it—"

I gasped. There, surrounded by sheets of paper crammed with drawings of human figures made of circuit boards and concentric circles, Alex sat crouched on the floor, his arms locked over his head.

"What's the matter?" I asked.

"I can't do it," he whispered.

"Why not?" I asked too loudly, not able to hide my annoyance, refusing to let in the fact that there was something much scarier than moodiness going on.

"All those people," he said, as he began to rock back and forth on his knees and shins. "It's not a good day."

Tears fell, and my stomach turned as I backed out of the room and leaned against the wall, still trying to drive away the dawning realization that something really scary was happening, or had already happened, to Alex.

I hurried downstairs, pulled Sammy away from his video game, and drove off to the Getty. Along with ignorance, there was a fair amount of denial evident in my behavior toward Alex. In fact, each of our actions and reactions toward each other that day spoke to the way denial works in a family coping with mental illness: my insistence that an art outing would help Alex snap out of his illness, if only for the afternoon; Sammy's acceptance of his role as the sainted "little prince" who quietly goes along with Mom and compensates for his older brother's weirdness; and my rapidly dimming wish—that we were a "normal" family, that going to the Getty on opening weekend proved it; and simply because I had gone to all this trouble to get us there. *Oh, poor me.*

As his condition worsened, Alex slept less and less. Most nights, he paced in loopy patterns around our apartment. That was when Alex's refusal to wear shoes began to be a real problem. I'd get a call at work from the Concord School principal explaining, "It's our insurance, with all the broken glass he can't walk around here in his socks." But that was exactly what he continued to do, day after day, no matter how many times he was suspended from school.

I pleaded with Alex to cooperate, appealing to his sense of fairness around the school's financial risks, and, when that didn't work, his questionable fate if he were cast out of another school. He listened patiently but explained over and over the impossibility of any compromise, repeating that he needed to feel his feet on the ground. *At least we don't live in New York,* I remember thinking, where his feet would freeze in the winter. In Southern California, all we had to contend with was the rain and broken glass.

That's when the Concord principal referred us to Steve, the psychotherapist who began working with Alex at that point. After several sessions, Steve called me to say he saw signs of a schizoid personality disorder in Alex, and he strongly suggested Alex be examined by a psychiatrist. It wasn't easy getting Alex to go see Dr. M. It took Steve, with whom Alex had closely bonded, telling him that it was essential to their continuing in psychotherapy for him to finally agree. Alex went by himself, and a week later I heard Dr. M.'s evaluation.

I remember sitting in his drab office in west Los Angeles, pen in hand and ready to write down his instructions, to do whatever was necessary to "fix" my son. What I heard next gave me chills. When Dr. M. asked Alex what he would choose to do if he could do any three things he wished (apparently a standard diagnostic question), Alex said he'd paint a purple stripe down the middle of the street, take a nap every afternoon, and be very wealthy and powerful.

The part of me still clinging to denial about Alex's problems did not want to hear these admittedly strange answers characterized as anything other than evidence of my son's artistic and eccentric nature. But Dr. M. quickly dashed those hopes, pointing out that Alex's *grandiosity, immaturity, disheveled appearance*, and *flat affect* were all symptoms of a "schizoid personality disorder." Later I would learn that this diagnosis frequently comes right before full-blown schizophrenia. In fact, 21 percent of adolescents diagnosed with this disorder or two others (schizoaffective, schizotypal) in what is called the "schizophrenium spectrum" will go on to develop schizophrenia.[1]

At the conclusion of our session, Dr. M. wrote out the prescription for what he described as a "promising new, second-generation antipsychotic medicine." Meaningless to me at the time, he had just described the same antipsychotic drug, olanzapine (Zyprexa®), that Thomas McGlashan would use in his early psychosis study at Yale; a medication in the same category as risperidone, used by Patrick McGorry in his Melbourne clinical trials.

In 1997, when Alex refused to take the Zyprexa, I didn't push him to reconsider his decision. I had my own doubts about psychiatric medications at that time; after all, I'd managed to avoid taking Prozac® for the entire decade it had been on the market—even after I'd seen it help people close to me who'd been struggling with their depression.

After that, Alex's symptoms got worse. One of the criteria that mental health practitioners suggest parents use when deciding about treatment for children and adolescents is to take a look at how far off the normal developmental track the child has gone; that is, from the normal milestones of social, emotional, and cognitive growth for his age. Is he mastering his basic academic lessons? Does he have friends outside of school? Is she prone to staying locked alone in her bedroom for long stretches? How depressed or anxious does he appear? If there is enough evidence that he is seriously off track, the priority for treatment is to try whatever evidenced-based approaches that can bring him back on track soonest, without causing unmanageable side effects. The goal is to give a child back as much of his childhood or adolescence as is still possible.[2]

Around the time Alex refused medication, I received word from the Concord School principal that Alex couldn't return in the fall—leaving him again without a school. This was a huge disappointment for both of us. It seemed to make Alex pull farther into his shell. As a last resort (in my mind), I scrambled to get the late admission for him at the aforementioned public high school for the visual arts, Fairfax High School. He started there in September 1997 and attended sporadically for three months until his eighteenth birthday. At that point, it was no longer possible for him to sit in a classroom with forty other students, walk in a bustling hallway, or perform the school-work he'd been assigned.

—ᴍ—

THE LIST OF EARLY WARNING SIGNS OF PSYCHOSIS

The negative (cognitive and behavioral) symptoms:

- difficulty concentrating
- less energy
- nervousness or a short temper
- increased sensitivity to sounds or light
- a strong desire to be left alone

The positive (psychotic) symptoms:

- you can hear or see things that others don't
- you can't trust anyone
- your food may be poisoned
- someone is watching you
- people or places you know seem different
- you have a special ability or powers
- your thinking is unusual or frightening
        —*From the PREP Clinic Self-Test for Signs of Psychosis*[3]

For a parent with a pubescent child experiencing any psychological disturbances, lists like these can be alternately terrifying, reassuring, or just plain confusing. If only it were as simple as checking off each item with a simple yes or no. A good doctor can explain the symptoms and diagnoses, but the only thing I've found to help navigate the emotions that accompany these difficult situations is to talk to other parents who've been there before you.

THE PLASTIC BRAIN IN ACTION

One of the key scientific rationales for early intervention is the plasticity of the brain. The brain is a malleable organ. It becomes what we make of it. If we worry too much, we turn into worry machines. If we remain depressed for too long, it's harder to bring our fried limbic system back to a baseline that isn't depressed. If through psychotherapy, or psychiatric medications, or a strong emotional support system we coax the brain into righting itself, the symptoms and—if caught early enough—the disease process itself can be stopped. One scientist studying early intervention for schizophrenia compared this process to the prevention of pneumonia by antibiotics in the early stages of a bad cough.[4] Neurons that fire together, wire together is the shorthand often used by neuroscientists. The brain, it seems, is a creature of habit.

We also now know that the two most active and therefore critical periods for brain changes to take hold—meaning those times when environmental events have the keenest opportunity to change the expression of our genes and mold our brains—are the first trimester of pregnancy and adolescence. Talk about inopportune times: the first four to eight weeks of pregnancy, when most women don't even know they're pregnant; and then at the most challenging child-rearing time for most parents, when our kids become teenagers. I couldn't think of worse times for the developing brain to be so vulnerable.[5]

The argument for treating early psychosis with "everything we've got," as opposed to waiting, is that by doing so we keep the adolescent's brain from dwelling too long in a diseased state marked by paranoia and skewed thoughts, and we halt the equally habit-forming negative symptoms of lost motivation and social withdrawal.[6] Because every brain, and every individual's environment, is different, I suspect that the threshold separating prepsychotic symptoms from full-blown psychosis will remain a moving target—open to interpretation—no matter how many studies, screening tools, and diagnostic labels are added into the mix.

FINDING THE CLIFF'S EDGE

Despite the evidence for schizophrenia as a long-term neurodevelopmental process, PREP medical director Demian Rose is concerned about the way his profession and the culture deal with psychosis as an all-or-nothing state. As it turns out, psychotic experiences such as hearing voices are a relatively common *human* experience, especially among adolescents: at from 14 to 25 percent.[7] In Rose's view and that of a growing number of research psychologists, a psychotic state exists on a continuum with "typical" sensory experience, with only some of its heightened, extreme aspects presenting a problem—and even this is a subjective assessment. A problem for one person is not necessarily one for another. For example, Alex's refusal to wear shoes only progressed to a critical state when it became part of a socially unacceptable set of behaviors that separated him from his peers and got him suspended from school.

Using the same cliff metaphor that Demian Rose employed to describe the conversion point for psychotically symptomatic youth, evolutionary psychologist Randolph M. Nesse coined the term *cliff-edged* to explain necessary aspects of human behavior that exist on a continuum with psychotic symptoms such as paranoia, extreme nonlinear thoughts, and heightened sensory perceptions. Nesse says it's the usefulness of certain cliff-edged behaviors that explains why psychosis remains ever-present in our human species. An example of this is the human ability to put ourselves in another's shoes, called "theory of mind" by psychologists.

Addressing the continuum, Nesse wrote, "Strong tendencies to use meta-representation [a representation of a representation] and theory of mind can increase the ability to predict other people's behaviors and discern their intentions, but it is only one step further, over the cliff 's edge of psychotic cognition . . . to find secret meanings and evidence for conspiracies in other people's most casual gestures."[8]

Theory of mind as a concept can refer to simple leaps in thought and communication such as the comparison between the two comments "The moon is made of green cheese" and "Tom says the moon is made of green cheese"; the latter being a meta-representation of the former representation of the moon. By developing an advanced theory of mind, the human species set itself apart from other animals, gaining the cognitive skills needed to reflect on such abstract things as life and death and forming cultures. The subsequent faculty to manipulate (adopt and reuse) ideas or representations that arise in the minds of others for one's own purposes is thought to account for the burst of creativity that marked the beginning of human art, culture, and religion at the beginning of the Upper Paleolithic period sixty to thirty thousand years ago.[9]

Many millennia later, this same ability enables us to tell reality from flights of fantasy or paranoid delusions, making it relevant to our understanding of when a mind is working well and when it isn't. Every child develops her own theory of mind—that is, an ability to discern that another person's thoughts are different from hers, and to begin to wonder what the other *might* be thinking—by about age three. It's an ability that is often markedly missing or weak in autistic children, making their ability to communicate with others difficult.[10] Applying this same premise to the population of young people at the PREP clinic, it is then the clinicians' task to keep their prepsychotic clients from jumping off the proverbial cliff and to learn how to hold on to their ability to discern so that they can continue to interact successfully with their fellow humans.

ALEX ON AND OFF MEDS

As the weeks went by, like the majority of young people with his diagnosis, Alex only grudgingly took his medication. The side effects of Zyprexa— weight gain and lethargy, among others—were odious for him as they are for anyone who takes it.

Still, when I asked if he felt different after being on medication, Alex described the changes he felt with profound simplicity, saying, "Well, yeah . . . now, sometimes instead of having three hundred thoughts at a time, I have one or two." We all noticed how much more present he appeared; nearly gone was the wall of fog that had separated him from the rest of the world. From his work with Steve in therapy over that same period, Alex seemed better able to express more feelings; a major point of healing for him.

After he left UCLA, Alex got all his remaining treatment from the Didi Hirsch Community Mental Health Clinic in west Los Angeles. When he and I talked about it not long ago, Alex said he had felt very positive about his one-on-one contacts with the UCLA psychiatric residents at Didi Hirsh. He said they were willing to engage with him about the nature of his psychological difficulties and described these conversations as often veering into art and philosophy—which, for Alex, added up to the very definition of respect.

I should say at this point that despite everything that happened to him in and out of treatment, Alex has never accepted his original diagnosis of paranoid schizophrenia. At one point, he described what had been disturbing him in those years as a "problem of the heart." I think his refusal to buy into his diagnosis of schizophrenia was probably very adaptive and a good defense against self-stigma. The two of us have agreed to disagree about this. Still, in my heart of hearts, and with everything I've learned since his one and only hospitalization, I believe that if it wasn't full-blown schizophrenia that struck Alex at seventeen, he came within a hair's breadth of it.

When he was twenty, Alex completely stopped taking his antipsychotic medication, announcing simply, "I'm okay now. I don't need it." Besides, he explained, "As an artist, I need all of my brain."

But what will happen to you without the medication to keep you stable, we pleaded—to no avail. Only time would tell. We collectively held our breath.

Chapter 6

MY LITTLE PRINCE COMES UNDONE

You have how many other children?
Just one, Sammy, but he's fine.

In 1998, when Alex was hospitalized, I did think Sammy was fine. His deeper problems would not become apparent until four years later, during his junior year of high school. And then he was like a wind-up toy whose battery simply gave out. This is how Sammy described what it felt like in an essay for his college application, the same application in which he checked neuroscience as his choice of a major.

> *It was a fog that had been coming closer and closer. I wasn't sure where it came from and it was so subtle I don't think I even noticed it until later on when I looked back. It divided the world from me. At home I couldn't muster the strength to get out my homework. At school when we were assigned to write in our journals, I stared out the window at a big tree.*
> *Sometimes I couldn't take the silence in the classroom. All I could hear were the pencils and pens churning like furious mechanical devices I couldn't understand. I would go sit on the sidewalk and look up at this tree that was at least forty feet tall and watch rays of sun reflect through the leaves. Their green and red colors were like my memories, there, but not there. I felt like there was nothing I could do but sit there. Later I would label all these feelings as depression, but then it was just the passage of time.*

In 2004, Sammy dropped out of college just two months after he got there. I found out later that he'd spent the majority of his brief time on campus playing poker, or just sitting alone, in the dormitory lounge. When I picked him up on the Tuesday before Thanksgiving break, he wouldn't look me in the eye and offered only monosyllable answers to my questions. By the time we were halfway home, he admitted he hadn't been to class in "a while." When I asked him why, he couldn't explain. I didn't push him any harder. I could see he was in enormous pain and confusion.

It wasn't as if I didn't already know Sammy was in trouble. Finishing high school had been a struggle for him. Two years before, he'd started taking Effexor®, an SSRI antidepressant. (*SSRI* is an abbreviation for the class of antidepressants known as selective serotonin reuptake inhibitors. SSRIs have the effect of keeping more of the mood-regulating neurotransmitter serotonin in the synapses between brain neurons, thus enhancing communication between them.) But Effexor never really worked well or consistently for Sammy. His failure to sustain the pressure of even one semester away at school was shocking to me—although it shouldn't have been. I'd allowed him to stay—for two years—on a medication that clearly wasn't working. When I described this period later to Columbia University depression researcher Myrna Weissman, she shook her head and said simply, "Two years is a long time."[1] Once again, a son of mine would have to create enough drama for me to drop the veil of denial.

Part of my problem in coming to terms with what would ultimately be diagnosed as Sammy's social anxiety disorder and major depression was his previous position in the family as the "good son." Even after growing up boxed into the role of good daughter in contrast to my sister Rita, my urge to believe that at least one of my sons was "normal" kept me from seeing who Sammy really was and what he needed.

Alex always received the majority of parental attention from Geoff and me, both positive and negative. Sammy never gave us any trouble—at least, not until Alex got well enough (at age twenty-two) to begin attending community college. Then, like clockwork, Sammy fell apart.

As I've come to understand this family dynamic, both siblings—the one who openly acts out his problems and the other who quietly keeps everything in—suffer by becoming trapped in rigid roles. It's easy enough to see the trials and tribulations of the "problem" child. But the same dynamic makes it harder for the "good" child to admit to having any trouble with the normal challenges of growing up since it might require admitting a "failure" and disappointing his parents. To this day, one of Sammy's biggest challenges is his perfectionism. He'll stare at a blank screen for half a day lest he begin an essay with the "wrong" sentence.

When I learned how this typical scenario works in families, I immediately saw that I'd repeated with my Sammy and Alex exactly what I had experienced growing up. Throughout my childhood and teen years, my sister Rita's antics inevitably took center stage. As the good daughter, I had had to wait another two decades for my turn to fall to pieces. Sammy, at least, had waited only two years.

—ɯ—

After taking a medical leave from college, Sammy went through fourteen antidepressant and antianxiety medications over a one-and-one-half year period—all in search of the right treatment for his anxiety and depression. Among them were two different mood-stabilizing medications to address what his then-psychiatrist thought might be Sammy's bipolar tendencies— rapid cycling between modestly high and very low states—with no success. Throughout most of this period, Sammy took one or two courses per semester at a local community college, but keeping even that together was a struggle for him as his moods fluctuated wildly in response to side effects caused by each of the medications. Then, as each drug failed to work, he was forced to face the return of even worse depression.

THE LOWDOWN ON MILD AND MAJOR DEPRESSION

Mild depression or **dysthymic disorder** is diagnosed when someone has a depressed mood for most of the day for two years or longer, plus at least two of any of these symptoms:

- Poor appetite or overeating
- Insomnia or extreme sleepiness
- Low energy or fatigue
- Low self-esteem
- Poor concentration or difficulty making decisions
- Feelings of hopelessness

Major depression is the diagnosis given when someone's depressed mood or loss of interest or pleasure in ordinary activities lasts for at least two weeks, accompanied by at least four of the following symptoms:

- Significant weight loss when not dieting, or weight gain, or change in appetite
- Insomnia or extreme sleepiness

- Activity level slows down or increases
- Fatigue or loss of energy
- Feelings of worthlessness or excessive guilt
- Diminished ability to think, concentrate, or make decisions
- Recurrent thoughts of death or suicide, or suicidal ideation, or a suicide plan or attempt

These symptoms cannot be due to a grief reaction or the direct effects of medications, drugs, or a physical condition.[2]

After what turned into two years of raised and dashed hopes, Sammy's psychiatrist, the same one he saw upon leaving college, concluded (prematurely, as it turns out) that Sammy belonged to the minority of depressed patients, one in three, who don't respond to antidepressant medications. The term used to describe this group is *treatment-resistant*.

The cycle of promise and failure required to get to this apparent dead-end was extremely difficult to watch and far worse for Sammy to experience. The worst point came when Sammy stopped taking four very powerful medications all at once, cold turkey, on the same day. He then fell into a month-long stupor that was by far the worst depressed state I'd ever seen him in, obviously aggravated by his sudden withdrawal from all the medications. You're not supposed to quit taking psychiatric medication the way Sammy did; doctors warn patients to very gradually taper off by a steady and incremental reduction in dosage, and it's best to do it under a doctor's supervision.[3] I knew that, and so did Sammy. But there was no talking him out of it. Finding the right medication can sometimes be a long and painful process. It certainly was for Sammy.

ADOLESCENTS AND ANTIDEPRESSANTS

What works? What are the dangers?

In 2007, researchers at Duke University Medical School, in cooperation with the National Institute of Mental Health (NIMH), released results of a major study they'd carried out to establish the best treatment for adolescents with depression.[4] Randomized and controlled (meaning it was double-blind; the students didn't know if they were getting an antidepressant or a placebo), this study—called TADS, for Treatment for Adolescents with Depression—tested the effectiveness of each of the following treatment options: an antidepressant alone (Prozac®), an antidepressant with CBT (psychotherapy), CBT alone, the placebo alone, and the placebo with CBT. The population tested included 327 adolescents (ages thirteen to seventeen), all of whom had moderate or severe depression.

By the end of the thirty-six-week trial, 82 percent of participants who received active treatment (not a placebo) had improved, and 59 percent had reached full remission. Four out of five teenagers in the study recovered completely either by taking an antidepressant, or through the CBT talk therapy, or a combination of the two. Medication worked fastest in this study. But antidepressants and psychotherapy together worked best and produced the least risk of suicidal ideation.[5]

THE ANTIDEPRESSANT-SUICIDE LINK INVESTIGATED

Because the treatment of adolescent depression is such a contentious area of mental health science, I've include the results of the TADS study below. The percentages measured the rate of positive response by the adolescents—meaning remission of most of their symptoms and a return to functionality—for each treatment approach.

At week twelve:

- 73 percent for combination CBT and antidepressant
- 62 percent for antidepressant alone
- 48 percent for CBT alone

At week 36:

- 81 percent for combination CBT and antidepressant
- 81 percent for antidepressant alone
- 86 percent for CBT alone
- Suicidal ideation decreased with treatment, but less so with antidepressant therapy than with combination therapy or CBT

> • Suicidal events were more common in patients receiving antidepressant therapy (14.7 percent) than combination therapy (8.4 percent) or CBT (6.3 percent)[6]
>
> The study's bottom line according to its lead author: "In adolescents with moderate to severe depression, treatment with antidepressant alone or in combination with CBT accelerates the response. Adding CBT to medication enhances the safety of medication. Taking benefits and harms into account, combined treatment appears superior to either [alone] as a treatment for major depression in adolescents."[7]

As with most psychiatric diagnoses, there are subtypes of depression and differences in the treatment of depression for people of different ages.

Mild Depression. Improvement from taking an antidepressant is not as consistent with mild depression as it is with moderate or severe depression. In one 2010 meta-analysis, the improvement rate for mild or moderately depressed adults (this "meta" did not include youths under eighteen), taking an SSRI antidepressant was no better than the improvement shown by those who had been given a placebo. (The same analysis showed "substantial improvement for severely depressed individuals taking the same antidepressant.")[8]

Lifestyle changes can help depressed people in every age group. The chief of the Mood Disorders program at NIMH, Dr. Husseini Manji, recommended for the alleviation of symptoms of depression in bipolar disorder "Avoiding simple carbs, like bagels and soda, which can cause fluctuations in blood sugar and worsen depression, and stimulants like caffeine and alcohol, which can destabilize moods."[9] Other known mood boosters include exercise, taking omega-3 fatty acids as a food supplement, use of stress-reduction techniques, and the practice of mindfulness, yoga, and meditation.[10]

Antidepressant Side Effects and Risks. No medication is without risks and possible side effects, and that includes antidepressants. Minor side effects include sexual dysfunction, dry mouth, sleeplessness or sleepiness, gain or loss of appetite.

After scattered reports surfaced of an increase in suicides among adolescents taking antidepressants, the US Food and Drug Administration in 2003 issued a warning that antidepressants could increase the chances of suicidal thoughts in children and teenagers. It warned that this effect was most noticed in the first two months after starting the medication.[11] After the warning, the number of antidepressant prescriptions issued to youngsters ages eleven to nineteen dropped by 22 percent. Within a year, this reduction in the use of antidepressants was followed by an alarming 8 percent increase in suicides among children and young adults (in 2004).

A subsequent analysis of the antidepressant-suicide connection released by a French and Canadian team concluded: "Prescribing antidepressant therapy (ADT) to all patients diagnosed with depression would prevent more than one out of three suicide deaths compared to the no-ADT strategy, irrespective of age, gender or history [of suicide attempts]." These researchers observed that noncompliance—meaning getting on and then off antidepressants—raised the risk of suicide.[12] Others expressed concern about the absence of a replacement form of treatment, for example, psychotherapy, if adolescents and children are taken off an antidepressant therapy regime.[13]

—∿—

I fully understand a parent's fears about the effects of psychiatric medications on their young children and teenagers. When Sammy was taking four prescribed drugs at a time and showing no real improvement, I rarely left him alone for more than a few hours. I took on only freelance writing work I could do at home so as to stay close by him.

I'd occupied this state of hyper-awareness for years, ever since we'd gotten Alex's diagnosis. I could rarely shake my fear—more like a constant low-grade fever—of *the other shoe dropping*. There was a shadow trailing first Alex's and now Sammy's every move and mood, God forbid, if one of my sons should appear momentarily unhappy; then surely he was about to do *something foolish*. It was a great relief when, a year later, we found a psychiatrist who believed in trying one medicine at a time until he found the right one for Sammy, but there would be more scary lows to go through before we got there.

"MOM, I'M JOINING THE MARINES"

Sammy and I had just finished eating lunch at a café in San Francisco, enjoying a pleasant conversation. Being together had gotten easier since I'd acquired the self-discipline to stop talking about "Sammy's problem," unless he brought it up. After strolling around the bookstore attached to the restaurant, we went out onto the sidewalk to part ways, me to my condo, him to get on the BART and return to the house he shared with Alex. But as I turned to go, he stood still and shifted awkwardly from one foot to the other.

"Is something wrong?" I asked, ever vigilant.

He looked away and said, "Ummm . . . Mom, I'm joining the Marines."

No. I didn't just hear that, I thought, while my mind flooded with images of legless, lifeless boys being carried out of Iraq in body bags. The date of this conversation matters; it was May 2007; "the surge" just barely under way, with fighting at its bloodiest. I simply couldn't, wouldn't stand for it.

"Mom?" Sammy pressed, now making uncomfortable eye contact.

"How could you possibly do this to me?" I asked.

I'm not proud of this response; it was a low and manipulative mother ploy, but I'd panicked. "It would kill me if anything happened to you," I said, going still lower. Then it occurred to me that my protests might be too late.

"What have you done about it?" I asked him.

"I just talked to this guy at the mall."

"Oh, my God. You didn't sign anything, did you?"

"No, not yet."

By now I saw that Sammy understood what I was up to; that I wasn't going to let up on the guilt trip, and he got pissed off.

"Mom, this really isn't fair," he said, giving me a disgusted, disappointed look.

"I don't care," I said, meaning it. "You just can't do this to me."

I knew I couldn't keep using this line of attack. If I kept it up too long, I risked pushing him away from me and into the arms of the Marines.

"Just tell me why you would do this?" I pleaded.

And then he leveled. "I'm just sick of feeling so rotten about myself."

"Oh, so you think fighting in an unjustified war will make you feel better about yourself?"

"I don't know," he said, struggling. "I just can't keep going on like I am."

"I understand," I answered, trying to bring the conversation to a more positive place. "But let's try and figure out something besides war to help you get out of it."

"No, please . . . just let me do this," he said, backing away, clearly not wanting to talk any longer. "I gotta go."

"No, not yet . . . I know we can think of something."

"Like what? I'm sick of therapy."

"How about the Peace Corps?"

He did a double take, clearly considering the notion, then shook his head. "They wouldn't take me. I'm a college drop-out."

"Then something *like it*, for kids who haven't graduated from college."

He looked at me skeptically.

"Just give the whole thing a couple of weeks, and we'll see if we can find something better."

He sighed and agreed that he would not talk to the recruiter again; at least not until after we looked into other options. Then we hugged good-bye, and I hurried back to my condo, shaking.

After that, I scrambled, using my frantic search for something to steer Sammy away from the Marines to avoid feeling any more fear about it than I had to.

It took a few weeks (with the recruiter calling Sammy daily), but I did find something that appealed to Sammy: a group out of the United Kingdom that arranges "gap-year" volunteer projects for eighteen- to twenty-five-year-olds. Sammy signed up to help build a school and to teach war orphans in an NGO-sponsored humanitarian project in Uganda. He spent four months there in the summer and fall of 2007, and it proved life-changing in all the best ways. As Sammy explained it, helping other people who were materially so much worse off than he was got him completely "out of his head." His tangible contributions—raising the new school building and working with the kids—had been the best possible medicine for him. Being part of a team of twelve men and women his own age also gave him something he'd been craving: that camaraderie that's so hard for young people to find when they're out of school and newly making their way in the world.

I'm not proud of how I got Sammy out of the Marine recruiter's hands and off to Uganda; however, I have no regrets about making it happen. We dodged far more than a bullet in that moment. It was so clear to me that being as depressed as he was made Sammy extremely vulnerable to the fantasy that he could get "fixed" by joining the Marines and going off to war.

Sammy came back from Uganda stronger and clearer. He found a summer job in retail and a lovely girlfriend, to boot. He then thought he was ready to make a return to college. But without a medication, his fluctuating moods still subjected him to sporadic days of being down and without motivation—and that gave us both pause. That's when he decided to try working with a new psychiatrist who put him on Zoloft®, an SSRI known to treat symptoms of both depression and anxiety. Sammy has been on it ever since, for three years now, and it works well for him.

That doesn't mean that he doesn't occasionally have his down days—and times when he makes things harder for himself. Unbeknownst to me, Sammy decided at the end of the last school year to take a "summer break" from his antidepressant. The thinking, he told me later, was to give his brain "a rest." Well, it didn't quite work that way. After returning to school, Sammy discovered there was a six-week wait to get a counseling center appointment, necessary to renew his prescription. In the meantime, he relapsed into a full depressive episode, becoming despondent and sleepless and rarely leaving his dorm room. I eventually heard about this episode when Sammy called me late one night in mid-November to say he was afraid that he'd flunked out. Fortunately, this wasn't yet true; he was able to get back on track, make up incomplete work, and slide through.

Sammy now says that with the stress of a full load of classes in front of him, he knows he can't afford to put his brain on another roller coaster. He's decided to keep taking the medication so he can to hang on to the stable moods he needs to accomplish his goal. His plan, he says, is to get his BS in molecular biology, a heavy-duty academic schedule that requires wall-to-wall math and science classes with labs five days a week, with the hope of getting into medical school.

A LEG UP OR DOWN

Just recently I got wind of a new study that shed light on this sort of downward cascade that can go on for students like Sammy who are under such relentless stress—but with a fascinating twist. Researchers at the University of Michigan monitored 740 medical school interns during their residencies at thirteen hospitals. From a baseline of 3.9 percent who were tested and found to be moderately depressed at the start, the proportion of those meeting the criteria of moderately depressed rose to 25.7 percent by the end. The factors most likely to raise the interns' risk for depression included working more hours, experiencing medical errors, and adding other stressful life events— nothing surprising so far.

But then investigators found a risk factor that trumped all the others and appeared to wield enormous influence over which students succumbed to depression under high stress and which didn't: their genotypes. Controlling for environmental factors such as work hours and medical mistakes, those medical students who carried a short allele, meaning a lower-functioning version of the 5-HTT serotonin transponder (serotonin is a neurotransmitter that, when scarce, is thought to cause depression) had a 43 percent higher risk of depression than those who had a higher-functioning version of this gene transponder.[14]

This gene × environment (G × E) finding tells us that although the playing field may look even, we each bring liabilities and strengths to the starting line of every task we undertake. And while for the time being these advantages and disadvantages remain invisible to us, this may not be the case for long. For the science of mental illness, this newfound ability to telescopically zero in on an individual's genetic risk factors opens a pathway for research that could fulfill the promise of personalized, better-targeted therapies, such as antidepressants. I can only hope these improved pharmaceuticals arrive in time to help one future doctor I know fulfill his dream.

—⁓⁓—

With Sammy back in school and Alex more or less managing on his own, I was freer to focus on my own life—with plenty of unresolved issues waiting for me to look at. It was also time to pick up the journey into my family's past that I had begun years earlier and had not yet completed.

PART 2

REVISITING THE FAMILY ILLNESS: GENERATIONS TWO AND THREE

Ar séath a chéile a mhaireas na daoine.
In the shadows of each other we must build our lives.
—Celtic proverb

Chapter 7

THE DEPRESSED MOTHER

Have you had any serious health conditions?
No, none.
All right, Dr. C. said, shall we go on to your siblings?

I felt torn: I had just told her I was healthy. Of course I didn't say I'd been depressed for as long as I could remember. Nor did I mention my drinking. *I'd always worked around it, hadn't I?* Dr. C.'s expression was sympathetic. Clearly she was throwing me a lifeline. Still, I was afraid—*what if I allowed the truth about me to come out, and my whole fragile house of cards came tumbling down?*

"I'm just wondering," I said. "This might not be the right time to ask, but do you think I might have . . . could I have a problem with depression?"

I flashed on the debris I'd left at home after staying up all night waiting for word of Alex's whereabouts and then rushing to get out to the hospital first thing in the morning. The empty bottle of cheap chardonnay on my coffee table; the expensive concealer I'd used to cover the dark circles under my eyes left on the sink; the flinty smile still imprinted on the bathroom mirror, the one I'd practiced in hopes it would disguise my pain when I delivered my firstborn son to this state-of-the-art kiddie psyche ward.

"Without a thorough interview," Dr. C. began. "I can't diagnose you."

Of course, stupid me. She's not going to want to mix it up here.

She then continued. "But I do see indications . . . certainly with your family history. If you would like a referral—"

"No, not yet," I interrupted.

"All right," she said, as we moved on to the next chapter in our family medical history.

It would take me another six months to pick up the thread of that conversation.

—⚏—

Bouts of depression hit me soon after I turned eleven and then worsened quickly. I remember putting one foot in front of the other without feeling my body, watching, listening, even laughing with my friends but not truly participating or engaging with school. Day after day, I was underwater, rarely coming up for air, most of the time not even thinking it possible. The strangest thing (looking back) was that this default state of mind felt *normal*.

I'd been aware of the antidepressant option since Prozac® came out in 1986. A close friend, Carol, was one of the first to go on it and swore by the changes in her life. Perhaps looking for reasons not to consider it for myself, I saw only what looked like a new flatness in Carol. Gone were our late-night anguished conversations about a failing relationship or her fading chance to become a mother. I missed the drama we'd always shared.

Broke, alone, and drinking, I was feeling increasingly scared—not just for Alex and Sammy, but for me, too. I wasn't working and had no health insurance, so my only option for getting help when I finally decided to seek it was to go to the nearest public mental health clinic. Sitting in the clinic's hot and crowded waiting room at the far end of a Van Nuys strip mall in the San Fernando Valley, my worst expectations were quickly fulfilled. Every chair was filled, the stench of homelessness, unavoidable. In one corner, a boy Alex's age talked to himself emphatically, while an older man paced jerkily from one end of the long room to the other. It was hard to know where to look with so much misery surrounding me.

Then the clinic door opened, and a woman whose age I couldn't guess entered. She had matted hair and wore a heavy coat, despite the warm temperature. The agitation in her gait and her heavy breathing immediately drew attention as she crossed the waiting room and went right to the Plexiglas® window that separated patients from clinic staff. But instead of ringing the buzzer as the sign instructed, the woman banged on the glass with her fist. Tension notched up as a male receptionist opened a speakeasy-style window and asked for her identification.

The woman handed over a laminated card and shifted her weight impatiently while the attendant checked a computer screen—only to be told that she didn't have an appointment. Cursing, she turned her head and, with a contorted mouth and squinted eyes, fixed her gaze in my direction. I felt like I'd been slapped. I couldn't help staring right back as she simultaneously glared at me while searching every pocket of her coat, pants, and shirt.

How dare I take time with a doctor away from this pathetic woman? I thought, as I watched her put an unlit cigarette in her mouth and walk to the exit. As she fussed with the door handle, pulling rather than pushing, I forced myself not to jump up and give her my appointment. But then a realization came to me. Take away the funky clothes and surly attitude, and she and I were the same; both of us there because we could no longer fake it out in the "real world."

When my name was announced a minute later, I got up and walked through the now unlocked door into the entrails of the clinic. I was led to a windowless, utilitarian office filled with metal furniture, books, and piles of files. Dr. B. didn't get up or smile; he just pointed to the lone chair opposite his desk. While he read over my intake sheet, I noticed the framed photo of him standing in hiking gear on a mountain next to a teenage boy and a woman, presumably his wife, with snowcapped peaks behind them. I found myself wondering whether she minded his working in this place rather than a private practice where he could be making the big bucks.

When he asked my reason for coming, I told my story as briefly as I could. He asked questions, took a handful of notes. I half expected him to tell me to just cut the booze and get out of there. Instead he put down the file and made eye contact.

"There's no question you have dual depression," Dr. B. said.

"Can you explain that?"

"It sounds like you've had mild depression since late childhood. As you get older, you're having longer episodes of major depression, which your alcohol intake is only making worse. The crisis with your son has pushed you into the severe episode you're dealing with now."

I was startled by how quickly and efficiently he delivered this diagnosis to me. *I guess there's simply no time to waste in a clinic like this one*, I remember thinking. But on reflection, it came down to this: all the high-priced psychotherapy I'd done over the prior two decades paled in comparison to the quality of care I received in that one, forty-minute session with that kind, understated man. Getting a diagnosis for something that has been part of you for your entire life is truly a strange experience. Ironically, the fact that mild depression is so chronic—like a personality trait—keeps many people from getting treatment, according to national surveys.[1]

THERAPY IS NOT A CAREER

Unlike the therapists I'd seen for months or years at a time since my early twenties, Dr. B. was willing to name my problem and respond to my need to function better—immediately. Previously, following the lead of my psychodynamic therapists, the kind who plumb childhood for causes to current personality problems, I had viewed the symptoms of my depression as the initial obstacles in a field expedition to a "higher purpose." It was a Freudian construct: believing that my task was to excavate nuggets of gold, those elusive insights that lay at the bottom of my psyche. Once I found them, so the construct went, I'd be free of symptoms and the emotional baggage I'd been carrying around all my life. Or at least I'd be wiser for having searched for them.

As it happens, talk therapy alone didn't work for me. Not if success is defined as becoming a self-sufficient, functional person and parent. Oddly, the first health provider to tell me in no uncertain terms that I was dangerously depressed and needed to be on an antidepressant was an obstetrician who saw me for a follow-up appointment after an abortion I had at age forty-one—two years after my divorce while in one of a succession of dead-end relationships. I remember telling this doctor, "No. I don't believe in psychiatric medications." I also remember her concerned expression and the long silence in the room that followed my refusal to consider her advice. That was 1993; it would take five more years of severe depression, and Alex's hospitalization, to get me to reconsider and get help.

People who speak negatively about antidepressants often complain that they mask your deeper issues and treat only symptoms. As if this is a bad thing. When I hear this line of argument, as I still frequently do, I detect in it the unspoken message that depressed people are getting off too easy, presumably by skipping over the hard stuff in life with the help of a drug. To me, this criticism doesn't add up. The *only way* I was ever going to blast through the Berlin Wall of fear and hopelessness separating me from my true feelings was with the help of an antidepressant.

Myrna Weissman, in answer to a consumer question on the Columbia University Department of Psychiatry website, said, "Psychotherapy is not a career path. . . . [When you're in therapy] you have a contract as to how long you're going to continue and what you're going to achieve."[2] I think Weissman's comment gets right to why my own earlier attempts at psychotherapy were relatively unproductive. I had used my weekly sessions as a comfort and a means of coping—a "career path," if you will—not as a route to recovery.

Before I left the San Fernando Valley clinic, I asked Dr. B. if he wouldn't mind explaining to me how someone first develops dual depression. By then, I'd read some of the science, but I still wanted a real human being to explain it to me. What I got felt more like redemption than explanation, which probably says as much about my state of mind as it does about his words. I wrote them down verbatim as soon as I got home.

"Experiencing the early loss of your father, and not having an emotionally trustworthy relationship with your mother, you came to believe you had to avoid feeling of any kind, good or bad. You shut down your feelings and survived on will power. That causes a lot of stress and compensatory chemical reactions in a child's brain. It's like living in 'fight-or-flight' state all the time. As time goes on, the brain habituates, and you become depressed."

Dr. B. handed me my first prescription for an antidepressant. "This should help. Give it a few weeks." Leaving the clinic that day, I felt seen and heard as I'd never been before.

—⁂—

My first antidepressant medication was Paxil®. It was everything I'd hoped for, at once subtle and magnificent. In this initial period of near-euphoria, I woke up feeling optimistic and stayed that way most of the day and into the night. Dealing with difficult things and people became easier. I went back to work and reconnected with friends.

After six months on Paxil, I switched to Bupropion, brand name Wellbutrin®. It produced the same positive emotional lift without the sleepiness I eventually experienced with Paxil. Today I remain on Bupropion and plan to stay on it indefinitely. The data on getting off an antidepressant after lifelong major depression is not very encouraging. Most people relapse within a year.[3] I don't plan to be one of them.

Eventually, as I improved, the "good news" of this new, improved "me" presented an unexpected challenge. I faced enormous guilt over my prior poor performance as a mother. I can vividly remember being awakened at dawn by Alex's cries after a few hours of sleep and wishing me (or he) dead; then, later, sitting on the carpet staring at the neon colors of a Candy Land® game board feeling immobilized and exhausted. I was unable to throw the dice or move my silly little plastic figure another inch—and I hated myself for it. Ironically, because I'd heard about postpartum depression being a "normal" part of the childbirth experience, I hadn't sought treatment for these debilitating feelings that followed both Alex's and Sammy's births.

MOTHERS, CHILDREN, AND DEPRESSION

Myrna Weissman has spent three decades researching exactly how depression runs in families, first at Yale, and now managing multiple studies and clinical trials while serving as a professor of epidemiology in psychiatry at Columbia University and as chief of the Division of Clinical and Genetic Epidemiology at the New York Psychiatric Institute. In 2009, she accepted my request for an interview and invited me to her Upper East Side apartment where she was working at home on a holiday. She offered coffee, warning in a no-nonsense manner that I'd have to take it black, before leading me to her living room.

While waiting for her to return with the coffee, I reread a profile of her I'd stuffed into my notebook. In it, she reminisces about managing the three-generation family study on depression with which she made her mark as a young clinical researcher at Yale while raising four children. Given the titles and awards she's racked up since then, there's irony in Weissman's account of how she ended up with this massive job as a young newbie researcher in part because at the time funding was easy to get and not many investigators were doing epidemiology in psychiatry, making studies of high-risk families quite novel. Weissman re-joined me and immediately apologized, saying she could spare only thirty minutes for our conversation, noting several imminent NIMH grant deadlines but then proceeded to give me an hour. I explained the premise of this book and asked about her ongoing study measuring the effects on children of treating their mothers' depression, which, as mentioned previously, has produced some elegant results with huge implications. Of those children who shared a diagnosis of depression with their mothers at the beginning of the mother's treatment, remission of symptoms was reported in one-third of cases when their mothers' treatment worked, compared with only a 12 percent remission rate among those whose mothers' depression did not improve after treatment. All children of recovering mothers who themselves did not begin with a diagnosis for depression remained free of psychiatric diagnoses at three months, whereas 17 percent of the children whose mothers remained depressed acquired a psychiatric diagnosis. "If the mother is depressed and just one other close relative in the family has a history of depression we know the children are likely to show up with either anxiety or depression by the time they're fifteen," Weissman told me.[4]

—⁓—

When a depressed parent raises a child who is at genetic risk for depression, the blurred line between nature and nurture becomes harder to find. How much does the depressive personality of a mother or father shape the child who takes her emotional cues from that parent? When "normal" in a family translates into a state of depression, how does a child overcome his expectation to be like Mom or Dad? The research tells us that a child in that position has got a lot stacked against him.

One study involving a community sample of 812 fifteen-year-old depressed and nondepressed adolescents with depressed and nondepressed mothers living in Queensland, Australia, parsed the issues of nature and nurture in depressed families using a set of intriguing and testable hypotheses.[5] After getting a baseline reading of the presence or absence of depressive symptoms in each participant, researchers measured both the chronic and short-term "episodic" stresses that had been experienced by the adolescents during the past six to twelve months and correlated these events to their depressed or nondepressed states.

Their first question was: Is a fifteen-year-old boy with a depressed mother (versus a nondepressed mother) more likely to respond to life's stressors by getting depressed? The answer seemed like an easy yes, and it was. After that, the researchers' questions got more interesting; the answers less predictable. They wanted to find out what kind of stressful events were most likely to trigger either the initially depressed or nondepressed adolescents into a severe depressive episode. Would the worse stressor be a chronic condition of his life; for example, living in a poor, crime-ridden neighborhood? Or was it more likely to be a one-time traumatic event, such as getting dumped by his first love?

In their results, researchers found that all risks for depression, even among children of depressed mothers, are not alike in their capacity to make life newly miserable for these adolescents. The chance of a teenager going from "at risk" to having depression was significantly higher in children of depressed mothers *when the stressful event was of a chronic nature*—the poor neighborhood example.

However, for the sons and daughters of nondepressed mothers, the risk for depression was higher after they experienced an episodic stress, like a romantic break-up.

With further scrutiny, these researchers concluded that the decisive factor increasing the risk of depression for the adolescents with depressed mothers was their mothers' chronic social difficulties. Another factor contributing to the worse outcomes for children with depressed mothers, investigators concluded, was the weight of negative self-beliefs they carried. These beliefs, investigators said, made them more vulnerable to problems in their social relationships.[6]

These results strongly suggest that having a mother who is not depressed and who thus can better navigate those aspects of day-to-day living over which we have little control, like poverty and joblessness, can make the difference between a child succumbing to depression or not—especially when the stresses are chronic, as so many in life are.

The unavoidable message of this epidemiological and clinical research is that we are taking a huge and unnecessary risk if we skirt our responsibility as mothers (and fathers) to handle our own depression, addictions, or other mental disorders. The pathways by which we transfer unresolved mental health issues from one generation to the next are no longer mysterious; children acquire our genes just as they internalize our everyday behaviors. We've even got state-of-the-art brain images to show us how one such transfer works.

YOUR BRAIN AT RISK FOR DEPRESSION

In 2009, neuroscientists at the Columbia College of Physicians and Surgeons working with epidemiologists at the New York Psychiatric Institute married behavioral observations and MRI scans and came up with a stunning result: photographic evidence of significant deterioration in the brains of children and adults who were only *at high risk for depression*—meaning those who *did not* yet have depressed symptoms.[7] Under the direction of Dr. Bradley Peterson, brain scans of 131 individuals, ages six to fifty-four—half of whom were offspring of a parent with major depression—revealed that those with a family risk of depression had a 28 percent average reduction in the surface of their left cortical hemisphere—the main thinking center of the brain.

In his comments, Dr. Peterson compared these reductions in gray matter to the most extreme abnormalities seen in neurological diseases such as Alzheimer's disease. He wrote, "These are all the more remarkable because this thinning is present in persons who have never suffered from major depression or anxiety disorders, but are biological descendents of a depressed relative."[8] The at-risk descendents in this study who already manifested symptoms of depression showed more brain thinning than those who were at genetic risk but not (yet) affected. The more severe their depressions, the greater the thinning researchers found in their right hemispheres, a thinning that extended into the left hemisphere in some of the more depressed individuals.

When tested, the study participants who showed this cortical thinning in their brain scans also had deficiencies in their ability to sustain attention and in their visual memory of social and emotional cues. Together, these biomarkers and behavioral traits point to what Peterson calls a "common, final disease pathway" for depression and a mechanism for its inheritance. How so? The ability to pay attention, to see and remember people or emotional cues is an important social skill that, when diminished, can lead someone to greater social isolation and depression.[9] In other words, the neurobiological cause of the poor social and coping skills evident in the Australian study of depressed mothers that researchers found made their kids' lives so much harder, have, in this brain-imaging study, been photographed in the brains of similarly depressed parents and their at-risk children. We can now see nature and nurture as constantly interacting influences manifesting in the same neural pathways and behaviors. The fluidity of this disease process, scientists working in G × E research suggest, may provide cause for optimism. More and more, we're seeing that brain health is something that can be restored as well as taken away.

THE RISK OF DOING NOTHING

In 1995, when I was forty-three, there was a night when my depression crossed the line to *suicidal ideation*. This is the point at which you begin to imagine not *if*, but *how*, to plot your escape from this life. I'd just returned from making a film in Wyoming and was staying at the Pacific Palisades home of a friend while she and her husband were out of town. Alex and Sammy, then fifteen and nine years old, were with their dad while I tried to get my life together.

I'd been living in Wyoming on the edge of Yellowstone National Park for four months, existing on a diet of coffee and wine while trying to keep a shaky film project alive. That documentary, *Wolf Nation*, tells the story of the return of the endangered gray wolf to the national park. The wolf was and still is a much-hated predator for many ranchers in Wyoming, making their government-mandated restoration a volatile subject for anyone to tackle.

All the controversy surrounding the issue caused financing for the film to fall through at the last minute. Nonetheless, in a fog of grandiosity, I charged ahead on a shoestring and my credit cards, incurring over $50,000 worth of debts along with the wrath of the Arapaho Indian Wolf Clan and a dozen production people who'd agreed to work cheap, who I then couldn't pay more than ten cents on the dollar. The chaos eventually pushed me into personal bankruptcy. It also brought me to a brink of a despair I could no longer escape.

But on this particular night in my friend's empty house, my sins as a financial deadbeat hadn't yet turned into full-fledged lawsuits, leaving me that night to focus only on being broke and lonely. While out of town, I had broken things off "for the last time" with a man (I'll call him Aaron) with whom I'd been involved for three years—a married former network television executive who'd swept me off my feet soon after my divorce. He'd deserted me for another woman who was not his wife. Even as I shed tears over this abandonment, I knew my wound was about so much more than Aaron. But he was the last suture to come undone. And now all I wanted was to make the pain go away. I found myself contemplating how I should kill myself.

I had no interest in physical pain. An overdose was the way to go, I remember thinking, as I stood in the bathroom, evaluating which of my friend's prescription bottles in her medicine chest would produce the quickest result. I found Valium®. I picked it up and brought it, along with an open bottle of chardonnay, out into the Asian-inspired garden filled with statuary, fountains, and small-scale plantings. Welcoming me was a life-sized Shakti, the Hindu goddess, with her eight flailing arms for slaying dark forces. A smiling Buddha flanked her.

As I lowered myself into a teak chair next to a red Chinese maple tree, my breathing became difficult. I thought I might be having a panic attack. I took some deep breaths, poured a glass of wine, and swallowed two of the Valiums in one long gulp just as a start. When I opened my eyes a minute later, Buddha seemed to be mocking me from across the fountain. To avoid him, I leaned back in my chair and stared up at the sky. And that's when my doubts arrived in earnest.

Did I want to down the whole bottle of pills? Undecided, I went back inside and got the portable phone to call my friend Racine. Racine earned her living as a "psychic to the stars" and by dispensing advice to all of us Hollywood wannabes. I quickly filled her in on all the things that had led me to this place, ending with my heartbreak about Aaron. She quickly and coldly offered her opinion that the relationship was a nonstarter and I was a love addict. Not exactly what I wanted to hear. She then moved on to the tough-love part of the conversation, warning me of the problem with suicide; her spiritual belief, she explained, was that if I killed myself, my soul would not move on to some heavenly rest home. Rather, I'd be immediately directed into a new incarnation where I'd face the same knotty issues all over again only somehow worse.

"So you see there's no way out," Racine said firmly. "Victoria?"

"Yes. I'm here."

"You've got to think about your boys."

Remarkably, over the previous hour, I'd actually forgotten Alex and Sammy even existed. This, from a mother who normally wouldn't allow them to walk ten blocks from school to home alone.

"Oh, my God," I said, feeling thoroughly ashamed.

Racine seemed to sense I'd made it back to more solid ground. She advised me to act as if things were getting better, assuring me that if I kept acting optimistically, they would actually improve. She told me to call her later if I needed to. But, by then, the two Valiums and wine had kicked in. I made my way to the guest room and crawled into bed, thoroughly spent. Now, when I'm asked why I take antidepressants, I often give as an example that night in 1995, when I came a step closer to suicide as a touchstone. I try to find adequate words for how lonely, scared, and desperate I felt; how close to giving up I was before I started taking the right medicine for what ailed me.

MY LITTLE YELLOW PILLS

I'm a poster child for the emotional and practical benefits of antidepressants. Within a year, my income tripled. I moved from Los Angeles to my present home in San Francisco, leaving behind Aaron and years of underemployment in the chaotic television business. In San Francisco I worked for several web businesses in the heyday of the Internet boom—which you'll recall didn't last long. I then decided I really wanted to write fiction as well as creative nonfiction, so I returned to finish my creative writing degree (dropped in 1975 with two semesters to go) at Mills College.

I found out that I could live and be happy on my own, and that, probably as a result, my relationships with men gradually got better and longer. For the last two years, after a healthily slow courtship, I've shared my life and home with Tom. Interestingly, we're both grandchildren of Irish immigrants and New York transplants, having come to California to escape the drama of our families of origin, which we soon discovered were equally chaotic and tragedy-filled. What I appreciate most about Tom is his sense of humor. I often listen and marvel as he uses it as both a sword and a lubricant for sticky situations in his business as a general contractor, and then again at home, where living with a writer can be equally challenging.

I've been asked several times if I miss my pre-antidepressant self. Do I miss days and weeks of despair? How about the sleepless nights? I believe the real question many people are asking is whether I've become a flatter, duller version of myself. And the answer is probably yes, but I'll take it.

Andrew Solomon describes the journey from depression to recovery exquisitely in his classic *Noonday Demon, An Atlas of Depression*. "Drug therapy hacks through the vines. . . . You can feel the weight going, feel the way that the branches can recover much of their natural bent. Until you got rid of that vine, you cannot think about what has been lost. But even with the vine gone, you may still have few leaves and shallow roots, and the rebuilding of your self cannot be achieved with any drugs that now exist."[10]

Solomon's last sentence speaks volumes to me. After my first three years on antidepressants, I found myself getting confused and worried that I'd lost touch with my core identity. It was as if my stable mood was eclipsing my former sense of who I was. I eventually went back to psychotherapy to do the necessary internal restructuring. Interestingly, this time, I was in and out of therapy in six sessions.

Doing therapy this time while on antidepressant medication helped me finally let go of that old baggage (in a nutshell, my "Daddy's girl" thing) and acquire some new ways of thinking and behaving that I then had to integrate into my old self: having an expectation that I would be liked, doing my taxes or the dinner dishes; returning a difficult phone call. When you've rarely if ever done these things easily, getting through them without trauma can be jarring—and, eventually, joyful. I am a much calmer, less melodramatic and self-pitying person than I used to be, and I'm also a more trustworthy friend, less susceptible to collapsing into despair and social isolation. I can look back and see my principal life accomplishments—mainly keeping my sons alive and finishing some films and books—as massive and largely successful efforts to compensate for these same tendencies. But these "successes" came at a great cost. In order for me to make a film, pull Alex out of a deep hole, or even sustain a love affair past a few weeks, it took so much energy that collapsing after reaching the finish line was all but guaranteed. The level of effort required for a depressed person to do something "big" is so huge it can produce a high level of success. But it's not a sustainable way to live or work. Eventually, a flatter curve looks awfully good.

Chapter 8

MY SISTER RITA: MENTAL ILLNESS AND SELF-MEDICATION

Rita Laurie Costello

(1953–1992)

> *My sister Rita died in 1992.*
> *Her cause of death?*
> *Her death certificate read "cardiac arrest."*

When spoons began to disappear from my mother's silverware drawer in the late 1960s, neither my mother nor I suspected my sister Rita's dope use. It didn't dawn on us that heroin had to be mixed with water and cooked over a flame before it was injected.

My friends and I smoked pot regularly, and we had also tried psychedelics, mushrooms, and acid—*tried* being the operative word. Since we still got good grades, held down after-school jobs, and didn't flaunt the behavior, our drug use stayed under the radar of parents and teachers—and the local police. Rita went further and did it much faster, and more overtly. She flew through pot and discovered barbiturates, speed, and cocaine. Heroin was too pricey without an older boyfriend, but by the time she was sixteen, it had nonetheless become her drug of choice. She started stealing to get it: Mom's wedding band was one of the first casualties; soon, cash could no longer be left in a drawer or purse.

This was before drug rehab as a concept had entered the American cultural lexicon. Mom didn't understand what was happening to her youngest, prettiest, and heretofore easiest child; and there was no one in our white, middle-class New York City suburb to help her sort it out. And so my mother routinely nagged and criticized Rita and bailed her out of trouble. In a letter she wrote to her sister Lillian during Rita's senior year of high school, Mom described the aftermath of Rita's first, near-fatal overdose:

> *When she passed out at the party, three men took her to Grosvenor Hospital in Lower Manhattan and just left her on the sidewalk. The cops took her in. She was hardly breathing, the doctor said. They had to give her an adrenalin injection to the heart and slap her back to life. When she got home after (she called it the "accident"), she was afraid to be left alone. She even slept with me last night. She seems ashamed of herself, but let's see what happens when the fright wears off.*

My mother had been an unknowing foot soldier, more like a guerilla fighter, drafted into a war she only learned about near its end.

A WAR ON DRUGS

Until the late twentieth century, with the exception of those talented, rich, or royal enough to be granted the license of eccentricity, an individual's addictions to alcohol, opium, and the like were seen as his private moral lapse, perhaps the work of the devil. When President Richard Nixon declared his war on drugs in 1971, it helped create a new and favorable climate for research into the causes of addiction. This research gave birth to the field of drug rehabilitation, and out of that treatment came the theory of self-medication—the idea that addiction comes about because people are attempting to alleviate the distress of preexisting mental disorders. The concept had come originally from Freud, in 1884, after he noted the antidepressant properties of cocaine.[1]

This theory immediately caused a storm of controversy because it challenged views then held by the medical community and law enforcement that attributed drug abuse to peer pressures, family breakdown, affluence, escapism, and lax policing. For the first time, the nation's newly minted suburban drug addicts (typified by my sister) were joining their less affluent urban counterparts, who were already populating US jails and hospitals. Junkies—hippies, rich and poor, black and white, addicts and alcoholics—constituted an equal-opportunity mental health crisis for public health doctors on the front lines of treatment in big-city hospital emergency rooms.

The father of the self-medication hypothesis is Edward J. Khantzian, a founding member of the Psychiatry Department at Harvard's Cambridge

Hospital. Khantzian, writing in 1985, believed addicts weren't victims of random selection but instead had a *drug of choice*: a specific drug affinity dictated by "psychopharmacologic action of the drug and the dominant painful feelings with which they struggle." For example, he observed the energizing effect of cocaine and other stimulants in response to the depletion and fatigue of addicts dealing with preexisting depression. In his patients who abused opiates, Khantzian noted the calming effect of heroin on the addict's typically problematic impulsivity.[2]

The idea that human psychological vulnerabilities had anything to do with addiction was a brand-new piece of the puzzle, and it reflected Khantzian's psychoanalytic background as much as his clinical work at the Cambridge Clinic. As a clinician, he saw the important roles played by what he called the damaged "ego and self structures" in his addicted patients. He then identified the following four common areas of psychological problems that led his patients to addiction: a lack of affect (as noted, refers to low emotional expression), damaged self-esteem, inability to form and maintain relationships, and lack of self-care.[3]

Three decades later, Khantzian's hypothesis is accepted medicine; one psychiatrist, reviewing a textbook edited by Khantzian, referred to the "simplicity and beauty of the self-medication hypothesis, and its usefulness in the clinical situation."[4]

—ⱳ—

Rita's flirty, fun-loving ways masked a deeply insecure self. My sister, who never went beyond a few community college classes, once visited me while I was a student at American University in Washington, DC. One night, to get away from my housemates who seemed to intimidate her into silence with their talk of culture and politics, we went to a neighborhood bar. When we sat down with our drinks, I enthusiastically shared with her my interest in a new form of psychotherapy called primal therapy. I explained that it involved a three-week intensive group experience. Knowing she'd just received a $10,000 settlement from a car accident, I was hoping she might loan me $1,000 to help me pay for an upcoming group I wanted to do. As I made my request, I referred obliquely to our early family sadness, especially losing Dad when we were so young. She startled me with her answer.

"Yeah . . . it was like growing up in a concentration camp," she said, before averting her eyes and gulping her whiskey, straight up, no ice.

I thought it an absurd overstatement, but it made me acutely aware of how much pain my sister was hiding behind her "I just want to have fun" exterior. When she dug into her purse and wrote me out a check, I knew all too well that my sister needed therapy as much or more than I did. But the only time Rita got any psychological treatment was when it was court-mandated as part of a sentence for a drug bust.

We were both in our midtwenties when my sister began her fast downward spiral. Her behavior alternately saddened and enraged me, as I carried an ever-growing wad of survivor's guilt over the fact that even though I had used every drug Rita had used—even heroin—I never became addicted. The first, and last, time I had tried heroin was in the late 1960s when I'd come to stay for the weekend in Rita's apartment on Prince Street. She lived there with her boyfriend, Frank, who, within hours of my arrival, brought home a small plastic bag of white powder and unceremoniously dropped it onto the kitchen table. Rita grabbed the bag and went straight to the sink. Using a spoon, she added a few drops of water and cooked the heroin over a gas burner. Then she leaned over the stove with a syringe and deftly injected the liquid into a vein on her arm. When she stood up straight again, she flashed me an impish grin, as if we shared a new secret. "You want to shoot it?" she asked, nodding at a tin can on the stove.

"No, I'm bad with needles." I said, feeling helpless to stop what was happening.

Rita shrugged. She brought the bag over to the kitchen table and drew two parallel lines of white powder directly in front of me. Then she pulled a dollar bill from the pocket of her jeans, rolled it up into a tight coil, and handed it to me.

In what I can only describe as a twisted attempt to bond with my sister, I took the bill and inhaled a line of heroin into each nostril. In the time it took Rita to pick out an album and put it on the stereo, I felt seized by a rush of the fabled, no-one-can-hurt-me bubble that drug users talk about. The feeling stayed with me for several hours as I lay on Rita's beat-up old sofa, listening to her music, each of us in a perfect world of our own making. Even coming down from heroin wasn't bad. As I told her afterward, it was—as she had said it would be—fabulous; so good I knew I would never, ever do it again. That comment didn't please Rita. She felt I was judging her one more time.

—m—

When my sister fell in love with heroin, illegal drug use by American teens was just a skirmish in the looming showdown between the establishment and its counterculture over the Vietnam War, the sexual revolution, and civil rights. For most of us who participated in these protests, there were no lasting negative consequences from the drug use that helped fuel much of our youthful rebellion. However, for some, including Rita, the repercussions were deadly and long lasting.

Today's teenagers still binge drink and experiment with the same illegal drugs—marijuana, speed, prescription painkillers, cocaine, and heroin—that a number of their parents did a generation ago. While the overall rates of illegal drug and alcohol use have gone down, those who do the illegal experimenting today tend to start earlier. The other important difference between then and now is the availability today of conclusive science that allows us to identify those young people whose drug use is five or ten times more likely to trigger a psychotic episode or a pattern of addiction based on their family history.[5]

I didn't have any inkling of this unequal effect of alcohol and drugs on different people back in the sixties when my friends and I started with booze and marijuana, and then went on to try every other drug out there at least once. I do recall being puzzled about one male friend in the eleventh grade who seemed unable to stop smoking pot on a daily basis, arriving at school stoned and ending each day the same way. Since I could take it or leave it, I wondered why he had so little control over his pot habit. I was stumped about the same thing in my sister Rita when I witnessed her powerless relationships with heroin and alcohol.

I suppose I went no further than thinking they were weaker than I was in some fundamental way. It wasn't until after Alex was treated and diagnosed at UCLA and I started reading about inherited risks for different mental disorders that I began to comprehend "genetic loading."

—⁊⁊—

In 1982, I was working as an independent video documentary maker in Washington, DC. In March of that year, I took Alex and a video camera to spend a week in Pearl River, the town where I grew up and where my mother still lived. While Mom doted on her grandson, I trailed Rita around and videotaped our conversations. We spent several nights hanging out at her favorite bar. During the day, I accompanied her to the Rockland County clinic so she could pick up a dose of methadone, and I went along with her to meetings with her parole officer and public defender.

The focal point of our conversations soon became the mandatory one-year drug rehab program she would soon be entering after she'd gotten stopped on a local highway and then, as the cop saw it, resisted questioning.

"What happened when the cop pulled you over?"

"I got outta the car, and he got out and we were walking towards each other. I said 'What's the matter?' and he said 'I stopped you for no tail lights.' I said, 'Come on, I've got tail lights, what are you messing with me for?' He said, 'Don't talk to me like that or I'll get you for driving while intoxicated.' I said, 'Come on, stop fucking with me.' Then he said, 'All right, if you want to play like that. . . .' Then he turned me around and cuffed me and slammed my head on the hood of the car. Then I got a little upset. . . . He put me in the back seat of the car, still handcuffed, and he takes out a billy club. I put my feet up to stop the club and he cut his thumb on the heel of my shoe."

"Then what happened?"

"He charged me with assault, resisting arrest, and driving while intoxicated."

After all that, a judge gave Rita the chance to go to rehab instead of doing more jail time. To my mother and me, this appeared to be nothing less than a miracle. Rita was acting like the worst of two options had been offered.

"Why don't you want to go to rehab?"

"I'm scared. I'm trying to stall the whole thing. I know I gotta do it. But it's Christmas, I want to be home, here. Yeah, I'm scared of that intense, long-term therapy. They're going to tear me apart."

DENIAL AND DECEIT

When she got out of rehab, Rita began using heroin again almost immediately. During the week, I videotaped her; Rita consumed a large amount of alcohol—a state she defined as *sober*. In fact, it was the most coherent condition I'd seen her in for quite a while, and I was desperate to use this opportunity to better understand the hold that heroin had on her. Looking back, I appreciate that Rita was as candid as I'd ever heard her be about her life as a junkie, while I, her codependent big sister, was still in denial.

"You never really did it every day, did you?" I asked.

"Oh, yeah, I did."

"Like when?"

"Many times."

"For how long?"

"It would usually only last about two or three months."

"Every day?"

"Yeah. Until it got stopped."

"Why would it get stopped?"

"Something would happen. I'd get robbed. Or I'd get really sick. Something to make me come to my senses. Or, I just couldn't get any and I'd have to kick cold."

As I watch the video now, I wonder if most of my sister's adult life wasn't one long play to be rescued. As sad and desperate as she was, she was also insincere and manipulative since she had no real intention to stop what she was doing.

This apparent contradiction is the central message offered by Robert L. Dupont in *The Selfish Brain*. Dupont holds that addicts often see themselves as victims, never as perpetrators, of pain and suffering. The addict is both aware and unaware of this self-deceit as well as of his attempts to deceive others. He notes that an addict will do virtually anything to pursue his drug of choice even as he assures you that he can, and will, stop at some future point, just never today.[6]

Dupont argues that an addict needs to take responsibility for his own actions, explaining that the crux of that responsibility comes at the point where the addict must decide whether to take another drink or do a drug when he has full knowledge of its potential lethal impact on him and others. Dupont compares this choice point to that of a diabetic who must take a daily dose of insulin and curb his intake of sugar or else risk a host of complications including blindness, diabetic coma, or death.[7]

This means the addict's desire for wellness, and her experience and memory of positive life events, must override the temporary, habitual pain-blotting reward provided by her drug of choice. Something has to call out to her in the darkness to help her turn away from the habit. However, if the baseline of the addict's preaddicted life was depression or another mental illness at a young age, she has less to work with. Certainly, she has little experience with coping with stress.

From Dupont and other researchers, we know that an individual with a family history of addiction has a *biologically based reward reaction* to the addictive substance—in other words, a genetically bestowed predisposition for addiction, which, after being activated by sustained use anywhere from several months to a period of years depending on the person, becomes a relentless craving.[8] The addict's age is also a key factor. Most addictions take hold in the person's adolescence and early twenties.

Coming from a family culture that allows, even encourages, self-medication makes it harder to see a loved one's addiction for the death dance that it actually is, especially when there's a hidden mental illness driving the behavior. Once dependence takes hold and becomes an addiction, *it* tends to look like the person's primary problem. Individuals with a mental illness and an addiction nowadays are said to have a "dual diagnosis."[9] Nancy Piotrowski, a clinical psychologist and former researcher in the Alcohol Research Group at Univerity of California–Berkeley, says, "About 50 percent of people getting treatment for alcohol and drug abuse have some kind of mental illness. Conversely, 50 percent of the people with mental illness have a substance abuse problem." The frequency of dual diagnosis varies, she says, from 45 percent of people with a diagnosed anxiety disorder to 65 percent of people with bipolar syndrome."[10]

WHICH COMES FIRST?

Is it the chicken or the egg; the mental illness or the addiction? For many inside and out of the mental health establishment, this fundamental question remained unanswered up until the 1990s. As always, there were some pioneers who caught on well before their peers—because they had to. In the 1970s, one group of clinicians and researchers at the Philadelphia Veterans Administration (VA) Methadone Clinic evaluated the effect of an antidepressant given to heroin addicts who were also diagnosed with depression and anxiety. After one year, their results showed a significant reduction of symptoms and less drug use for the addicts whose treatment included the use of the antidepressant. In subsequent follow-up studies, they found that the additional use of psychotherapy added even more significantly to their patients' recovery rates.[11]

The degree to which these clinicians were able to diagnose the multiple conditions their patients were contending with was extraordinary at a time when the medical literature lacked any coherent theory to explain the workings of comorbid mental illness in alcoholics or drug addicts. In the mid-

1980s, the Philadelphia VA staff said that 80 to 85 percent of their heroin-addicted patients were comorbid; more than half were afflicted with major depression. Other common diagnoses included antisocial personality disorder; a history of alcohol dependence; anxiety disorders; and other disorders of mood, such as manic depression (now known as bipolar disorder).[12]

And then there's this startling statistic: according to the National Institute of Mental Health (NIMH), nearly half (45 percent) of Americans with any mental disorder meet criteria for two or more disorders, with severity increasing with each additional disorder. As noted, the technical term is *comorbidity*: having more than one mental disorder at a time. *That's me and my family*, I remember thinking, *comorbid and counting*.[13]

In 1992, a first-of-its-kind national survey of the state of the nation's mental health called the National Comorbidity Survey (NCS) evaluated 8,098 people, ages fifteen to fifty-four. These individuals were interviewed in face-to-face home settings by trained laypersons—making them far less able to lessen or deny symptoms and patterns. Among the striking results of the NCS survey: 45 percent of those people with an alcohol-use disorder and 72 percent with a drug-use disorder also had at least one other mental disorder. Perhaps more important, at a time when the self-medication theory was still under attack, the NCS survey provided a concrete and comprehensive answer to the chicken-and-egg question about addiction and mental illness.[14]

So which is it? The NCS showed that when an alcohol disorder accompanied another mental disorder, the alcohol abuse began *after* the individual was suffering from symptoms of the other mental disorder, *usually one year or more after*. Not including other forms of substance abuse, the most common preexisting mental disorders reported among those interviewed were anxiety, depression, and, for men, conduct disorders.

When an updated NCS survey was done with a new group of ten thousand people in 2002 (called the NCS-R, for "replicated"), its findings were strikingly similar to the first.[15] Fifty-five percent of those interviewed had one mental disorder (two-thirds of these either severe or moderate cases); 22 percent had two; and 23 percent had three or more comorbid disorders. Faring worst by age group in the 2002 numbers were thirty- to forty-four-year-olds, among whom 37 percent had anxiety disorders and 24 percent had mood disorders in addition to their alcohol abuse issues. Depressed women in their thirties and forties have a 2.6 greater risk for heavy drinking, compared to those without major depression. It occurred to me as I read these numbers that age thirty to forty-four, when comorbid disorders are highest, are also our prime childbearing years.[16]

—⚋—

In 1982, Ronald Reagan moved into the White House, and the tone of the capital, where Geoff, Alex, and I still lived, changed dramatically overnight. Fortunately, Geoff, working as an engineer at the television network that would broadcast the 1984 Olympics from Los Angeles, and I, with a staff position managing television/video production at the American Film Institute, both had an opportunity to transfer to the same new city and keep our jobs. So we happily fled DC for LA. But it wasn't just about our careers. I had a keen desire to escape my sister's cycles of dope, bust, and rehab, which, though they played out mostly in New York, still felt too close for comfort. Southern California represented all the Northeast was not, a warm, flat climate that took the edge off—well, everything.

Having Rita show up on our Hollywood Hills doorstep three years later pretty much defeated my purpose in moving west and soon took over our lives. On most days, my sister's drinking would start right before or after lunch, lasting until she fell into bed well past midnight. I was six months pregnant with Sammy and still working full time.

Desperate to get her out of our house before Sammy's arrival, I rented and furnished an apartment for her six blocks away. In typical fashion, Rita busied herself finding a new drug dealer and cultivating friends in the neighborhood who shared her "interests."

One night, when Sammy was about eight weeks old, our shared bubble burst wide open. It was a weeknight. Geoff was working late. Alex, then six years old, was fast asleep in the room next to mine while Mom was sleeping in the guest room downstairs. At three in the morning, I was in my bedroom nursing Sammy, when I heard Mom's scream. I rushed downstairs carrying a wailing Sammy and found her standing in the hallway.

From the bathroom, I could hear Rita retching and coughing.

"There's blood!" Mom said in a ragged whisper.

Rita was holding onto the toilet and gagging up blood, spitting it into a circle of yellow vomit. Desperate to get my puking sister out of my house, I threw on some jeans and dragged Rita from the bathroom into the car.

It was a thirty-minute drive to the public hospital in South Central LA, the only place I could imagine that might take her in for a detox. Rita continued to throw up in the back seat all the way. By the time we got to the hospital, she had regained enough of her wits to resist the idea of going in.

"You're either coming in with me or I'm leaving you here in the parking lot," I said.

People in wheelchairs and on stretchers lined the hallways, many seemingly unconscious or, if awake, contorted in pain. The few visible hospital staff sat behind glass sliding windows. Rita took her place on a hard plastic chair, nodding off while I forced myself to stay awake long enough until it was her turn for an intake interview.

I told the admitting nurse that she'd attempted suicide.

Rita perked up at that, but I shushed her before the nurse could respond to her protest. This was a game we'd played before. Finally, Rita was admitted for a three-day detox. I left. I made it home before dawn and crawled into bed.

Before Rita was released to me to live in our house until she recovered enough to move back to her own apartment, I attended a meeting with a doctor who apparently wanted another family member to hear what he had to say when he told Rita that her liver was close to destroyed. Plus, she had hepatitis C and needed to stop drinking if she cared to live much longer. I was stunned; I suppose I was still young enough to not have taken in the accumulated destruction she had done to her own body solely at the hand of her addictions. Before night fell, Rita had somehow slipped out of the house to buy a bottle of whiskey. When I checked on her before turning out the lights, she had finished off half of it and was passed out on the sofa in front of the television.

COLLATERAL DAMAGE

Rita continued her binge drinking for a month until, to my relief, she returned to New York. It was there, while she was living at Mom's house, that Rita's luck finally ran out. She had overdosed again, this time on a combination of cocaine, downers, and alcohol. Her brain had been deprived of oxygen for five or perhaps seven minutes, and she was comatose for three weeks. Upon waking, she couldn't walk, and her speech was seriously impaired. From Nyack Hospital, she moved to a rehabilitation center in western Massachusetts, although no one predicted her condition could measurably improve.

Visiting her once at the rehab center, with Alex and Sammy in tow, I was shocked by a change in her personality. Gone was my sister's junkie persona, the manipulative part of her that was always playing you for money, a ride to her dealer's house, or your silence. It was replaced by a cheerful, carefree thirty-seven-year-old woman who no longer seemed to need anything—apart from twenty-four-hour medical care. With the nurses, she took on the demeanor of an eager-to-please child with an easy laugh, as if her demons had finally been chased away.

When I mentioned this to my mother, she said, "That's what she was like before. You just don't remember."

She meant *before* the age of fourteen. Twenty-four years ago.

Rita died in December of 1992.

The nightmare year that ended Rita's life also led to my divorce. At the time I remember a fatefully skewed logic driving my actions. It boiled down to my realization that life could be over so quickly, therefore I "deserved" to feel loved and to be happy while there was still time. I promptly fell for a man with whom I'd recently done a video project, another charming, morally chal-lenged user who was, at the time, living with and off another woman. Still, this man (whom I won't name) gave me the high that reliably came to me from a new romance—my own former drug of choice. Now it helped me get through (meaning "avoid") grieving my sister's death and the end of my marriage. Nat-urally, the affair ended fairly quickly, just three months later. What I'd done is clear to see now: I dumped my own unhappiness—and untreated depression—on Geoff. I regret the timing of the divorce and the fact that I delayed getting treatment for so long as to make fixing the marriage impossible.

While packing my boxes to break up our household, I found a letter I'd received from Rita, written during her first stint in Rockland County Jail a decade earlier, dated March of 1982:

> *I should have known I was heading for trouble again. I was having black outs from small amounts of liquor (small amounts for me). But I went on another drinking binge and now I'm back here again. I guess I've hit the pits this time. I just finished speaking to a woman from the jail ministry. She's quite sure that God brought me back here to save my life or try again. She may be right. I just feel really bad now that I won't be home for Easter when you come. So much for all that. Meanwhile pray for me, forgive me for letting you all down, try to talk to Mom for me and take care of my beau-tiful nephew. Love, Rita.*

Although she never gave up on dragging me and the rest of the family into a series of futile codependent attempts to save her, at heart, Rita knew she was the only one who could have saved herself. Recovery is always an individual struggle, but there are points at which family and friends can intervene and provide crucial help. These are brief windows of opportunity when a loved one is calling out for your help, whether or not he or she knows it.

When I finally woke up and sent Alex to wilderness therapy at age fourteen, it was an intuitive reaction that sprang from the years I'd spent watching Rita's slow, tortured decline.

Looking back now, it's easier to see that the clearest sign indicating the presence of an underlying mental condition in any member of my family was the degree of their self-medicating behaviors. It has been three decades since my sister's heroin and alcohol use blinded us to her deeper emotional problems and led us to focus only on her relentless addictions and the deceitful behaviors they produced. In that time, the self-medication theory had been upheld and strengthened by new evidence.[17]

The important thing if you have an adolescent going down this road is to act. Don't wait. And don't think the substance abuse has to be gone before someone can deal with a mental disorder. As noted, the standard of care now is treating both at once.[18]

Chapter 9

MY FATHER RED: "THE HEART-ACHE AND THE THOUSAND NATURAL SHOCKS THAT FLESH IS HEIR TO"*

John Michael Costello
(1914–1960)

You said your father was an alcoholic?
Yes, he was.
Did he have any other mental health issues?
He was always sad. But he had good reasons to be.

Dad put out his cigarette in the ashtray on the frayed arm of the stuffed chair we shared, me on his lap. His cough jostled me with its intensity as he rose to open the front door. Swollen from the humidity, it needed a firm tug. A cool breeze snuck in, raising goose bumps on my arms, a cacophony of crickets announcing the end of our daylong downpour.

He took a deep breath and ran a hand through his hair. Like mine, Dad's hair curled and sprung forth in every direction in this weather. Dad told me our curls would bring us the luck of the Irish. I was still waiting to see how this luck might show up for Dad.

"I'm going down to bail," he said. "You stay put, princess."

I was relieved not to make another trip to our flooded basement. I could still feel the warmth of Dad bulk on my bare arms and legs as I lay cuddled on his well-worn seat cushion, lulled into a half-sleep by the hypnotic slowness of the Yankee® game still on television.

143

But after a half hour had gone by without any of the usual sounds—no shovel scraping against cement or water splashing into pots—I got worried. Mom's snores from down the hall told me no one else was awake, so I decided to go check on Dad myself.

I hated how the cold air hit me when I opened the basement door, and how the stairs creaked when I walked on them, but I kept going. Midway down, I saw Dad lying by the water pump. I ran down the rest of the stairs, my sock-covered feet splashing in the rising water until I reached him. I stroked his forehead and pale, freckled cheeks. "Daddy . . . wake up." He didn't open an eye or make a sound. I saw that his chest was moving up and down, so I knew he was just asleep, probably drunk. So I sat down in a dry spot determined to wait.

Near Dad's shoe, I spotted an empty bottle. When I smelled its rim, I noticed Dad smelled just like the bottle, as if he'd poured it over himself. It was the same smell that filled the car when Mom picked Dad up at the tavern where he went most nights after getting off the train. He just wanted one or two drinks, he would say. If he didn't call by eight, Mom would put me, James, and Rita in the car and drive downtown to get him. She'd park in one of the spaces halfway between the bar and the green-roofed, paint-peeling-off train depot. I hated waiting in the car. But I hated more those times when Dad wanted to drive home himself. Then I held my breath and closed my eyes, bracing against James's knee for the eternity it took to reach our house on the edge of town.

But on that night, even with Dad passed out drunk on the floor, I felt protected, which was odd only for someone who knew more about safety. After awhile, I put my cheek on his chest. That way I could close my eyes and still hear his heart beating. I must have fallen asleep. Maybe he awoke and carried me away to bed. Another bedtime recovered. More likely Mom finally came and found us, and he hollered at the indignities.

—ɷ—

My father commuted by train to work in New York City. Both my parents grew up in the Bronx—Mom in the Italian neighborhood, Dad among the poorer Irish, side by side, but separate. Dad was a WWII hero. In 1946, he brought home a Distinguished Flying Cross and a battered body. The way Mom made it sound, when Dad got back, she was the last unmarried girl in the neighborhood.

They'd known each other since elementary school. After the war ended, they kept the party going with jobs in Manhattan and nightly trolling among the city's nightspots. In old photos from that time, the two of them are sitting on barstools in a crowd, everyone laughing like the good times would never end. Nobody thought their marriage was a good idea, not even Mom, she assured me later. When she wasn't mad as hell at him, Mom would say that Dad's failings weren't really his fault. He was an orphan; besides, all the Irish drink themselves into the ground. By the time I turned six, all the laughing had stopped.

Dad never drank on the job, nor had he ever missed a day of work. Mom told that to everyone without either question needing to be asked. Many years later, I would learn about the time Dad drank away the mortgage payment, forcing Mom to borrow the money from Nana, and explaining why Dad never came with us again to visit Nana.

FROM VICE TO DISEASE

In 1952, a public health official wrote in a pamphlet "Alcoholism is no more a disease than thieving or lynching."[1] It would take until the mid 1970s for the words *disease* and *alcoholism* to be positively paired in the same sentence and to enter the *DSM-III*. In *The Natural History of Alcoholism, Revisited*, published in 1995, Harvard psychiatrist George E. Vaillant reported on the drinking habits of the 660 Boston-area men he tracked over four decades. Comparing an alcoholic to the driver of an automobile who knows his brakes are defective but chooses to drive down a busy highway, Vaillant writes: "Genetic loading is an important predictor of *whether* an individual develops alcoholism, while an unstable childhood environment is an important predictor of *when* an individual loses control of alcohol."[2]

The study found three factors to be reliable predictors of future alcohol abuse:

1. A family history of alcohol abuse
2. Anglo/Irish ethnicity
3. Adolescent behavior problems[3]

Someone with an alcoholic father but with an otherwise stable family was five times more likely to develop the disease of alcoholism than someone from a problem family without an alcoholic parent. So with alcohol abuse, this study suggests, genetics trump environment.

—⚋—

My father's given name was John, but everyone called him Red. I don't recall my father ever talking about his father; Mom said it was because he was ashamed of him, but I'd always figured it was just too painful for Dad to remember Grandpa and how he'd died. In the course of writing this memoir, while searching for traces of Grandpa in New York's public records, I came upon a surprise having to do with my father. I'd always believed that, after his mother's death from influenza in 1918 had made Dad an orphan at age four, his own blood relatives had taken him in. So I was stunned when I found my father's name in the 1920 US Census listed as follows:

John Costello, age 5, adopted son of Michael Murphy.

It turned out that Dad had been given up for adoption outside the family. I couldn't help but wonder if Grandpa's siblings, three in the United States at this time, did not take in their nephew because of the suspicions surrounding Michael's death. Once again, with all the principals gone, there was no way to know why Dad was given over to be raised by the Murphy family, but something about it felt very wrong to me. It was as if Grandpa and his descendents—my brother, sister, and I—had been cut out of the Costello family tree.

When I located Dad in the next US Census done in 1930, he was sixteen years old and had an occupation listed next to his name: bank messenger. He still lived with the Murphys at the same Bronx address, but there was now a husband for Nora: George Quinn. And Quinn had replaced Murphy in the space reserved for "head of household." Dad was no longer identified as an "adopted son"; he was now a "cousin" to George, presumably by way of George's marriage to Nora. It was at this point that I recognized the names: they were Dad's "cousins" whom we knew as Aunt Noni and Uncle George.

Noni, an immense woman with washboard frizzy hair, was a marginal, though contentious part of our lives. At least she was until Dad's death; after that, it was as if she and Uncle George dropped off the face of the earth. The way my mother told it, Noni forced Dad to quit high school so he could help support *her* family, depriving him of a scholarship to a prestigious Catholic high school. As much as Noni angered Mom, she scared the wits out of my brother, sister, and me. I remember one Easter Sunday morning, sitting on the front steps of our house waiting for Noni and George to arrive for a visit. Dad examined his watch while Mom kept track of how late they were.

"They did it again," she declared. Noni and George had made the two-hour drive from the Bronx a handful of times before, and each time had showed up hours late.

"Sit down," Dad said when James got up from his place on the top step.

"But I'm thirsty," James said.

"Red," Mom hissed with a sharper edge in her voice, as she opened the door for James to go in. It went on like that; my skirt sticking to the under-side of my legs; Dad lighting another cigarette; Rita whining, and James punching his fist into an open palm.

Finally, Noni and George pulled up in their sky-blue Cadillac®, sounding a long honk as the front end of the car scraped onto the steep driveway. Dad went down and opened the passenger door for Noni. She stood on her tiptoes to give him a sterile peck on the cheek. Then Dad went around and shook hands with George. Mom sighed as we watched Dad and Noni walk up the driveway as if in slow motion, with Dad holding Noni's elbow so she wouldn't topple over. When they turned the corner onto the front sidewalk, Uncle George became visible again, and I was amazed to see that he carried a brightly colored basket in each hand.

"Don't you both look pretty," Noni said to Rita and me in our matching Puritan dresses and caps, ignoring James when she finally reached us.

"Here, give me those," she said to George, reaching for the baskets, handing one to Rita and the other to me.

"What do you say?" Dad asked.

"Thank you," Rita and I chirped in unison.

My eyes were fixed on the bed of green plastic grass, where a cellophane-wrapped chocolate rabbit sat surrounded by yellow marshmallow chicks and jelly beans. But I knew something was very wrong.

"What about Jimmy's?" I heard Mom ask. *Uh-oh*, I thought, stealing a peek at Noni and catching her snarl.

"The boy's too old for an Easter basket."

"He's six, for Christ's sake," Mom said. But before Noni could answer, Mom grabbed James by the hand and pulled the screen door tightly into place behind them. Dad kicked the ground. "Come on inside," he said to Noni in an apologetic tone.

"Didn't I tell you your life would be miserable if you married that woman?"

To be honest, I doubt Noni said those exact words. But the feeling of it was that mean and angry—and mainly so sad for Dad. I watched his face fall as Noni turned and walked away, George at her side. Her backside jiggled as she scrambled back down the driveway and climbed into the Caddy. The front end of the car scraped the driveway again as they backed out and sped away, never to return.

That day serves as a talisman for my father's seemingly endless sorrows; the *reasons why* he drank. However unsatisfactory they may have been, they were the unspoken answers to my mother's litany of complaints about his failings as a husband and father.

THE LOWDOWN ON MULTIPLE GENERATIONS OF DEPRESSION

The results of the groundbreaking family depression study done by Myrna Weissman and her colleagues at Columbia University and reported in 2005 strongly suggest that as successive generations accumulate mental illnesses, especially moderate to severe depressions that remain untreated, the level of impairment for the youngest generation becomes increasingly severe, and the onset of their disorders occurs earlier. The study involving 161 grandchildren and their parents and grandparents was done over twenty years. Among the study findings:

- There was a threefold higher risk of depression for grandchildren who had a depressed grandparent and depressed parent.
- The severity of the grandparent's depression, as measured by impairment, significantly increased the likelihood and impairment caused by a mood disorder in the grandchild.
- But when the children had depressed parents but not moderate or severely depressed grandparents, the grandchildren's impairments were fewer.

- A full 59 percent of grandchildren (with a mean age of twelve) who had two generations of major depression preceding them had either depression or an anxiety disorder. Anxiety disorder appears to precede depression in young children.
- The rates of psychopathology (childhood depression and anxiety) are highest in grandchildren of parents and grandparents with a moderately severe depression.

Each of these results was compared to a control group of three-generation families without depression.[4]

It was June, and Dad had already spent three months that spring in the VA hospital for lung cancer. Back then, children weren't permitted in hospitals, not even to visit dying parents. I remember sitting with my brother and sister in the car in the parking lot at the VA Hospital, waiting for Mom to finish her visits with Dad. Those endless hours—the throbbing in my throat, the blank look on my sister Rita's face, my silent tears—became my permanent shorthand for the experience of loss. I never thought I'd see him again. But then Dad surprised me by coming back home once more—for my First Communion.

Dad loved the Church. Growing up, it was his substitute family; at least that's what Mom said. That day of my Communion, I knew he was there in church somewhere, but I hadn't seen him during our procession into the chapel. When I finally caught up with him outside the church, I had only a few precious minutes to hold on to his bony leg.

After telling me I looked like an angel in my frilly, white balloon of a dress, Dad stood silently looking at me for several more minutes before he touched my cheek. "Pray for me," he whispered. I nodded and put my hands at my side. Then I could only watch as he walked away, arm-and-arm, with Father Anthony. Although I hated my father leaving, I also felt like he'd just given me a new kind of power—that if I prayed hard enough, everything would all be okay.

That must have been when I acquired my conviction that the truth was whatever I needed it to be. Thereafter, everything I thought about Dad was fused with Father Anthony in his black robe and wherever it was I imagined the two of them went that day; often, I was convinced, they went straight to heaven.

Dad died in the hospital one month later.

After that day, if I went to church at all, it was with neighbors, since Mom never took us back. Nor did she ever mention Dad's name again in my presence. Much later, she told me how she'd gone to Father Anthony when she was worried about Dad's drinking. He told her a man needed his drink, so she should leave him alone. Although she'd been a lifelong Catholic, that was it for Mom and the Church. Mom was like that; she held a grudge.

What is death to a seven-year-old? Since nobody in my family could figure that out, they decided it was best for us kids not to go to Dad's funeral. I remember lying on the bottom bunk that night, feeling a sharp, throbbing ache from the top of my chest down through my thighs; I thought it was going to cut me in two. I stared at the dark hallway outside our bedroom and felt as if I was stuck in a ditch, like one of those drainage channels where the new houses were being built in our neighborhood. If the water kept coming in, I would likely die, but either I couldn't get out or I just didn't want to. Not going to the funeral, not seeing Dad put into the ground, and then no one talking about it after that day—all that made it a lot easier for me to come up with my own, preferable ways of seeing, hearing, and understanding.

RAISED BY ALCOHOL

I had no unmet physical needs growing up; we were middle class in every way. But the visceral experience of growing up in my family consisted of thousands of small moments of bone-chilling fear with no adult to help me cope. To hold onto someone who is committed to his own self-destruction is not a choice a child makes consciously or willingly.

So I created an imaginary world to replace the things and people that were missing in my family. Several times after he died, I dreamed or imagined that my father came to me. It was always at night. My bedroom would be pitch-dark, but he'd have a light inside him that allowed me to see him and the space immediately around him. I wasn't scared; in fact, I'd prayed for him to come. I would wake up and sit on my bunk bed and just look at him for minutes at a time. My brother and sister, who shared my room, never once woke up during Dad's "visits," which continued for about one year.

After they ended, I retreated even further inside myself. Sometimes, in my mind, Dad wasn't dead; at other times, I wasn't alive. My preference, I think, was to stay in a space between life and death. Then I didn't feel pressed to make a decision.

For many years, I truly believed I could save my father—oddly enough, even after his death. Children of alcoholics often develop grandiose ideas of their responsibilities and abilities. As flawed as my thinking was back then, I suspect this childhood belief in my power to change reality probably also gave me strength to do whatever it took to "save" my children when they were threatened by mental illness.

As I got older, the trouble came for me when I finally couldn't tell the difference between what was real and the things I made up to comfort myself. I was swimming deeper and deeper underwater, not wanting to resurface—even when I could feel myself running out of breath. This system of denial that helped me to cope as a child outlasted its purpose by adolescence. By then my depression had taken firm hold, even if I denied its existence. And it might have stayed that way too, if not for Alex's disintegration that night in the high school parking lot.

SCREENING AND PREDICTING DEADLY FAMILY PATTERNS

Although Alcoholics Anonymous had been around since the 1930s, my father never attended an AA meeting. When I told my mother about the first Al-Anon (Adult Children of Alcoholics) meeting I'd attended in my thirties, she looked at me with disbelief. Her response, "You say things about our family in front of complete strangers?" indicated to me that she'd never heard of it.

According to Robert Dupont, "Recovery most often comes from participation in the lifelong fellowship of a Twelve Step program such as Alcoholics Anonymous and Narcotics Anonymous."[5] I've read success rates for people in AA reaching sobriety ranging from 5 to 95 percent; I have a dozen or more friends who say they've been saved by "The Program." If nothing else, twelve-step groups have performed two important functions that I've experienced directly. First, they introduced the concept of recovery to a wide public. Then, ironically, given the principle of anonymity that informs everything they do, AA and its associated programs have made it "okay to tell." As a result of this massive cultural shift, we can now speak openly about our own or a family member's problem with addiction and, by extension, also mental illness.

Not everyone is happy about this. A chorus of complainers, many of them book critics who've apparently been forced to read too many memoirs, have taken to decrying our confessional, narcissistic culture.[6] Beneath the intellectual sniping, I detect the opposite cultural extreme creeping back in; the propriety that would have us hush up about the strange and sordid behaviors committed by alcoholics, addicts, and the mentally ill, and push these deviants back into the closet. By the sheer volume of testimony, this book included, it appears too late for the culture to revert back. Personally, if I had to choose between the old system of secrets and lies and the current spate of narcissism, the choice is an easy one to make.

—⚏—

Work by Terrie Moffitt and other behavioral scientists doing long-term family studies may eventually push the culture to catch up with its science regarding how we think and speak about the gamut of mental disorders, including addiction. Much of Moffitt's groundbreaking research derives from duties as codirector of the New Zealand Dunedin Cohort of 981 individuals (referred to in chapters 3 and 4), members of which have been followed for some forty years. In June 2009, I went to interview Professor Moffitt in London about the latest report out of the Dunedin study, "The Predictive Value of Family History on Severity of Illness," which was to be published the following month.

In the article, researchers explain how they were able to accurately predict the degree of mental illness an individual study participant would face by computing the sum total of his individual and family risk factors. Called the Family History Screen, or FHS,[7] this score produces a prognosis for the individual based on known and suspected mental disorders in his extended family. *Suspected*, since—even though these families have been tracked for decades—researchers still do not assume they've documented all the mental disorders or addictions that may be present.

The results demonstrated the predictive value of the FHS tool. Moffitt and her researchers found that the more relatives a person had with substance use disorder, depression, or anxiety disorder, the more likely he was to have that condition, too. And the stronger that family history was, the greater a person's risk of having recurrent bouts of the disorder and of reporting that it impaired his ability to function. These individuals were also at greater risk of being hospitalized for that condition and to take medication to treat it.

Here's how the FHS screening process works: First, a family member is considered to have a history of disorder if one or more of the disorder's primary symptoms are endorsed by at least 50 percent of family members interviewed (for example, two of three "informants"). Then, to avoid underreporting, or, in lay terms, finding what's hiding in plain sight, interviewers ask a pair of questions to get at each major point of inquiry. The first is more general, for example, "Has anyone in the family ever had a sudden spell or attack in which they felt panicked?" If answered affirmatively, this question would be followed by a much narrower one, "Did this person have several attacks of extreme fear or panic, even though there was nothing to be afraid of?"

Given the efficacy of this approach to taking and using family history data, it seems antiquated to operate without it in an initial mental health evaluation. What will it take to put this tool in every mental health practitioner's office? According to Terrie Moffitt, "There's nothing about family history in the *DSM* even though it may be the most important."[8] She adds that health professionals have tended to avoid questioning people about their family history of mental illnesses because of the stigma attached to these illnesses. "There's a sense that many families are not as open about mental disorders. That people may not know or may make incorrect assumptions."[9] The idea that any of the dozen mental health providers I've consulted for my sons might have had this tool at their disposal to systematically add up their "genetic load" before making a diagnosis and treatment plan is truly mind-boggling. And what if I had had my own FHS score; how much sooner might I have treated my depression?

A SAMPLE SEQUENCE OF QUESTIONS FROM THE DUNEDIN FAMILY HISTORY SCREENING TOOL

The following questions, concerning symptoms of bipolar disorder, are asked of a study participant about himself and then about anyone he's put on a list of biological family members, including siblings, parents, and grandparents.

1. Has anyone on the list ever had a period of feeling extremely happy or high?
2. I mean "high as a kite," so that other people worried about them, or so that it interfered with carrying out normal responsibilities. Has anyone been unusually happy or high, not because of drugs or alcohol, for two days or more?
3. Has anyone on the list ever had a period in which they were more active or talkative than normal?
4. I mean extremely overactive or talkative, so that people worried about them, or so that it interfered with carrying out their usual responsibilities. Has anyone been like that, without being under the influence of drugs or alcohol, for at least two days?
5. Has anyone on the list showed inappropriate behavior such as spending too much money, having more frequent sex than usual, talking too much or rarely sleeping?
6. Has anyone showed these inappropriate behaviors for two days or more and not because of alcohol or drugs?

—*Taken from the Dunedin Family Health Study "Parent Family Health Interview—Whole Questionnaire"*[10]

The well-established use of family history in primary-care medicine compared to its tiny role in mental health care is striking. On this point, Terrie Moffitt comments, "Family history is an essential part of every cardiologist's interview of every patient. But contrast this with practice in psychiatry. Although family history could be one of the most effective tools in mental-health care, it is often asked in only the most cursory way, and it is seldom used seriously by clinicians to help patients and families understand their risk situation."[11]

Chapter 10

THE FIRST GENERATION, MY GRANDFATHER

Michael John Costello
(1887, Galway–1913, New York)

Has it ever occurred to you that your grandfather's remaining on the rail-road track may have been an intentional act?
  No, never. I said. Not until you just asked me.

The three-generation family mental health interviews carried out since 1972 in Dunedin, New Zealand—and many other studies like it—have enormous significance for the science of mental illness. But their value is greater still in light of the secrecy and shame surrounding mental illness in most families and cultures around the world.

As I've been working on this book, I've been struck by the number of people who, after I explain my subject, launch into their own sad accounts of a "weird-acting" aunt, cousin, or grandfather who had been shunned from the family because of unacceptable behavior. Though long gone and never known by anyone living in my family of origin, my grandfather Michael was oddly present. Like a phantom, he hid in my mother's cocked eyebrow when she wanted Dad to quit the booze. He held forth in the empty space on the mantle next to Dad's only photo of his mother in her frayed Sunday best, looking so young and hopeful yet, I would discover, a year or two from widowhood when it was taken.

I've come to think that whoever is denied their rightful place in a family's collective memories will possess the hearts and minds of those left behind, unless and until he is acknowledged. In aboriginal cultures, this psychological exchange takes the form of ancestor worship. In the culture of my Irish forbears, the same impulse is expressed through storytelling.

The unthinkable manner of Grandpa's death put a shroud over his life.

According to *his* Church, which was, of course, still *our* Church while I was growing up, his death by suicide would have prevented his entrance into heaven and excluded him from the burial ground of his parents. Maybe that's why Grandpa couldn't leave us. It was as if he remained a permanent occupant of the border regions—until Alex's illness turned the secret he carried into information of vital important for us, Grandpa's descendents.

I'm not suggesting that a distance of four generations between Grandpa and Alex makes his genetic influence akin to anything like that of a first- or second-degree relative. But looking at my family lineage from the perspective of the sheer density of undiagnosed mental illness that has been present, Grandpa's life and likely death by suicide becomes one more integral part of the story. More so if he took his own life. As we know, the inheritance of mental illness doesn't happen entirely through the mechanisms of our genes. Equally important are the habits of mind and behavior that are culturally endowed to us—across oceans and centuries.

THE IRISH FACTOR

While pursuing the issue of Irish ethnicity as a factor in my grandfather's life, I came upon the work of Nancy Scheper-Hughes, chair of the Medical Anthropology Department at the University of California–Berkeley. In her book *Saints, Scholars, and Schizophrenics: Mental Illness in Rural Ireland*, Scheper-Hughes weighs cultural factors affecting the rural Irish to draw a collective psychological portrait. She demonstrates how rural Irish styles of family life and community mythmaking, child rearing, and religious practice contributed to a strong vulnerability to mental illness in the several decades leading up to the 1970s. Her fascinating central theme in the book is that the Irish "mad" act out the emotional ills of the entire society—especially its family dysfunctions.[1]

The fact that my grandfather, Michael Costello, came to America as a young farm laborer from Galway piqued my interest in Scheper-Hughes's book. In her portrait, the conflict-laden meeting of the individual and the group is but one of several critically important intersections; hers is a list of meeting points that includes nature and nurture, mind and body, science and culture, even paganism and Christianity. Scheper-Hughes's book zeros in on how the messy interplay of all these forces in Western Ireland helped form troubled individuals within a distressed community. I immediately saw the implications of this model of the cultural roots of mental illness for my family and others like us with multiple generations of mental illness, including addictions.

In the mid-1970s, Scheper-Hughes arrived in Ireland as a newly minted anthropologist in search of a field project. An Irish colleague encouraged her to take on the twentieth-century Irish epidemic of mental illness and its concentration in the western counties. She accepted the challenge and then narrowed her gaze to one town in County Kerry she called Ballybran in the book.[2]

First, some brief backstory: In the 1960s, when Ireland began to count its mentally ill, the official census of hospitalized psychiatric patients revealed that Ireland's rate of "first-admission" hospitalizations for mental illness, particularly schizophrenia, was the highest in the world.[3] From this research, one county stood out: Roscommon, a stone's throw from Michael Costello's ancestral farm in western Galway. In these lightly populated 984 square miles of wooded green pastures edged by stone-walled, one-lane roads, researchers found 258 cases of schizophrenia from searching hospital records.

Even if, as many now suggest, there was a considerable amount of incorrect diagnosing of schizophrenia going on,[4] the prevalence of schizophrenia among Roscommon residents was still arguably much higher than normal and has remained so for their descendants. In 1993, the Roscommon Family Study found that the overall risk of schizophrenia in all first-degree relatives of schizophrenics was found to be thirteen times higher than in the relatives of controls.[5] Irish neuroscientist Dara Cannon, whose imaging studies at the National University of Ireland in Galway draw heavily from the population of Western Ireland, told me that the rate of schizophrenia in Roscommon remains notably higher than elsewhere in the country.[6]

Nancy Scheper-Hughes's 1977 analysis of the cultural risk factors for mental illness, along with her portrait of how these factors played out among real people living several hundred miles south of Roscommon in a County Kerry village on Ireland's southwestern coastline, offered a medical anthropologist's perspective on the same phenomenon that had been isolated a decade earlier by the Irish government.

Scheper-Hughes was not the first to ask "Are the Irish susceptible to schizophrenia, depression, alcoholism and suicide *wherever they live?*"[7] The same observation of the Irish people has been made since the early part of the nineteenth century. But with her composite portrait of the residents of Ballybran, Scheper-Hughes illustrated the psychosocial risk factors that could very well have contributed to their historically high risk for mental illness. For example, she notes the characteristic Irish evasiveness in speech and body language. While this same indirectness has contributed to Ireland's venerable vocal repartee and literary culture, the dynamic she points out can put impenetrable walls into social relations. She cited the tendency of the rural Irish to react to disappointment and sadness with anger, denial, and withdrawal as inherently corrosive of mental health.

Here she describes the complex role of the village alcoholic in rural Ireland:

> A certain amount of mental illness and "abnormal" behavior (by village standards) is tolerated when disguised in the cloak of alcohol. In this regard I might note that alcoholics find themselves far less often hospitalized than do schizophrenics in Ireland—alcoholism is, as such, a "safer" form of pathology. Since alcoholism is, to a degree, an accepted part of masculine role behavior (especially among bachelors) it is not recognized as abnormal. The common Irish defenses of denial and scapegoating also serve to protect village alcoholics from recognition and public shame. A "community myth" perpetuates . . . the village view denying alcoholism as a widespread mental and social problem by acknowledging the existence of only one village alcoholic."[8]

The flip side of this ready acknowledgment of "the" village alcoholic was an adherence to a standard of normality for male behavior that was to be at all times reserved. "Uncontrolled excitability is noted as abnormal behavior, and 'manic' persons are more likely to be recognized as mentally ill than are extremely depressed and quiet ones, who are more rarely hospitalized."[9] Reading this, I felt awash in my father's interminable sadness and my familiar childhood urge to "save" him.

In the fieldwork she did for her book, Scheper-Hughes shone a spotlight on one character type in the rural Irish family, one that, she observed, appeared to carry the brunt of mental instability that in fact belonged to the whole community: the "bachelor gentleman farmer." He was usually the youngest son who stayed behind to run the marginally viable farm while his older brothers and sisters left for better opportunities elsewhere. His particular double bind was to be the one chosen for this "special" role, with the unspoken message that he was too weak to do more with his life. He remained a bachelor largely because most of his potential brides had also flown the coop.[10]

Writes Scheper-Hughes, "The older, rural system of match-making controlled by the elders had since given way to a free market in which younger men were now expected to manage their own marital and reproductive affairs counting on their own personal assets of including their symbolic capital: the ability to dress, to dance, to present oneself, to talk to girls and so on." The new system, she explains, "completely disenfranchised the 'shy bachelors.'"[11]

From this description, and given the factors that have been identified by psychiatric researchers as raising one's risks for schizophrenia, it's not difficult to imagine how the negative cascade of effects that began with a "gentleman farmer's" social awkwardness and social isolation could have tipped the scales for him toward greater vulnerability to psychological problems.

Scheper-Hughes's insights enabled me to form a conceptual bridge between my personal family history and the science of mental illness that I'd been accumulating for over a decade. As Scheper-Hughes points out, we cannot overlook the fact that the majority of rural Irish were "invulnerables," meaning they fit the accepted definitions of healthy, sane, well-adjusted individuals. Still, it's difficult to imagine that the same cultural patterns did not increase the collective vulnerability toward mental illness in the entire, far-flung community.

My grandfather was an eldest son who left the West of Ireland at a socially turbulent time when it was estimated that half of Ireland's population had either crossed the Atlantic or fled elsewhere. From epidemiological data collected on the mental health of Irish emigrants in the United States and Canada comes evidence of their shared vulnerability. Psychiatric treatment rates were far higher for Irish immigrants and their descendents than for those of other ethnic groups. In 1903, the Irish made up 13 percent of the white population of the United States and 29 percent of those in mental hospitals.[12] In East Coast US cities where Irish immigrants converged between 1850 and 1920, mental wards were swamped with the so-called Irish lunatics, most of them hard-drinking laborers.[13]

The same vulnerability was still apparent back home when researchers looked for it in a 1993 follow-up study in Roscommon. It included 534 people with schizophrenia, of whom 415 were personally interviewed, and 2,043 living and traceable relatives, of whom 1,753 were personally interviewed. Study results showed that these residents carried a significantly higher risk for any of the several diseases classified as part of the schizophrenia spectrum of personality disorders: schizoaffective disorder, schizotypal/paranoid personality disorder, and schizoid personality disorder.[14] Reading this finding, I felt as though I'd come full circle; the last disorder on this list—schizoid personality disorder—was Alex's first psychiatric diagnosis back in 1997.

THE FIRST LETHAL GENE IS FOUND

In 2002, a joint Irish-American team of geneticists with $50 million from the National Institute of Mental Health (NIMH) stepped in to carry out the Irish Study of the High-Density Schizophrenia Families—focusing on the genotypes of the residents of Roscommon: those with schizophrenia, their relatives, and a group of normal controls. In the process, researchers uncovered the world's first evidence of an altered gene that, due to its significantly higher presence in the Roscommon schizophrenics and not in the control group, could be identified as conferring susceptibility to schizophrenia. The culprit was an abnormality in the dysbindin gene,[15] which is thought to play a role in the speed of information processing in the brain. More recent genetic analysis of descendents of these study participant genotypes has shown that schizophrenic patients who displayed strong negative symptoms, among them social withdrawal and isolation, were more likely to inherit this particular dysbindin variation.[16]

When the altered dysbindin gene finding was replicated in several other European studies of concentrated schizophrenic populations, researchers zeroed in on common risk factors that might be interacting to play a causative role in schizophrenia. One factor they found was migrant status, discovered after analyzing strongly elevated prevalences of the disorder in first- and second-generation African Caribbean migrants in the United Kingdom,[17] a finding that has since been replicated in other poorer migrant communities.[18]

Out the window went any intrinsically special relationship between the Irish and schizophrenia. Instead, researchers have isolated sociocultural and historical forces that can raise an individual's and an entire people's risk. Among them: emigration, famine, armed conflicts, poverty, and social instability. Not a snapshot of a single cause; from the Roscommon, Dunedin, and other single-population family studies we end up with a moving picture of diverse risks manifesting as tragic consequences in the weaker members of a larger group. There's an inherent unfairness to who is stricken, but we now know that the victims of schizophrenia are not random. Only those with a genetic vulnerability who chance to experience certain events—with those events multiplied and reinforced by imbedded cultural patterns—will find their lives reshaped by this, like any other mental illness.

—ɱ—

While I was in Ireland two summers ago, I paid a visit to a fascinating character whom I'll call Mr. B. He's a self-described bard and modern-day Druid, who lives "off the grid" on a farm in Roscommon. I found Mr. B. through reports of his public appearances and writings as a proponent of the Gaelic revival movement. One area of his work focuses on reinterpreting the history and meaning of the Irish diaspora. Mr. B. chooses to remain anonymous because, as he explained before our visit, he's also an activist who lobbies to preserve ancient Celtic sacred sites, a campaign that puts him at odds with urban developers and the country's Catholic leadership—and occasionally upsets his rural neighbors.

We sat in front of a fire in the great room of the farmhouse that Mr. B. built himself. Between his leather pants and vest, long beard, and the melodic lilt of his voice, my encounter with the forty-something Mr. B. had a timeless quality to it. He talked about Western Ireland at the turn of the last century, when, he explained, farmers faced some of the most brutal British repression in the long, tortuous history of their occupation of Ireland, with the appropriation of native Irish lands and farms still commonplace.

This struck a chord, as just days ago at the Irish National Library in Dublin I'd learned that my grandfather Michael had been the oldest of four boys among seven children born to John and Bridgett Bourke Costello. At the time of the 1911 census, just one child, named Patrick, remained in Galway and lived with his parents and two sisters in the family's two-room farmhouse—located fewer than fifty miles from where Mr. B. and I now sat.

I asked my host his opinion of what might push a young man of that time to make either fateful decision: to go or to stay behind. Mr. B. offered the view that there were no "good options" for Irish men coming of age in the first decade of the new century. "It was a myth that the ones who left found a pot of gold at the end of the rainbow in America," he said with a new intensity. "On either side of the Atlantic, it was a holocaust for the Irish. Some were simply stronger than others. It sounds like your grandfather was one of many who fell to the darker forces."

It's another perspective to add to that of Nancy Scheper-Hughes and the small army of psychiatric researchers who've made their way to Roscommon over the past three decades—each in their own way searching for the underpinnings of the "dark forces" that occupy every mind—but manifest only in some.

DESPERATELY SEEKING ANSWERS

It took me until the mid-2000s, after Alex, Sammy, and I had stabilized in our recoveries, to pick up the task of settling accounts around my grandfather's life and death.

Grandpa died on a railroad track. Drunk. He was lying there and got run over by the train. It was a terrible accident.

I can still hear the thinly veiled disgust in my mother's voice as she spoke those words. I also remember the image that came into my mind after she stopped speaking: a train screeching to a halt before it struck Grandpa as he lay limp across the railroad tracks. I remember asking Mom just one question.

"Why didn't he hear it?"

If she gave an answer, it escapes me. My guess is she didn't.

Mom died from a heart attack in 1993, five years before Alex's hospitalization. Her death was sudden, but I suspect the reason I'd never raised the subject of Grandpa with her again was that it had long before been made taboo. A *family secret* is called that for a reason. Not necessarily because it's *never* spoken about. The term can also describe an alternative interpretation of events—or a deliberate lie.

But now it was time to find the answer without the benefit of my mother's memories. Learning the ropes of genealogy, I did the easy things first. On a lunch break, I would go to the Ancestry.com website. It's the McDonald's of genealogical research, giving you the exhilarating feeling that you're just a click or two away from filling in a slew of blanks on your family tree—each oscillating leaf on the computer screen signaling another nugget of heretofore unknown information delivered to your personalized "family tree" home page. Victory feels imminent; that is, until you discover the relatively small number of popular names used by an ethnic group in any single historical period.

I went to the Ellis Island Museum website, a marvelous place—with an abundance of riches that can soon become overwhelming: steamships arriving monthly between 1900 and 1910 from Irish ports alone, each carrying more than four hundred passengers often with one dozen Michael Costellos among them. I had to narrow my search, so I worked backward from my father's date of birth. I figured that in order for Grandpa to get to America, marry, and have a baby by 1914, he'd have immigrated prior to 1910—maybe.

As I continued searching the Ellis Island database in this narrowed range, I quickly found a passenger named Michael Costello, twenty-one years old, arriving in May of 1906. *Hmmm. Don't get too excited*, I told myself. Checking August of the same year, I found another one. This Michael Costello was nineteen years old, his ship, the SS *Majestic*. I dutifully printed out the *Majestic* passenger list, stuck it in my file with all the other candidates, and forgot about it. Here's what it said.

Passenger name: Michael Costello. Age: 19.
    Nationality: British/Irish. Read/Write English: Yes. Marital status: Single.
    Last Place of Residence: Ballenstock, Tuam.
    Occupation: Farm laborer.
    Final destination: Jersey City, N.J. Relative: Sister, Mrs. P Fergus.

The evidence to corroborate that this last of the Michael Costellos to arrive at Ellis Island in the summer of 1906 *was* indeed Grandpa surfaced three months later and was found by my brother James in a paper bag full of memorabilia in his basement.

—⁓—

Despite the fact that we were the last of our family still living, during the years of Alex's troubled adolescence, my brother (who lives in New England) and I were rarely in touch. I think I didn't want to create the impression that there was another Rita in the family—only this time the "troublemaker" was my kid. I also didn't want to risk his judgment or criticism; no doubt a projection of my own self-doubt as a mother. So I gave my brother only the barest outlines of what was going on during our twice-a-year conversations. Besides, I rationalized, James had never shown any interest in interior things.

When I went alone for a visit to his home on a November weekend in 2007, the closest I came to sharing what I was up to was to mention the family "genealogy project" I'd undertaken in advance of a planned trip to Ireland. Then again, I had an ulterior motive: James's basement had become the repository of our family archives; everything that Mom had kept from her's and Dad's lives was now his.

ARTIFACTS IN SEARCH OF FACTS

After the breakfast dishes were cleared, I asked James if he'd found anything interesting in his basement since we talked on the phone. He admitted he hadn't yet gotten around to looking; he was hoping, I suspect, I would drop the idea. When I didn't, he rose from his chair, offering only a roll of his eyes in half-hearted protest before descending downstairs. When I volunteered to help, he urged me to stay put, saying, "It's a mess down there . . . one of these weekends."

"Close the door—it's cold!" yelled my nephew from the sofa where he was watching college football.

Still at the kitchen table, ostensibly reading the Sunday newspaper, I felt increasingly apprehensive. *What would he find?* I wondered. My worst fear was that there would be nothing at all saved of Grandpa. Half an hour later, James emerged carrying two dust-covered paper grocery bags. A quick glance in one suggested they'd been filled in a hurry, probably before Mom's house went up for sale. With a grimace, James unceremoniously dumped the contents of both bags onto the kitchen table.

With James's shrug signaling I should do with this stuff whatever I wished, I dug my hand into the pile, picking through old bankbooks, Mom's driver's license, dozens of vintage grocery coupons, and yellowing greeting cards. James was more selective, pulling from his side of the pile Dad's army release papers and his Distinguished Flying Cross, still in its original case.

"This I'll keep up here," James said, putting the case on the empty chair beside him.

We dug for a few more minutes before James made a big find. "Here you go," he said, handing me a diploma-size piece of wrinkled parchment.

"I don't believe it," I said, as I read Michael Costello's naturalization certificate, issued by the state of New Jersey on February 15, 1911. It gave Grandpa's age as twenty-five.

"I didn't know they lived in Jersey City," James said, leaning over to take another look.

"Not they, just him," I said pointing to the check mark next to "single" on the document. More fine print told us that Michael had met the minimum requirement for residence in the country and state of five years. His street address in Jersey City followed, written in elegant cursive.

"Hmmm," I said, thinking aloud, "1911 minus five years is . . . oh, my God, he could be one of the Michael Costellos from 1906."

"Huh?" James wasn't following me.

I went to my suitcase in the family room and pulled out my file of Ellis Island records. When I showed James the stack of ship passenger lists I'd collected, his eyebrows shot up, perhaps just then taking in the intensity of my obsession. Every page had a line with yellow highlighting where there'd been a Michael Costello onboard the ship. It took only seconds for me to locate the Michael Costello who'd arrived in August of 1906 with the stated intention of joining his cousin, a Mrs. Fergus, in Jersey City.

"It's Grandpa!" I said, and then reading aloud, "He was nineteen years old when he got here. He came over on the SS *Majestic* by way of Queensland. His home town was Tuam, in County Galway; occupation, farm laborer. And he had six dollars in his pocket."

"How do you know all that?"

"It's right here," I said.

"No shit," James said, grabbing the ship manifest.

Just to be sure, I did the simple math on a scrap of paper. Adding five years to the age of Michael Costello on the *Majestic* made him twenty-five, same as Grandpa's age on the naturalization form. The match was perfect.

Later, this trail to Grandpa's first home in Jersey City would be corroborated by a 1910 US Census putting him at the same address with a brother, Thomas Costello, and sister Ann, married to a James Fergus. And then I found an official New York City record documenting his marriage to Ellen in a Manhattan civil ceremony, just three weeks from the day he received his citizenship.

"You actually had this," I said, still amazed at our luck that Grandpa's proof of citizenship had survived all the years, with the many moves and neglect it had endured.

Although my father had the one torn sepia photograph of his mother Ellen, he'd never had a picture of his father. Now the certificate offered a physical description: five-feet-eight-inches tall, hazel eyes and red hair. It could have been a description of Dad, nickname Red.

I felt as if a curtain had parted, and I'd made contact with the dead.

"Yeah. That's great." James said, sounding relieved as he gathered the papers and photos and started dumping them back in the bags.

I, too, was ready to wrap things up. It had already been a remarkable morning. After carefully putting the certificate in my "Official Documents" file, I noticed James puzzling over another piece of parchment. He handed it to me without comment.

The single-folded, larger parchment page was decorated with cherubic angels flying over a row of tombstones. "St. Raymond's Cemetery" was printed in old English lettering across the top. The address at the bottom of the page read "Bronx, Westchester." *How strange*, I thought, *the Bronx isn't in Westchester County*. But stranger still were its contents: A forty-dollar St. Raymond's receipt for the purchase of a four-by-six-foot burial plot, with room for two. The signature on the document belonged to "Ellen Costello."

James appeared to be waiting for me to say something.

"Grandma Ellen bought a burial plot," I said, stating the obvious.

"Looks like it."

"I wonder why Grandpa didn't sign the receipt. And why they bought a burial plot in the first place."

"Why wouldn't they?"

"The date on the receipt is August 13, 1913. He would have been, what?" I got the naturalization certificate out of my file and sat the documents side by side. "Twenty-eight."

"Yeah?"

"I don't know about you, but I'm fifty, and I don't have a burial plot. Forty dollars. Think about it, James. They were dirt-poor."

He shrugged, clearly not getting my point.

A major roadblock had been thrown onto the neat trail I had only minutes before drawn for Grandpa: setting sail from Ireland in 1906, landing on the tip of Manhattan, making a detour to Jersey City before getting his citizenship, hooking up with Ellen, and moving back to Manhattan, ready for his new married life, and soon, a son.

"Not only that," I said. "On August 13, Dad's birth was less than seven months away."

James looked perplexed. "Maybe they just wanted things set."

"Set?"

"You know, for the future."

I sat waiting for my brother to see the obvious gap in his logic. But he'd already turned his attention to the football game in the next room. My mind, however, was stuck in quicksand. The St. Raymond's receipt just didn't make sense. By the time I left James's house the next day, it had become a physical talisman for me. I fingered it, held it to my cheek, searched for its smell, savoring whatever essence of Michael and Ellen it carried. What continued to bother me was the absence of a date for an actual burial in either of their plots, and the dreadful possibility in my mind suggested by this absence.

Okay, I reasoned, *they were each buried at some point after these plots were purchased, but how long after?* The date I couldn't get out of my mind was March 9, 1914, my father's birth. I refused to consider the possibility that Ellen had delivered her son alone. That she'd lost Michael seven months before, and that this was why she alone signed the St. Raymond's receipt.

—ᴟ—

One week later, I was in the Millstein Division of United States History, Local History, and Genealogy at the main branch of the New York Public Library armed with two new artifacts. I'd found a line outside the library's main entrance by ten thirty for the branch's eleven o'clock opening. Hurrying down the marble stairs, I secured one of the last available computers, removed my coat and scarf, and walked back to the front of the room to wait for my turn at the librarian's desk—behind one-half-dozen other customers. Anyone who loves research is in heaven in this place. Most of the floor space is taken up by homely metal shelves holding oversized tomes, records of the millions of people who'd ever lived in the city of New York—Michael and Ellen Costello among them. Mobile ladders provide easy access for the searcher needing an upper shelf to find a given year or neighborhood. I've always loved the sense of timelessness I feel there, of past and future fused. On this personal mission, that sense of time standing still gave me hope that I wasn't searching in vain.

When it was my turn for help from the reference librarian, I showed him the St. Raymond's receipt and received a contact phone number. He gave me one for an archivist associated with the cemetery. Then I walked out of the Millstein Room into the cavernous hallway to place the call to St. Raymond's on my cell phone.

I asked the receptionist who answered the phone for the occupants of burial plot fifty, section ten, range forty, graves one and two.

"Hold, please," she said with a disinterested tone.

I felt dizzy and put my hand on the cold stucco wall for balance. She came back on the line. "Plot one . . ." A long pause followed. "Plot one is Michael John Costello."

"When was he buried?" I asked, barely able to contain my frustration.

"The same date you have, dear," she said, "August 13, 1913. He was twenty-eight years old."

"Is there a cause of death?"

"No, none given," she said, and hung up the telephone without another word.

As I walked back to my chair in the Millstein Room, my stomach tightened as it dawned on me that this latest discovery would necessarily dislodge one of my long-held assumptions about Grandpa. It was my belief that Ellen had died before her husband. This had been the "reason" I'd allowed for Grandpa's despondency and likely suicide. I had rationalized that, as a lonely, likely unemployed widower with a young son to care for, he had lost all hope. This scenario that I apparently created out of whole cloth had served to take the edge off his suicide. Now the edge was back. Grandpa had died some six years earlier than I'd thought, leaving Ellen alone to raise her son in New York City—in 1914—until her own death from the flu in 1919.

After learning the date of Grandpa's death, I've tried unsuccessfully— searching county and city records for New York and New Jersey—to locate an official death certificate for Michael Costello. It struck me as very strange when I received a notice by mail from New York City Vital Records with a brief sentence stating: "No Record Found" and then listing each of the five boroughs by name, including the Bronx. I was stunned. In contrast, on my first try, I found Ellen Costello's certified record of death online in the Manhattan database, which I accessed instantly from the New York Public Library. It seemed like I'd arrived at a dead-end.

Watching *CSI* on television one night, it occurred to me that there were medical examiners and coroners in 1913, too. The next morning, I thought I might be close to finding something when I came upon thousands of turn-of-the-century records already digitized and available to the public on the Westchester County website: lists of almshouse and jail residents, wills and judgments filed, even autopsy records. But in a chilling close call, I discovered that coroners' records were not saved until 1914, one year after Grandpa's death. I felt teased by my new proximity to Michael Costello's life, but I was still unable to locate anything other than a burial receipt to shed light on his premature death. Assuming as I did then that a government-certified document provided a true cause of death, I feared the lack of an official document would leave my fundamental question unanswered, perhaps for good.

Grandpa died on a railroad track. Drunk. He was lying there and got run over by the train. It was a terrible accident.

Was Grandpa's death intentional or not? Within each possibility there were vast amounts of gray area. When does recklessness leave the domain of unintended mishap and become intentional self-destruction? Is a slow death by alcohol so different than lying in front of a train? And what if there really wasn't a train? Given the way the story first came to me, akin to a game of telephone, I've had to accept the possibility (more, the likelihood) that things were added or subtracted from the account of my grandfather's death told by my mother. So powerful was the force of my family's denial, there would have been no need for her to tell an untruth. Not when an unconscious, unspoken conspiracy of silence would have sufficed.

Chapter 11

GRANDPA'S PSYCHOLOGICAL AUTOPSY

Discovering how my grandfather may have lived during the decade he spent in New York after getting off a transatlantic steamship at age nineteen would eventually require going beyond the particulars of his individual life. As young immigrants living in New York in 1913, the notion of looking for professional help to solve a mental or emotional problem would have been completely foreign to my grandparents. If anyone outside the family was consulted about Michael's severe depressions, his alcoholism, or his reckless behavior, a priest would have been the only option.

The Catholic Church in its online New Advent Encyclopedia of Catholic teachings calls the deliberate taking of one's life an egregious and cowardly act against God.[1] It describes extreme despair as a "movement of the soul," which can be resisted if one accepts the help of religion. The technique recommended for this is "repentance and the practice of confession to relieve the moral suffering of man." This teaching goes on to assert that Catholic beliefs and practices "forbid and prevent to a large extent the disorders of life and prevent the causes which are calculated to impel a man to the extreme act [of suicide]."[2] For my grandfather's generation, the kind of "extreme despair" that might lead a man to bury himself in alcohol or to take his own life lay wholly within the realm of morality and sin. With its dual emphasis on confession and repentance, the Church obliquely recognized the traditional role played by the Catholic priest as a poor man's therapist.

Meanwhile, in an alternate reality populated by the upper classes and the educated, the century-long process of redefining the self using the new science of psychology had barely just begun. The creator of that distant universe, neurologist Sigmund Freud, had in 1911 defined melancholy, the disorder we now call depression, as an incomplete form of mourning.[3] Fast-forward one century, and more recent genetic research reveals that the same genes and neural pathways that can make one more vulnerable to depression are also implicated in anxiety, alcoholism, and suicide.[4]

—⁓—

To get inside the Michael Costello of 1913, I allowed myself to ask the first of many "what if?" questions. What if Michael and Ellen's two-year-old marriage was buckling under financial and emotional strains? According to the *Majestic* manifest, Michael left Ireland as a farm laborer. In a listing for him and Ellen in the 1913 Manhattan phone directory, Michael's occupation is given simply as "laborer." On Ellen's death certificate, she is described as a widow and a housekeeper. Irish immigrants in East Coast American cities during the decades before and after the turn of the twentieth century were at the bottom of the social and economic heap. Signs reading "No Irish Need Apply" hung on fences around construction sites and shipyards.

Any family members to whom my grandparents might have turned for help would have been in the same fix as they were. The census records of 1910 and 1920 showed tenement buildings in Manhattan and the Bronx typically filled with anywhere from six to twelve people, many with different last names, some identified as "boarders." It was not hard to get a feeling for the odds a young man may have felt were lining up against him, or the temptations of an escape.

All the "what if" questions I had about Grandpa ultimately came down to one: *Why?* Even with all the pressures and odds stacked against him, why did he put himself in front of a train and leave Ellen to fend for herself with a newborn baby? What was it that pushed him beyond despair to the ultimate act of suicide?

UNRAVELING AN UNTHINKABLE ACT

I found an analysis of the act of suicide from every possible angle in a meta-study from the McGill Group for Suicide Studies in Montreal published in 2004. These researchers looked at twenty-seven studies comprising 3,275 suicides that occurred in North America, Europe, Asia, and Australia. They found that the vast majority of these people who died by suicide, 87.3 percent, had a history of psychiatric disorders prior to their deaths, although 14 percent (of the 87.3) had not been diagnosed prior to death.

The means used in these studies to determine the mental disorders of those who had not been previously diagnosed was the psychological autopsy method—during which, like a forensic psychologist, an interviewer reviews medical records or physical evidence concerning the cause of death, then finds out if there are any diaries or correspondences written by the deceased and puts those together with the verbal testimony of family, friends, and coworkers about the deceased's recent comments and behaviors to re-create what may have been going on in that person's life and mind when he was alive. This is essentially what I've attempted to do with the life and death of my grandfather—although it is admittedly much more difficult after so much time has gone by.

The most common retrospective diagnoses of the suicides documented in the McGill study, at 43.2 percent, were the mood disorders major depression and bipolar disorder. The next largest categories represented in the suicides based on psychological autopsies included those persons suffering from a psychotic illness such as schizophrenia and an addiction.[5]

Psychologist Thomas Joiner has studied the records of hundreds of completed suicides including those of many of his own depressed clients and the death by suicide of his father to come up with a novel point of view on this subject, which he published in his 2005 book *Why People Die by Suicide*. In it, Joiner points to the overwhelming majority of seriously mentally ill people who don't commit suicide and asks what makes them different from the 20 percent of mentally ill individuals who take their own lives. He points to three key risk factors that he consistently sees in people who die by suicide.

First, they are socially isolated.

Second, they have a sense of personal inadequacy, often feeling as if this failure to succeed as a breadwinner or spouse makes them a burden to loved ones.

Third, and this is where Joiner breaks new ground, those who die by suicide have developed a comfort level with violence, meaning they've become habituated to the kinds of high-risk behaviors that lead to self-abuse.[6] This trait dovetails neatly with the symptoms of bipolar disorder, particularly those associated with manic phases. Notes Joiner: "Manic episodes frequently land people in jails, fights or accidents."[7] From there, he points out, it's not such a great distance to carry out an act of concerted self-harm.

It took me awhile to understand the implications of what Joiner was doing with his more nuanced picture of how someone gets to this most final of final decisions. He refutes the common belief that suicides are impulsive responses to socially determined setbacks—or, that suicide is a cowardly act committed by a weak person. Consider, he suggests, that suicide attempts outnumber completed suicides by at least ten to one. Among other things, this reveals that it's hard to kill yourself. Most people who have had what's called suicidal ideation (and I count myself among them), don't even try.

Joiner's third criterion sets would-be suicides apart from those who go through with it. That is, the individual's ability to administer intense physical self-abuse. These are people, Joiner suggests, who cut their own skin, appear addicted to covering their bodies with tattoos, or frequently get into physical fights. They push the limits with partying and recreational drug use. Drive fast. Ride a motorcycle without a helmet. Go for days without sleep. Fall frequently. Have accidents with power tools. And drink to oblivion.

—⟋⟍—

Joiner explains how reckless behaviors such as alcoholism allow the mentally ill person to habituate to reckless self-harm, making the completion of a suicide attempt more likely. He doesn't discount the role of alcohol in reducing inhibition and increasing the likelihood that the suicidal person will choose a particular moment and the closest opportunity to commit the final act. But he differentiates between that and a "spur of the moment decision to die by suicide." Joiner is adamant that mental illness alone is not enough to push someone over the line. Rarely, he says, does he see a completed suicide that does not include the three factors he cites again and again in his book: social isolation, a sense of personal failure where the individual feels as if he is a burden to loved ones, and a habituation to physical abuse.

FICTIONS AND FACTS ABOUT SUICIDE

There are many fictions about suicide. I found the following to be most in need of being brought to light—with the corresponding facts.

Fiction: People who talk about suicide don't do it; suicide happens without warning.
Fact: People do talk about it. Their statements should be taken seriously.
Fiction: Talking about suicide may give someone the idea.
Fact: Not true. See Thomas Joiner's research above: suicide is hard to pull off.
Fiction: Suicide rates are higher for people of low income.
Fact: No. Suicide shows little prejudice to economic status. It is representative proportionally among all levels of society.
Fiction: Once a person is suicidal, he or she is suicidal forever.
Fact: As noted, research shows a strong association between mood disorders (depression and bipolar disorder) and suicide. If an individual achieves remission from his depressed symptoms, the desire to die by suicide will usually fade.
Fiction: Most suicides are caused by a single, dramatic and traumatic event.
Fact: Precipitating factors may trigger a suicidal decision, but more typically the deeply troubled person has suffered long periods of unhappiness, depression, lack of self-respect, has lost the ability to cope with her life, and has no hope for the future.
Fiction: It's unhelpful to talk about suicide to a person who is depressed.
Fact: Depressed persons need emotional support and empathy; encouraging them to talk about their suicidal feelings can be a therapeutic first step.[8]

PREVENTING SUICIDE

There is a growing consensus that suicide is preventable by taking a fairly simple common-sense approach: making it harder to accomplish. A case in point: when the United Kingdom in 1963 (the year of poet Sylvia Plath's suicide) changed the type of household gas from a highly toxic coal gas formula to a less toxic natural gas, England saw a one-third drop in its suicide rate.[9]

Was there a note? It's the first question that comes to mind after a suicide. If the deceased leaves written or verbal evidence of her intention, and if she completes the act, we tend to view her intent as unequivocal. It was surprising, then, to read the contrary view of psychiatrist and medical director of the National Suicide Foundation, Dr. Herbert Hendin, who says that three-quarters of those who die by suicide (note or no note) are crying out for help and would rather live than die.[10]

How does he know? Apparently, there is substantial testimony available from individuals who survive or who are thwarted from completing their suicides.

The issue of suicide prevention has been at the root of a decades-old debate about whether the city of San Francisco should erect a suicide barrier on the Golden Gate Bridge, one of the nation's most popular landmarks, and the place where more people commit suicide than any other location in the world. Since the bridge was built in the 1930s, over 1,200 people have jumped to their deaths. The case against a suicide barrier comes down to the desire to preserve the bridge's unrivaled views for pedestrians who throng there every day of the year. Buttressing this position is the old argument about would-be suicides, that if denied the opportunity to end their lives one way, they'll just go elsewhere.

The counterargument has been made by University of Berkeley professor Richard H. Seiden, who followed the cases of over 515 people who (from 1937 to 1971) were thwarted (by park police or Good Samaritans) from making suicide jumps from the bridge. Of these, he found that only 6 percent went on to complete a suicide in the months and years that followed.[11]

In July of 2010, the Golden Gate Bridge Authority finally got the necessary support to erect a horizontal net under the bridge railing that would discourage jumpers. A compromise between utility and aesthetics, it is not unlike the safety net erected during the bridge's construction in the 1930s after eleven men fell to their deaths. As of March 2011, the final stage of the net's design was under way, but the project is still without the necessary funds to erect it; the cost is estimated to be $5 million. In the meantime, contributions are being sought from the public while the old deterrent system remains in place: emergency telephones posted across the bridge's pedestrian areas, the trained eyes of bicycle and motor vehicle patrols and bridge workers, and members of the traveling public who frequently report suicidal behavior they spot to authorities using their cell phones.[12]

SUICIDE PREVENTION FOR PARENTS AND TEACHERS

There are proven ways to support a young person struggling with depression and despair and to reduce the likelihood of adolescent suicides. There are also warning signs that someone is seriously considering suicide—and things to do that might stop them. The following suggestions come from San Francisco Suicide Prevention, the oldest community-based telephone crisis center in the United States.

WARNING SIGNS

Sometimes, as a parent, you need to be the person with the courage to bring up difficult topics such as suicide and self-destructive behaviors. A young person feeling suicidal might not have the courage to tell you directly, because these feelings are very difficult and confusing. If he brings up the topic, treat it seriously. Look and listen for these clues that may signal your child may be in trouble.

- Suddenly isolating from friends and family
- Talking about or expressing fatalistic statements
- Talking about or expressing death in unusual ways, including journaling or art
- Acting helpless and hopeless
- Tying up loose ends by giving things away or saying good-bye in weird ways
- Experimenting with acts of harm, like a sudden interest in guns, pills, or high places

- Suddenly acting very irritable, perhaps violently (adolescents often express their depression outwardly, not inwardly)
- Taking behavior risks that might not be fatal, but that might cause serious harm to their bodies
- Having erratic sleep patterns causing mood changes
- "Medicating" depression with alcohol or drugs, which amplify depression and impulsive behavior
- Acts of self-harm; for example, cutting

MAKING AN INTERVENTION

These behaviors and statements listed above may or may not be a sign that your child is considering suicide, but they are a sign that something is wrong. Your child may really want to talk to you about these concerns, but might not know how to approach you.

- Initiate a direct conversation. Find a time when the two of you can talk privately without interruption.
- Tell your child the behaviors you've noticed that cause you concern.
- Assure your child that you love him and that you want to hear whatever he has to say.
- Ask your child directly if she's been feeling depressed. How long has she been feeling depressed? Try to sense if her feelings have become more intense over time.
- Temper your reaction. It's okay to express your concern; however, anger may cause your child to become defensive. Avoid interrogating or accusing. Focus on your child's feelings rather than your own.
- Ask your child what his ideas are about how to get help and express your own ideas. Reassure him that you want to go down this road together. Reaffirm that you are available anytime he needs to talk.

> • Many young people resist talking to their parents. Perhaps you can get another trusted adult (relative, religious leader, friend) to talk with your child about his feelings.
> • Sometimes parents feel shame or guilt because their child is having mental health concerns. If you feel that way, don't let it prevent you from accessing help for your child.
>
> *Reprinted courtesy of San Francisco Suicide Prevention, http://www .sfsuicide.org.*[13]

Thomas Joiner says that many of the suicide survivors whom he's interviewed have admitted to him in subsequent treatment that despite what they told loved ones or emergency room doctors, their suicide attempts were *not* impulsive acts. Apparently, many survivors swear their attempts to die by suicide were impulsive actions simply because they are ashamed. In his book, Joiner includes a startling quote from a man who jumped from the Golden Gate Bridge and lived. "I instantly realized that everything in my life that I thought was unfixable was totally fixable—except for having just jumped."[14] What I recognized in this survivor's statement was the total loss of perspective that can occur when someone is in the depths of depression, making it terrifyingly easy to miss the most obvious truths, such as better options, and the pain our death by suicide will cause loved ones.

DEATH BY TRAIN

Bizarrely, the terrifying scenario of a loved one dying from an intentional confrontation with a train would come sadly close to me again, when, in early 2009, my sweetheart, Tom, lost his younger brother Kevin to suicide. But instead of the truth—that Kevin had walked in front of a locomotive of the Long Island Railroad—Tom was first told by the brother who gave him the news that a car struck and killed Kevin while he rode a bicycle on a dark road near their parents' North Shore home.

Since Tom knew that Kevin had suffered from bipolar disorder for over twenty years, he immediately suspected another cause of death. He then spoke to his mother, who, it appears, heard the same lie "to spare her the pain" of Kevin's suicide. She then repeated the bicycle accident story to Tom. The net effect of this confusing sequence of calls was to drag out Tom's painful process of discovering what really happened to his brother for another full day. In the end, he was forced to call the Nassau County coroner from San Francisco. When the coroner reported that there was no bike involved in Kevin's death, and then placed the location of his death on a rail-road track, there was no longer any question about the cause. When confronted with this information, Tom's brother finally acknowledged knowing of Kevin's suicide by train from the start. To his already complex emotions, Tom now had to add his hurt and anger at the lie he'd been told more than once.

It turns out that *how* someone we care about dies and the nature of their last moments of life matter a great deal to those of us left behind . . . especially for suicides. It's as if we want to re-create those final seconds, perhaps so we can imagine being with that loved one who, on some level, we feel we've failed by allowing their unnatural death to happen.

—∿—

One of the last things I did at the main branch of the New York Public Library was read the *New York Times* obituary index for the month of August 1913 (the month Grandpa died), a long list of names and causes of death with a smattering of suicides identified among them. After not seeing my grandfather's name on the list, I was ready to put the voluminous index back on the shelf when I caught the words "possible suicide" on an adjacent page. What I found after tracking down the full obituary on microfiche was a nuanced picture of how a suspicious death by train would have been treated in turn-of-the-century New York City.

Published on November 19, 1894, the article-obit offered four headlines: "SUICIDE OR AN ACCIDENT," followed by, "An Unknown Man Killed by a Third Avenue Elevated Train," then back to all caps for a third headline, "SEEN ON THE TRACKS, BUT TOO LATE," and, finally, the full obit was introduced with this: "Several Articles of Little Value and a Card Were Found, but There Was Nothing to Indicate Who the Man Was."[15]

Despite the question about a cause of death suggested by the first head-line, the statement "All the facts point to the theory of suicide" closed the article's first paragraph, putting all ambiguity to rest. By far, the most riveting element in this obituary was bystanders' accounts of the victim's final moments. With the few details I knew about Grandpa's death, I felt that these witnesses could just have easily been describing his death scene. Here was how the *Times* obit read on the day following the unidentified man's death.

> A little group of early passengers was standing on the up-town platform at Houston Street when a tall dark man walked quickly past the ticket chopper. He paced rapidly up and down the promenade, keeping away from the other passengers, who were gathered together near the ticket office, awaiting the train.
>
> It was just approaching, when one of them suddenly shouted, "Look out! there's a man on the track!"
>
> John McKeon, the ticket chopper, heard the shout, and, grasping a red light, he sprang forward and waved it in front of the approaching train.
>
> The engineer saw the lamp and shut off steam and applied the brake, but he was too late. The engine, when the warning was given, was almost on the man, who had jumped or fallen from the end of the platform. Before the brake could take effect, the engine had struck him. He was knocked down and carried along for nearly a dozen yards before the train stopped.

The obituary then goes on to provide details of the victim's appearance, describing him as "mustached" and "in his forties," "wearing a black coat and derby hat" and "carrying no identification." This incongruity of a gentleman not carrying an ID, along with the fact that his pockets contained a lady's intimate items, provided sufficient evidence for officials to declare this death by train a likely suicide. I can't help wondering whether "Miss Ada" was ever located and informed of the victim's death. There were clear intimations of unrequited love as the deceased's likely motive for taking his life. One would hope if the same suicide occurred today, we would look a little deeper into the man's behavior and psyche to determine cause. One would hope.

THE NEW "OFFICIAL STORY"

I was on the phone discussing some technical issues of this book with my neuroscience reviewer, Linda Carroll, when I idly picked up the day's mail. I'd long before accepted the likelihood that Grandpa's death had been a suicide by train when I saw the letter from the New York State Department of Health, Vital Records Section. I stared blankly at the envelope's return address, confused, not immediately recalling that six months earlier I'd filed a second search request for Michael Costello's death certificate through the department's genealogical unit. I told Linda I'd have to call her back later.

When I opened the letter, I was shocked to see an official copy of Michael J. Costello's death certificate, raised seal and all. I scanned down quickly, searching for the area where it listed his cause of death. The first thing I read threw me for a loop. "Body found in the Hudson River, opposite Newburgh, New York." And then, under "Cause of Death," the words "Accidental Drowning."

There was no mention of a train accident. The only link to a train appeared under the deceased's occupation, where it read "Fireman on the Erie Railroad." I learned later that this was the person who shoveled coal into the train's engine—not a fireman in today's sense.

But the bigger issue was the recorded cause of Michael's death, not his occupation. *How could this be?* Mom told the story as if it were absolutely true, an irrefutable given. Perhaps she, too, had been given the lie and simply passed it on to me. Or she'd made it up, perhaps to underscore the drunkenness of Grandpa's reputedly wild ways. Either way, it now struck me that this official document explaining Michael Costello's "accidental drowning" was no more reliable than if the State of New York had said he'd died in an "accident" with a train. People intentionally walk into bodies of water and step in front of trains every day. Most of these incidents are reported as accidents, whether they are or not.

There would be no official solution to the mystery of Grandpa's death.

At first, this absence of certainty around Grandpa's death felt so unworkable that I packed up the first fifty pages of this manuscript in a box and put them in a rarely visited storage space. It was like burying a freshly dead body in a remote shallow grave where I would not smell the odor or notice the dogs scratching at the freshly laid dirt. My life went on, and the compulsion to dig faded. But it never completely left me. It would flit through my mind each time I brought Alex or Sammy to a new doctor. But I could not seem to allow myself all the way back in until I got some help from a John Lahr essay in *New Yorker* magazine. Lahr's subject was Harold Pinter and his play *The Homecoming*.[16] The money quote from Pinter went as follows: "We are faced with the immense difficulty, if not the impossibility, of verifying the past," wrote

Pinter. "I don't mean merely years ago, but yesterday, this morning. What took place, what was the nature of what took place, what happened?"

I thought again about my mother's account of Michael Costello's death.

Grandpa died on a railroad track. Drunk. He was lying there and got run over by the train. It was a terrible accident.

How might Pinter apply the *truth* test to my mother's statement? Reading on, I found the beginning of an answer. "The speech we hear is an indication of what we don't hear. . . . It is a necessary avoidance, a violent, sly, anguished or mocking smoke screen which keeps the other in its place."

If you are newly confronting a family legacy of mental illness, you may find yourself in a situation similar to mine. Faced with a wall of silence and denial, your search for *a definitive objective truth* about your genetic roots may be, at best, a partial success. But that doesn't mean there isn't value in taking the journey. Especially if you keep in mind Pinter's admonition to value the silences you encounter as much or more than the words spoken aloud. At a certain point, the psychological autopsy requires that we come up with working answers using the best information we have available, including our best surmise of what is not said. The fact is, even if Grandpa's death by "accidental drowning" happened yesterday and not ninety-five years ago, I would still not know with certainty what happened to him, or why. That is the special problem of suicide—with or without a note.

One last observation. It came from a young man who served me the best shepherd's pie I'd ever eaten in the Eyre Square Hotel in Galway City, Ireland. We were the only two left in the dining room when I got to telling him the story of my grandfather's Galway birth and the "official story" of his death by drowning in the Hudson River.

"Ah, that's too bad," he said with a kind smile.

It seemed like the perfect opportunity to ask a question that had been gnawing at me since the day before when I took my first look at the beautiful vista that is Galway Bay.

"Something about it doesn't sit right with me," I began. "Wouldn't a young man who'd grown up here near the ocean be a strong swimmer?"

"Not necessarily," he said. "The tradition among the men who fished the waters off here was not to learn to swim."

That made no sense to me. "Why not?" I asked.

"Well . . . from what I'm told, they figured if they were going to go down with a vessel in rough weather, they wanted to make it a quick end."

"Oh, my God," I said, dumbfounded.

He gave me one of those distinctly Irish smiles that convey an unfathomable sense of tragedy, upheld by a bedrock of humor.

"I hope you're going to take the ferry out to Inishmore," he said before leaving.

"Yes, I think I will," I said, thanking him for the pie.

It was the last thing I did before taking the train back to Dublin.

PART 3

THE SCIENCE AND PRACTICE OF RECOVERY AND PREVENTION

A smart mother makes often a better diagnosis than a poor doctor.
—*August Bier, a German surgeon practicing at the turn of the nineteenth century*

Chapter 12

THOUGHTS OF ALL ORDERS

When I look at Alex today at twenty-eight, I can still see the dreamy little boy of three who would habitually drift off into a world of his own. Only now, he does it consciously to fuel the creative process behind his artwork. He's a painter and sculptor but in no way a tortured artist—even if he still likes his own company best and laughs too easily for some. I've heard more than one person call him *eccentric*. A very telling word, it derives from the Greek word for *elliptical*, *elleiptikos*, meaning "defective"; the verb, *elleipein*, means to leave out or fall short. An elliptical form with lines that don't make neat or conventional meetings works handily as a metaphor for the entire experience of difference in an unforgiving culture like ours. Interestingly, it also works for Alex's personality and equally well for his art.

In my son's sculptures, there aren't two adjacent straight lines to be found. Instead he displays a keen sensitivity for the vulnerability in all living things. Alex's first two gallery shows recently opened with a series of sculptures he described as "Living and dying expressed through the body language of animals." One reviewer noted the scarred, unsteady nature of his *Dying Deer*, *Pelican*, *Bull*, and *Blind Fish*. At the opening reception, I overheard a young man say, "Wow, what presence," as he eyed the bull. A little girl petted the deer's drooping head as if to encourage it to get up onto its wobbly legs.

Naturally, motherly pride informs my response to Alex's art—especially when I see the reaction of old friends and family who stayed close to us during the difficult years of Alex's illness. They, too, can appreciate the big and small things. "My God, he's already showing in a gallery. And he's wearing shoes!" effused one friend who came to the reception.

Sometimes I wonder about the price of sensitivity like Alex's. *Has he even paid the full price yet?* Despite all of Alex's successes in this past decade—finishing a prestigious four-year college with a bachelor of fine arts degree, working full time, and maintaining close personal relationships— none of it guarantees he won't have a relapse. I hesitate to even use that word, given how solid Alex is today—more so than many young people his age who've never dealt with anything like schizophrenia.

DEFINING RECOVERY

One thing I found troubling was when clinicians and laypeople who heard Alex's story would insist that his present level of functioning means he must have been misdiagnosed a decade ago. I've since discovered that this reaction is a common one, reflecting a widespread cultural unawareness of the possibility of recovery from severe mental illness. It's a new concept in psychiatry as well, in that it has only received serious attention since the late 1990s. In an eye-opening article in 2000 for *Monitor on Psychology*, a publication of the American Psychological Association, Patrick McGuire quoted one psychiatrist as saying, in response to a colleague who had dared to raise the subject, "Recovery from schizophrenia? Have you lost your mind, too?"[1]

A *New York Times* article on the current state of psychiatry reported that "a 2005 government survey found that just 11 percent of psychiatrists provided talk therapy to all patients, a share that had been falling for years and," the reporter surmised, "has most likely fallen since."[2] Neither do many psychologists provide psychotherapy to people with schizophrenia or bipolar disorder, according to Patrick McGuire, reporting from inside their professional association. McGuire also quoted consumers talking about where the mental health field needed to go. One echoed my own experience, saying, "People [tell me] 'Oh, you were misdiagnosed, otherwise, you couldn't be where you are now.' I mean, that's an impossible circular argument."[3]

McGuire also spoke to Patricia Deegan, who has a psychiatric disability and a doctorate in clinical psychology. Back in 2001, she was quoted in his article as saying: "There is no one out there teaching patients how to cope with stressing voices. Or how to avoid or get out of the delusional vortexes of thought that you slide into. I think psychologists are a decade behind."[4] Since that interview, Deegan has apparently stopped waiting for the field to catch up with patients' needs. With her company, PDA,[5] she's created a self-help course for schizophrenics on how to deal with their voices, and a computer application to enable mental health consumers to participate equally in decisions (with their providers) about psychiatric medications.

—〰—

Rehabilitation for those with full-blown schizophrenia frequently involves the use of cognitive behavioral therapy (CBT), as well as building in skills in employment, social interactions, and self-care within a family and community-based support system. The purpose of this rehabilitation is to help people in recovery navigate their psychotic symptoms using the strengths they still have and whatever abilities can be restored. Representing the new recovery-oriented paradigm of psychosocial rehabilitation in Patrick McGuire's report is psychologist Courtenay M. Harding, PhD, a professor of psychiatry at the University of Colorado, who says: "There appears to be a recalibration of the brain to fully function again. . . . I define recovery as reconstituted social and work behaviors, no need for meds, no symptoms, no need for compensation." For those dealing with severe psychiatric disabilities that don't make it to "full recovery," Harding offered "significant improvement" as the objective of rehab, defining it as "someone who has recovered all but one of those areas."[6] I'm guessing that the consumers I know who are dealing with schizophrenia or bipolar disorder would be delighted with the latter characterization of their recovery. Indeed, many of them are living it.

Harding bases her view—still uncommon among psychologists—on her own highly respected studies of long-term positive outcomes experienced by hundreds of formerly hospitalized patients in Vermont and Maine. All of these former patients whom she followed for one or two decades had suffered from severe cases of schizophrenia. Upon leaving hospitals, some received formal psychosocial rehabilitation; others did not receive those services but remained in their communities in some kind of support system. Courtenay Harding observed that the patients she studied who had fully recovered or who had made substantial improvement had one thing in common. "Someone who believed in them, someone who had told them they had a chance to get better."[7]

I don't want to oversimplify or overstate the odds of someone recovering from these serious mental illnesses. Recovery is different for everyone, depending on who you were when the disease manifested and who you wish to be now. I didn't know what normal felt like before I started taking antidepressants. Now I can say that I'm thankful for the severe episodes of depression that pushed me to do something about my chronic mild depression, which feels anything but mild when you're under its influence.

For many chronically mentally ill people, staying on antipsychotic medication and living in supportive group environments with the benefit of public assistance is the best long-term treatment. Their recovery *is* about managing symptoms and achieving a modicum of self-care; achieving those goals constitutes a major victory. Many have had their illness for a long time and have gone much of their lives without treatment. Far too many live on our streets. According to a National Coalition for the Homeless 2008 fact sheet, 16 percent of the single adult homeless population has a severe and persistent mental illness.[8] With public mental health services falling victim to budget cuts throughout the United States, I shudder to think of what will happen to those now barely hanging on with the minimum services available to them.

The equally important issue is *what kind of care* the chronic mentally ill receive, if they get any. Do we provide the means to make a meaningful recovery in a psychosocial rehabilitation model? Or will we continue the asylum-era paradigm of learned helplessness? This school of thought holds that because the severely mentally ill will never make full recoveries, there's no point in investing scarce resources in their partial rehabilitations.

Fortunately, California has taken a different, more evidence-based route to delivering services that improve people's lives and finding the money to pay for these services. With so many citizens outraged by the increasingly common sight of homeless mentally ill people receiving no care, the state's uniquely populist-approach response has been to tax its rich. Proposition 63, voted overwhelmingly into law in 2004, established a 1 percent tax on anyone with an income over one million dollars, with the money raised set aside to pay for mental health services. Since enactment, the Mental Health Services Act (MHSA) fund has accumulated seven billion dollars and counting.

As designated by law, this pot of money pays for direct services to the mentally ill in each of California's counties. It is also the primary source of funds for the UCSF PREP early psychosis clinic, with several more such clinics now slated to open in other locations.[9] The MHSA is a major accomplishment by any measure, especially in comparison to the estimated two billion dollars in funding cuts to other states' mental health budgets last year, with ten more states reportedly ready to slash their mental health services to the bone in the near future. Eduardo Vega, the executive director of the Mental Health Association of San Francisco and an activist who worked to pass Prop 63, has said, "The MHSA was viewed across the nation as the first real agent of transformation, the way one state would show that services and supports informed by a recovery model and strategically keyed to resiliency for children would help consumers move beyond even the most severe mental illnesses."[10] Like an army quietly preparing for war, the same activists who got the act passed stand ready to guard it from either a counter-proposition at the ballot box or an executive branch raid on the funds it has collected.

OTHER VOICES OF RECOVERY

Over the past two years, I've had the privilege of working with a group of twenty or so individuals, all of us in recovery from schizophrenia, bipolar disorder, depression, OCD, or another mental illness. We're part of the Mental Health Association of San Francisco's SOLVE program, short for Sharing Our Lives: Voices & Experiences. The goal of this campaign is to demonstrate that the mentally ill are everywhere among us, living, working, contributing, and in many cases struggling to do so because of stigma. SOLVE speakers tell their stories to anyone who will listen. Reliably, after every presentation, members of the audience will come up to share their own experience of mental illness or that of a loved one.

My fellow speakers' experiences with mental illness and recovery are very different from mine and my sons. Many have faced much tougher ill-nesses and obstacles to recovery. Here is one such experience from Erika Trafton:

> I have had bipolar disorder for as long as I can remember. At age five, I recall feeling intensely depressed. At age seven, I had a euphoria that could only have been manic. I literally thought I was going to rule the world. I didn't get diagnosed until I was twenty-five. . . . Stigma kept me from get-ting early treatment, which I completely regret. I didn't want to be seen as "crazy." Stigma I experienced in the medical/psychiatric fields was partic-ularly damaging. It made me feel worthless and lazy and culpable. One of

the most difficult aspects of the illness has been psychosis. Sometimes it was fairly benign, such as "receiving" messages from digital clocks, billboards, and television. Other times my thinking has become completely paranoid and disoriented, very scary. Depression is the symptom I wrestle with the most. I spend about 80 percent of the time at some level of depression. . . . I'm now thirty-nine, and I would say medication has helped to keep me alive. Recovery means achieving some peace and acceptance around my illness and regaining my ability to function. I wish that people understood mental illness is not the sufferer's fault. I wish they would approach us with compassion and respect.

From SOLVE speaker David Elliott Lewis, PhD, comes this story:

Two decades after having received my doctorate and building a high technology company, I found myself psychologically disabled by a mixture of anxiety and depression. I sat immobilized. . . . What finally woke me out of it was when the lights went out. That got my attention. Was it a power failure? No. I had not paid my PG&E electric bill. At the time, I had money. So why didn't I pay it? How did I get to this mental space? The first blow was the death of my mother. This loss, stressed further by a declining economy, eventually led to a divorce after a fourteen-year marriage. The loss of my wife, who was also my best friend and business partner, became overwhelming. I lost the ability to work and pay my rent.

After moving to a series of successively less expensive apartments, I eventually found myself on a friend's couch, then a series of homeless shelters. Finally, thanks to the Community Housing Partnership, I was able to escape transitional housing and move into a studio apartment. This was the first step in my recovery. The second step was seeking and receiving help through psychotherapy and also engaging with the lives and activities in my surrounding community. I am still trying to find my way.

—⁓—

Mental health practitioners who toil on the front lines of treatment are exposed on a daily basis to harrowing experiences of the sort my SOLVE colleagues talk and write about. This exposure leads many to recommend to those with similar diagnoses that they stay on their medications indefinitely, rather than risk a relapse. But even when people keep taking their medications as prescribed, avoiding relapse is far from a sure thing. Twenty percent of schizophrenics on medications will relapse within a year after successful treatment of an acute episode. Clinicians are also well aware that one out of every ten young males with schizophrenia commits suicide. Young people who are just developing psychotic symptoms are at the highest risk for self-harm.[11]

These statistics kept me up at night when Alex announced his intention to quit medication. Knowing our family history and the poor prospects for schizophrenics who go off antipsychotic drugs, Alex's father and I were terrified of what might happen to him if he went "cold turkey" as he intended. Of course, caution is not a quality most twenty-year-old males readily embrace. That's how old Alex was when he took himself off Zyprexa®. At the time, he said he was doing it because the side effects were interfering with his art.

THE COST OF CREATIVITY

Some recent science is demonstrating that Alex's conflict is one felt by other creative people with a severe mental illness. How far are they willing to tamp down their natural tendency to leave the grid of normalcy? When does stability interfere with art? By the time he quit taking Zyprexa, Alex's worst symptoms of schizophrenia—the thought disorders, sensory overload, and paranoia—had largely disappeared. Another remark he made at the time, an attempt to reassure me, was: "Mom, if I wanted to get an MBA, I'd stay on it. But as an artist, it's just not helpful anymore."

The links between creativity and mental illness raise tantalizing questions for researchers and for those of us who wonder when and why intervention for prepsychotic symptoms is justified. Does a vulnerability to psychosis always involve the same out-of-the-ordinary brain wiring used for creating art?

To examine the link between psychosis and creativity, Hungarian psychiatrist Szabolcs Kéri focused his research on neuregulin 1, a gene thought to play a role in strengthening communication between neurons. However, a variant of this gene is also associated with a greater risk of developing mental disorders, such as schizophrenia and bipolar disorder. For his study, Kéri recruited self-described creatively accomplished volunteers and put them through a battery of tests. To measure creativity, the volunteers were asked to respond to a series of unusual questions (for example, "Just suppose clouds had strings attached to them which hang down to earth. What would happen?"). They were scored based on the originality and flexibility of their answers. They also completed a questionnaire regarding their lifetime creative achievements before the researchers took blood samples. Their gene scan results showed a clear link between neuregulin 1 and creativity: volunteers with the specific variant of this gene were more likely to have higher scores on the creativity assessment and also greater lifetime creative achievements than volunteers with a different form of the gene.[12]

Kéri noted that his is the first study to show that a genetic variant associated with psychosis may have some beneficial functions. He observed that "molecular factors that are loosely associated with severe mental disorders but are present in many healthy people may have an advantage enabling us to think more creatively." In addition, these findings suggest that certain genetic variations, even though associated with negative mental health problems, may survive evolutionary selection and remain in a population's gene pool if they also have beneficial effects. It should be noted that the Hungarian researchers did not test psychotic people, only creative ones.[13]

—◊◊◊—

In another study exploring possible links between creativity and risk for mental illness, researchers at Stanford sought to find out whether the children of bipolar patients had any greater claim to creativity than their peers who were not at risk for bipolar disorder. Through the use of creativity tests, the researchers found that these children did, and researchers related this finding to the participants' "enhanced ability to experience and express dislike of simple and symmetric images." The researchers' reasoning was that with increased access to these negative feelings, the children could benefit from a greater reserve of emotional energy that they could then channel toward creative achievement. On the other hand, this same access could make them more vulnerable to depression.[14]

So far then, the evidence suggests a link between creativity and mental illness in terms of at least one altered gene and the brain wiring over which it appears to exert some influence. Meanwhile, garden-variety psychosis offers a window on supra-reality that everyday perception does not. As I would personally see in Alex's evolution as an artist, the ability to direct one's creative vision while steering clear of its outer edges is key to staying alive and productive as an artist—particularly one, like Alex, who has displayed a past tendency to jump off the proverbial cliff. Now I see that this nebulous intersection between the edge of sanity and the pathway of an artist's creative impulse is something that can actually be measured. Some methods are new, but others have been around for more than one hundred years—such as the early-twentieth-century inkblot test.

Of course, most brain and genetic research into bipolar disorder and schizophrenia is being done to understand causes, courses, and potential cures for these diseases, not to hunt for any compensatory reasons for their continuing presence in our species. But the two questions may be more related than they initially appear; if not the question of why these diseases are still around, then how they remain so steadfastly present among humankind. One clue may be the findings that show these diseases are *more present* among us than we like to think—albeit in different and less intense forms.

Chapter 13

FROM INKBLOTS TO ALLELES

"C onsider," says Deborah Levy of Harvard McLean Hospital, "the incidence of schizophrenia is stable at about 1 percent, and schizophrenics have very low reproductive rates. What is keeping those genes going?" It's the central question guiding Levy and her colleagues in a study focused on the genetic and behavioral traits, oddities, and even facial characteristics of severely mentally ill patients and their well relatives under way at McLean Hospital's Psychology Research Lab. The hypothesis guiding Levy's work is that the majority of people who carry the genes of severe mental illnesses—especially schizophrenia—are not afflicted with a full-blown case of the disease. They are well parents and siblings of these patients, most of whom never show signs of the illness.[1]

To find the elusive genetic underpinnings of schizophrenia, Levy is attempting to "intensify its signal" by testing these well relatives for a dozen different possible markers. Her hypothesis is that she can detect the genetic anomalies that transmit schizophrenia by looking for select physical and behavioral traits in a large-scale sample of first-degree relatives of patients with schizophrenia. Her study also includes subjects with bipolar disorder and schizoaffective disorder, as well as two disorders considered part of the schizophrenia spectrum: schizoid and schizotypal personality disorders.

In the course of this study, Levy is quantifying the most common of these traits in study participants and correlating their symptoms (phenotypes) with whatever common genetic anomalies (genotypes) show up in the same individuals. Levy's pairing of genomic scans of these diverse population samples with testing for physical and behavioral traits called "endophenotypes" that appear in relatives of affected persons represents an intriguing and relatively new region of research.

Levy is looking to match one or more of these traits with genes; not the only gene responsible for schizophrenia, something no one in psychiatry now sees as a viable research path, but any gene(s) that may have "large enough effects" to serve as a beacon to guide researchers to discover why some individuals fall into the 1 percent who develop schizophrenia and others don't. One of the novel features of this study funded by the National Institute of Mental Health (NIMH), begun in 2005 with a three-million-dollar federal grant, was its teaming of Levy's research team of psychologists at McLean Hospital with cutting-edge molecular genetics researchers at five major institutions around the country. This pairing of old and new research methodologies—putting patients and their families, inkblots and EEGs side by side with supercomputers—sets this study apart from many others.[2]

Dr. Levy points out that since 80 percent of all schizophrenics do not have a schizophrenic parent, that means many cases of schizophrenia might involve spontaneously mutated genetic expressions. It also means that there are likely to be many parents transmitting a genetic vulnerability to the illness to a child without manifesting any obvious symptoms themselves. Early evidence from Levy's study supports the 1999 NIMH finding, which pointed to the genetic presence of schizophrenia and bipolar disorder in family members who do not manifest either of those diseases, or who manifest other milder mental illnesses or traits associated with the pre-onset period of a major psychiatric illness.

TWO DAYS AS A LAB RAT

After a phone interview with Deborah Levy, I was intrigued and volunteered to serve as a well family member participant in her "Study of the Genetic Contributions to Schizophrenia." I figured that by undergoing the testing myself, I would get a much better idea of the subtleties of what Levy and her colleagues were searching for—and perhaps gain some more insights into what Alex had experienced with his symptoms. I made the trip there in the beginning of November 2007, after spending the weekend with my brother, James. It was during this same visit to James's house that we discovered the burial receipt for Grandpa's grave. I still had Grandpa very much on my mind when I drove into the McLean Hospital campus in Belmont, Massachusetts, on a rainy, cold Monday morning.

Built in 1865, McLean is the nation's oldest still-operating psychiatric hospital. Located thirty miles west of Cambridge, the hospital sits on a rolling multi-acre campus, its state-of-the-art research facilities interlaced with clinical treatment facilities throughout the complex of colonial brick buildings. As a visitor to McLean, you are as likely to pass a psychiatric patient on his way to a treatment appointment as you are to encounter a doctor, intern, or visiting family member.

The bucolic atmosphere and easy mixing of those working and living at McLean challenged my image of the genomic researcher as a blinkered scientist hunkered down over a microscope, interacting only with lab rats and far removed from the nitty-gritty challenges of human beings coping with mental illness, and the clinical psychologists and social workers who treat them. I came away thinking it was their proximity to real psychiatric patients that gave the researchers working at McLean their sense of urgency—and their obvious empathy.

Because I was at McLean in the dual role of journalist and research study subject, there was some added complexity to my participation. Aside from Deborah Levy and study coordinator Anne Gibbs, none of the other psychologists and technicians who tested me knew my name or whether I fell into the category of patient or well relative. Nor did they know I was documenting the experience for publication. As a well relative, I was one of approximately 350. The family member who qualified me in this capacity was, of course, Alex. As part of my participation, I gave a blood sample for a genetic scan, which Levy's molecular geneticist colleagues examined later to see if I had one or more of one-half dozen currently known chromosomal mutations that researchers suspect may confer a risk for schizophrenia or bipolar disorder. Although we do not receive our own individual test results, through our involvement, participants help build the database to assist Dr. Levy in her efforts to correlate any apparent anomalies in our genomes with those alternative traits that manifest in family members of schizophrenics.

In addition to drawing blood for my gene scan, over the two days I spent at McLean, I received ten hours worth of psychological and behavioral assessments. On my first morning there, I completed a standard family psychiatric history and a three-hour Structured Clinical Interview (SCID). For the latter, I answered several hundred questions about my psychiatric history, moods, drug and alcohol use, sleep and eating habits, and physical health. There were also questions I've seen since then on screenings for psychotic symptoms for children and adolescents: "Have you ever felt as though thoughts were being put into your head from someone or somewhere outside of you?" and "Have you ever felt as if your arm or leg did not belong to you?"—another example of a distorted sensory perception.

Later that day, I was sent to the McLean Psychology Lab, where a researcher, helped by two interns, pulled a soft helmet tight over my hair and scalp and then connected me to thirty electrodes and a wall full of computers. They did an EEG (electroencephalograph) recording of my brain waves and used a series of auditory and visual signals to test my "sensory motor gating." This is the technical term for our ability to screen out a sequence of background or otherwise irrelevant sounds after hearing the first such sound. Another aspect of the brain circuit that gives us this ability is called pre-pulse inhibition, or PPI, another term for "startle response."

When it's working normally in the brain, PPI describes when a weaker stimulus inhibits an autonomic muscle reaction like an eye blink to a subsequent stronger, startling stimulus, such as a bright light or loud sound. Impaired PPI is often present in schizophrenia (those affected with the disorder and their well relatives), as well as in people with attention deficit hyperactivity disorder (ADHD) and obsessive compulsive disorder (OCD), among other brain diseases. Antipsychotic medications have been shown to increase PPI in schizophrenia patients, with atypical antipsychotics having the most effect in replacing the missing response mechanism.[3]

Experiencing these tests myself and learning about the specific brain functions they measure helped me put together some pieces of the puzzle around Alex's early psychotic decline. It brought to mind his comment about the difference in his perceptions before and after taking Zyprexa®—the atypical antipsychotic medication he took beginning at age eighteen: "Now, sometimes instead of having three hundred thoughts at a time, I have one or two." If you consider "thoughts" to be in the same category as sensory perceptions and emotions—all of them functioning as stimuli to the brain—then impaired sensory motor gating and PPI were probably involved in Alex's feeling of being overwhelmed with stimuli. He was literally "under siege." It also explains why the medication was neuroprotective for him.

In another room, I took an eye-tracking exam to test my ability to make rapid corrective movements in pursuit of a dot on a screen. Schizophrenics tend to make erratic eye-tracking movements, as opposed to a smooth and controlled visual pursuit. Dr. Levy later explained that deficient eye tracking is present in only 10 percent of the general population, but it shows up in 40 to 80 percent of schizophrenics and in 25 to 45 percent of well relatives; eye tracking is linked to a specific region of chromosome number six.

On a computer screen, I was tested for deficiencies in my working memory, another brain impairment common to schizophrenics, measured by how well I saw and remembered the correct sequence of shapes on a monitor. This cognitive ability is linked to the prefrontal cortex and, upstream, to a genetic anomaly on a chromosome geneticists have named "number one." As I struggled to complete this task, I wondered if my clumsiness with it had anything to do with my difficulties in math, a subject at which I was so bad, I'd had to take both algebra and geometry twice in high school, since they were both required for graduation. I never got around to asking anyone about it though, probably because I didn't want to relive any of those dreadful memories from high school math class.

Although I was wilting by the end of day two when I got to Dr. Levy's windowless office for my scheduled inkblot test, I was looking forward to having the one-on-one time with her to ask questions. After listening to thousands of beeps and clicks and watching screen after monotonous screen of dots and squares, I felt in danger of becoming overwhelmed by the minutia of the science, unable to extract what I wanted to understand and apply to my narrower agenda. Dr. Levy began by explaining that an inkblot test is a way to detect thought disorders. A thought disorder can be revealed in a completely unintelligible sentence—less intelligible than the "rectangularly speaking" example Levy had given me previously. An example of an unintelligible response drawn from some of the classic psychological literature on inkblots by Paul Meehl, written in 1962, goes as follows: "Naturally, I am growing my father's hair." No shades of gray there.

Like most laypeople, I'd never actually seen a Rorschach® or inkblot test—a series of abstract black splotches with occasional smaller blobs of red, green, and yellow images; this is how psychological testers prefer it so they can prevent the formation of preconceptions about these images in their test subjects. Hermann Rorschach, a Swiss psychoanalyst, developed the inkblots in 1911 as an experiment in psychological testing. In the century that's passed since Rorschach's creation, his images have been used to screen for emotional disturbances and mental illness in patients around the world.

According to Dr. Levy, who, with her mentor, McLean Psychology Lab founder Philip S. Holzman, developed a scoring system for the inkblot test called the thought disorder index (TDI), there's a precise qualitative and quantitative process for interpreting a patient's responses to these cards.[4] By using the TDI, a tester can determine many finite degrees of thought disorder—a highly important point for Levy since she and her colleagues have now identified thought disorder as the single most significant marker for finding traces of schizophrenia in well relatives.

So, what do they look for in our responses? Dr. Levy characterized one (abnormal) response to the inkblot test as "thought slippage." Within the spectrum of deviance from the norm, there are the minor idiosyncrasies, exemplified by the term "rectangularly." At the opposite extreme lie wholly incoherent responses, illustrated by the schizophrenic man who said he was "growing his father's hair." But both of these are broad strokes in a much more finely tuned gauge. On the TDI scale, a 0.25 severity level identifies minor, often barely noticed breaks in ordinary conversation, for example, a word-finding difficulty. A TDI of 0.50 correlates with a loss of stable mooring in reality, such as an individual's use of a playful confabulation, defined as extreme elaboration without objective support from the blot; in other words, details in one area generalized to a larger area without representational support from the image. At the farthest extreme, a TDI score of 1.0 goes to those whose statements in which "reality constraints have collapsed" and display bizarre ideation. An example of thought disorder at the 1.0 level of severity is "contamination": the merging of two separate and unrelated percepts into one.

Levy and her colleagues explain: "Thought disorder can be inferred when two responses, each justified by reasonable formal resemblance to an area of the blot, are combined in a capricious manner, and it is the combination rather than either percept that violates reality constraints." I wondered, isn't what they're calling combinatory thinking the very state that creative people crave, whether writers in search of the perfect metaphor or painters seeking poetry in visual form? When I posed this question, Dr. Levy answered that yes, of course the psychotic person's sentences are more colorful and perhaps more artistic than the type of sentence we might score in the normal range. But remember, an artist can choose when and if he wants to see things in this more colorful way. The schizophrenic, or anyone else with a severe brain disorder, cannot freely make that choice. By way of example, one of the inkblots prompted the following three responses:

"Two women bending over to pick up baskets."

"Two crows with Afros and they're pushing their hearts together."

"Two bears on a coral reef."

When I looked at this inkblot, I easily saw two leaning stick figures, thus the first response seemed plausible. In comparison, the second and third responses incorporate two small red splotches (ignored by the first response) that lie between the two stick figures. They do so in a clearly fanciful way that one could say is pushing, if not violating what Dr. Levy called the inkblot's reality constraints. Acknowledging the superficial appearance of subjectivity in this scoring system, Dr. Levy says that any tendency toward subjective interpretations is countered by the fact that "normal subjects understand implicitly that they are to give responses for which "sufficient justification" may be found in the perceptual qualities of the inkblot; while "abnormal" minds presumably don't.

After doing this test, I saw her point. Whereas I could look at this inkblot, see the two stick figures and imagine the red splotches as two hearts beating together and suggesting love at first sight, my impulse to read them in a less colorful, representational fashion won out. And all my responses were largely in this vein. It struck me then that this pull toward normalcy is a strong, probably evolutionary human trait—for most of us. Interestingly, here I was at another intersection between the potentially at-odds demands of creativity and normal thought.

In an early finding from her study, Dr. Levy identified thought disorders in 35 to 39 percent of the well relatives of schizophrenics she tested. Why does this matter? It goes back to the study's main objective: to amplify the signal of schizophrenia so researchers might have an easier time locating any gene or epigenetic expression that may play a role in the disease process underlying this disease.

To get to this amplified signal, Levy started with the 35 to 39 percent of family members from her sample who demonstrated a thought disorder. Next, she added the 15 percent of study participants whose thought disorders could be attributed to schizophrenia, schizoaffective disorder (8.5 percent), or other non-affective psychoses (1.8 percent). Then, she added those participants who displayed any other schizophrenia-related clinical disorders, specifically schizoid and schizotypal personality disorders (5.7 percent). At this point, Levy reached a potentially significant threshold: a full 50 percent of study participants who showed some detectable degree of thought disorders.

To fully grasp the potential significance of a large amplification of the signal for this key aspect of the schizophrenic disease process—the fragmentation of the affected person's thinking—we must remember that the disease has a relatively rare rate of occurrence of 1.1 percent in the general population. With this amplified signal for thought disorder—hiked to 50 percent—the McLean Psychology Research Laboratory results, combined with the findings of molecular geneticists working the problem from their end, may yet help uncover a new part of the neurobiological and genetic pathway for schizophrenia. Other researchers can then search for a way to compensate for it, through new medications or some other therapeutic intervention.

COMPARABLE DISEASE MODELS: ALZHEIMER'S AND PARKINSON'S

Many hope that we may already be seeing some payoff for the strategy of using genetic research to steer the development of therapies capable of halting the progression of a psychiatric illness as scientists race to confront the scourge of Alzheimer's disease. More than one hundred years ago, Alois Alzheimer tracked down the cause of the disease that bears his name: clumps and tangles of protein were accumulating inside and in between neurons and eventually killing the cells. But it would take many decades before scientists figured out why the proteins piled up in only certain people's brains.

Clues to the mystery were eventually found when researchers started to look at the genetics of families in which the disease struck often and early. First, scientists isolated which genes were mutated in the families. Then they began to tease out what these genes did in the normal brain and how that changed when the genes mutated. What they learned was that the mutated genes, through a mechanism not yet understood, were associated with the tendency of certain proteins to become long and sticky, and that led to the formation of the clumps and tangles found in the brains of Alzheimer's patients.

Armed with those discoveries, drug company researchers thought they might have the tools they needed to design medications that might block the damage. Many such drugs are being tested in clinical trials. If any one of them turns out to be safe and effective, it may hold the key to halting the damage. But the promise of such medications is even greater: if people with high risk for Alzheimer's can be identified before any proteins begin to accumulate, then the hope is that the disease may eventually be eradicated.

Another relevant disease model comparison for schizophrenia may be with Parkinson's disease, a degenerative brain illness that causes problems including tremors, rigidity, and slow movements. High-profile sufferers include actor Michael J. Fox and former US attorney general Janet Reno. The disease affects about one in every five hundred people. For a long time, researchers thought Parkinson's was simply caused by exposure to toxic substances. But studies of families in which the disease appears much more frequently than in the general population proved that there were genetic mutations tied to the disease. And this meant that cases that popped up in a seemingly sporadic fashion were most likely an interplay between a genetic susceptibility and exposure to environmental toxins.

As is the case with schizophrenia, there is no cure for Parkinson's disease, making the control of symptoms the purpose of its standard treatment. Now, gene therapy is reemerging as a possible treatment that may radically reduce the presence of symptoms in people with advanced Parkinson's disease. Safety concerns have stymied this field, which first emerged some twenty years ago. An Arizona teenager died in a 1999 gene therapy trial, while in another, two people developed leukemia as a result of such treatment.[5]

"Gene therapy is no longer just a theory," said Michael Kaplitt, a neurosurgeon at New York-Presbyterian Hospital and Weill Cornell Medical Center and one of the leaders of a new Parkinson's trial whose promising results were announced in March 2011. "We are getting much closer to a reality where this treatment can be offered to patients." In the recent trial, a gene called GAD that is believed to foster the growth of a chemical called GABA was injected via a "harmless virus" into the brains of sixteen people. Without sufficient GABA, the brain produces a Parkinson's sufferer's debilitating movement problems.

Twenty-one "controls" in the trial received a sham surgery with neurosurgeons only making a minor penetration of the outer brain but providing the "double-blind" aspect of this trial. After six months, the treated group showed a 23.1 percent improvement on a scale of Parkinson's symptoms, compared with a 12.7 percent improvement for patients who received sham surgery, according to the published research. One Arizona man who participated in the trial said that before beginning the trial he had become essentially immobile. Afterward, he resumed playing the violin and had just returned from a trip to Brazil. According to the study authors, their participants had minimal side effects as a result of the gene therapy—mostly headaches and nausea.

The key to the trial's ultimate success will be the continuing safety of these patients and the longevity of its positive effects. Current drug treatments for Parkinson's all eventually stop working. The researchers involved with this newest trial indicate that it is not yet clear how long the newly injected genes will continue to do their job. Neurosurgeon Kaplitt says even these initial positive results might spur similar treatments for other brain disorders like Alzheimer's, epilepsy, and depression.[6]

To develop effective interventions for a mental or physical disease that is heritable—meaning one with a genetic component—researchers need a good fix on what an implicated gene does, and what happens when it doesn't carry out its assigned role. Then they must figure out how this altered genetic expression may be shaped by environmental factors, whether the culprit is a carcinogenic toxin in the local drinking water or the equally serious damage we now know can be generated by childhood maltreatment. The impact of what are undoubtedly multiple genetic and environmental interactions must be tracked to specific interactions between and within cells. Only then can scientists begin to design interventions like gene therapy, or a new medication to influence the actions of neurotransmitters, or a nonpharmacological therapy to help reverse or prevent the disease.

—⟶ഝ⟵—

Peter Jones of Cambridge University is a pioneering schizophrenia researcher. In an overview of more than twenty papers presented at the 2001 symposia on "Risk and Protective Factors in Schizophrenia," Jones emphasized the continuing importance of genetic research into mental illness— but *with a difference.*

> This [epigenetic] model leads us away from the model of "bad genes." Rather, different combinations of genes have different effects, and again, may interact with events, environmental or behavioral, that are themselves trivial, but in combination . . . lead towards bad outcomes. . . . An analogy might be genes as individual playing cards being dealt as a hand. None of the cards is, *per se*, good or bad, but their combination leads to a good or bad hand. Interactive effects, such as calling one suit of cards as a trump, can radically change the importance of individual cards, suits or combinations.[7]

Jones's likening of G × E (gene × environment) to a deck of cards calls attention to the subtle and myriad nature of how risk factors can join with each other and our genes to affect us epigenetically and then neurobiologically and behaviorally. They can have one value alone and quite a different one when they occur in tandem. In this sense, every risk factor we face, from the DNA we receive from our parents to the traumatic life events that can change us by altering our gene expression can be seen as "wild cards." Jones sums up by calling these G × E interactions the "new, new genetics."[8]

THE NEW, NEW GENETICS IN ACTION

On the day I arrived at the King's College London, Institute of Psychiatry to interview Terrie Moffitt, she and her research partner and husband, Avshalom Caspi, were in the midst of a media firestorm, which had ignited just the day before. The spark was a meta-analysis released in the *Journal of the American Medical Association* that had discredited the conclusions Moffitt and Caspi reached in an earlier 2003 research finding from the Dunedin family study. Now the critique made in the meta-analysis had landed in the *New York Times* with the headline "Report on Gene for Depression Is Now Faulted."[9] This was followed by an even more damning lead, which read, "One of the most celebrated findings in modern psychiatry—that a single gene helps determine one's risk of depression in response to a divorce, a lost job or another serious reversal—has not held up to scientific scrutiny."[10]

The research under attack was a G × E finding in which Moffitt and Caspi linked one allele (a shorter version) in the promoter region of the 5-HTT serotonin transporter gene—the gene noted previously that regulates transport of the mood-regulating neurotransmitter serotonin in the brain—to those in the Dunedin Cohort who showed a poorer ability to handle the stressful events that can lead to depression.[11] Individuals with one or two copies of this short allele exhibited more depressive symptoms, diagnosable depression, and suicidality in relation to stressful life events than individuals who carried the long allele of 5-HTT. This interaction, Moffitt and Caspi reported, also showed that childhood maltreatment predicted adult depression only among individuals carrying a short allele but not among those carrying the longer allele. It was the first study suggesting that a difference of one allele could result in someone possessing either greater vulnerability or resilience to life's hard knocks, and one of few since showing a significant interaction between this genetic variation and both the trauma of abuse that happened long ago and episodic stresses that happened six months ago or yesterday. These short and long 5-HTT alleles are not uncommon in the population, thus this finding would seem to hold large implications.

Even more provocative was the study's concurrent finding that those study participants with the longer version of this allele had a lower chance of developing depression after facing the same kinds and numbers of stresses. For those scientists seeking tangible proof of a meaningful gene × environment interaction, this discovery had been considered akin to finding the Holy Grail—with attendant and probably premature and unfortunate fanfare. *Science* magazine identified it as one of the reasons they chose mental illness genetics as a top science breakthrough for 2003.[12]

Now these conclusions were being discredited, with detractors pointing to the results from nine of fourteen studies that did not replicate Moffitt and Caspi's 2003 findings. I had seen the *Times* article the morning before my meeting with Professor Moffitt, so I knew to put aside our earlier agenda, at least until I got her response to this story. She readily agreed and offered a detailed defense of the earlier work, focusing on what she saw as an unreported problem in the critique—one that I then realized was highly relevant to the original subject of our interview.

One of the differences between the 2003 study and the nonreplicating findings, Moffitt explained, concerned the different methodologies used for collecting family mental health histories. These differences had special bearing on how researchers collected information on the stressful life experiences that were the basis for the environmental component of these G × E studies. Moffitt pointed to lower-quality interview techniques used when obtaining family mental health histories in many of the larger studies that were part of the meta-analysis.[13]

Out of the 14,000 individuals surveyed in the fourteen studies reviewed, a full 8,000 people had reported their stressful events and presence or lack of depression *over the phone or through the mail*. This would be like expecting someone to reveal an intimate, potentially embarrassing part of their lives to a telemarketer who's calling during the dinner hour with the entire family watching. I tried to picture that scene. The family is assembled around the table when the phone rings, and a stranger starts rattling off questions. "Have you experienced a divorce? Did you experience depression after this event; if so, was it mild, moderate, or severe? Okay, now let's move on to any lost jobs and deaths in the family. . . . How about child abuse?" It's hard to imagine responding with the whole truth and nothing but the truth in such a situation.

In contrast to the phone and mail self-reports used in most of the larger, mostly nonreplicating studies, Moffitt explained that her researchers conducted sit-down interviews scheduled in advance with willing individuals who were part of a long-term studied cohort. Eighty percent of her self-reports were corroborated by two other family members. Another deficiency in the critique from Moffitt's perspective was the greater weight given to larger studies over the smaller ones, which tend to do more in-person interviewing. Interestingly, the smaller studies were also the ones that reported results closest to Moffitt's.[14]

Beyond the fascinating science revealing a gene × environment interaction of potential relevance to me and my family history, what most stood out to me that day in Terrie Moffitt's office was that just as family mental health histories are routinely given short shrift when diagnosing and treating patients, they are also apparently undervalued in fieldwork for psychiatric research.

But there was more to the controversy than differences in interviewing methodology and data crunching. It also reflects the long-brewing battle over priorities for future psychiatric research dollars. Would the lion's share continue to go to the big genome studies, or would the field embrace G × E interactions and split its funding resources accordingly? The question is far from settled.

Dr. Caspi, who, as lead author of the 2003 study, added in a published comment after the critical review, "It would be premature to abandon research into gene-environment interaction, when brain imaging and other kinds of evidence have linked the serotonin gene [the short allele they linked to depression] to stress sensitivity." By this he meant that this same genetic anomaly has already been shown in laboratory testing using both animals and human subjects to be excessively vulnerable to stress.

Since the 2003 study that started all the excitement and the 2009 brouhaha that brought it to a fever pitch, other studies (some not included in the 2009 meta-review) have replicated aspects of the Caspi-Moffitt 2003 study—while others have not. This left the field of G × E research in a near limbo[15] until another much larger, seemingly definitive review came along at the end of 2010. Unlike the "discredited" story of the year before, this

NIMH-funded double meta-study went virtually unnoticed in the mainstream press, despite having the pedigrees of the Department of Psychiatry at the University of Michigan, Ann Arbor, and the Human Genetics Department of the University of Wuerzburg, Germany, Department of Human Genetics, behind it as well as a larger number of studies reviewed. These researchers reviewed the raw data from a total fifty-six G × E studies that had investigated how and if the 5-HTT serotonin transporter modified depression. Their finding: "Robust evidence that [the gene] moderates the relationship between both childhood maltreatment and specific stressors and depression."[16]

The reasons justifying this conclusion are fascinating in light of the previous controversies about methodologies, for example, the finding that the G × E association was strongest when researchers used in-person interviews rather than self-report questionnaires. Another finding, also involving methodology, was that the accuracy of studies measuring a grab bag of different "stressful life experiences," meaning different episodic (brief-duration) stresses (divorce, job loss) over a long period of time, suffered due to the study participants' insufficient recall, making measurement of stresses and their impact less reliable. So, too, did the mixing of too many different types of stressful experiences. More recent studies that zeroed in on a single type of stressful event—like experiencing a hurricane with low social support,[17] cancer treatment, Alzheimer's care giving, and childhood maltreatment— showed the strongest G × E associations. With a total sample size of 27,000 individuals and an average study sample of 961, this new meta-review represents a complete validation of the original Caspi-Moffitt finding, and offers the field a solid foundation from which to move forward, with clear preferences given to certain data collecting and assessment methods over others.[18]

Even before receiving this positive news, Terrie Moffitt and Avshalom Caspi published a commentary emphasizing the need for researchers—as well the media and public—to embrace the essential complexity of this emerging science. In one article they wrote, "We speculate that some . . . disorders, instead of resulting from variations in many genes of small effect, may result from variations in fewer genes whose effects are conditional on exposure to environmental risks."[19]

In other words, we should stop expecting simple answers or silver bullets to emerge from this research. At the same time, Moffitt, Caspi, and their colleagues are saying, don't lose hope or patience; there is solid science emerging that ultimately offers actionable guidelines for providers and consumers in mental illness recovery and prevention.

For an example of complexity and potential applicability emerging from G × E research, we need look no further than a 2005 Yale study in which the genotypes and emotional states of 196 children were compared: 109 who had been physically abused and 87 non-maltreated comparison children. After taking saliva tests to document their genotypes and administering psychological tests to detect any symptoms of mental illness, researchers found a "significant three-way gene-environment interaction" in these children between those who had been abused and were now depressed with two genes. One gene was BDNF; the other was the same 5-HTT featured in the Moffitt-Caspi study.

Children who had a certain allele of the BDNF gene and two short alleles of 5-HTT had the highest depression scores, but the vulnerability associated with these gene variations was only evident in the maltreated children. But then the Yale researchers added a fourth factor, another environmental variable, and came up with an exception to their own rule. They found that those abused children with the vulnerable genotype who *had had the benefit of social supports* displayed a lower risk of depression—compared to their counterparts who did not have the same source of emotional support in their lives.[20]

It's an example of the sort of simple beauty that occasionally arises from science and epidemiology. On one hand, we can read this result and say, *Well, of course, common sense tells you that an abused child is going to be helped by having a loving source of support.* But we should not forget that in order to change our current fragmented system of mental health services to a model emphasizing prevention and recovery, our national conversation has to be based on more than common sense. It has to include robust science and an up-and-down look at our public policy and budgetary priorities.

Of course, we'd also like to see scientific insights such as those generated by the Yale study used to actually prevent the problem of child maltreatment, which we know involves a cycle of violence handed down from one generation to the next. In that regard, it's reassuring to learn that the lead author of this study, psychologist Joan Kaufman of the Yale School of Medicine, Child Study Center, continues to study how genes and environment shape risk and resilience in abused children.

Chapter 14

PREVENTING MENTAL ILLNESS

We've now arrived at the how-to part of this long and winding story. How do we as individuals and parents work with known risk factors to prevent mental illness?

We start where the scientific evidence is strongest. It's clear that a baby's prenatal experience and the quality of parental care received during the first five years of life top the list of significant environmental risk factors. When there's a family history of mental illness, the research tells us that a high level of stress for a mother during the first trimester of pregnancy can raise a child's risk for schizophrenia—as can obstetrical complications and a baby's low birth weight.[1]

There's now no doubt that physical abuse and bullying,[2] and ingesting cannabis[3] can do great damage to a genetically vulnerable prepubescent child. We understand that conduct problems in early childhood and adolescence can lead to antisocial adults and raise the risk for psychosis.[4] There's also convincing science to show us that if aggressive and antisocial behavior starts in a young elementary-school-age boy, he's at highest risk. Further, we know that *where* we live and the quality of children's schools can also impact one's risk for psychosis.[5] Finally, we are very aware that the level of chaos in our household and the presence of untreated adult psychiatric problems can also negatively affect any child's mental health—but particularly that of a child carrying a higher genetic risk.[6]

If it's beginning to sound like I'm getting dangerously close to the historical tendency to blame parents for the psychological ills of a child, my answer is that, to a certain degree, I am. In so far as I believe we've gone too far in the direction of "blaming" biochemistry and not taking responsibility for our own roles in shaping the health of our children's brains, I think we have to back up and reconsider. I'm advocating transparency and the taking of greater responsibility by everyone—parents, extended family members, mental health practitioners, and our larger communities, including corporate healthcare and government-administered services—for the mental health of our children and future leaders. For grandparents, that may mean giving up an old family secret over which you still carry considerable shame. For parents, it means first becoming more educated about what factors contribute and detract from a child's positive emotional growth.

To make it happen, our public and private institutions need to give parents more, not less support. To those who say we can't afford it, the obvious answer is that we can pay now or pay later. In any given year, approximately 17 percent of Americans under twenty-five have a mental, emotional, or behavioral disorder. (Over our lifetime, 46 percent of us will receive such a diagnosis.) If we reduce the proportion of young people who become mentally ill by even one-quarter, that would mean about 3.8 million saved each year from what can turn into a lifelong and expensive struggle. How expensive? The National Academies estimates that the total economic cost of mental disorders just among Americans under twenty-five was $247 billion in 2007. Another 2007 study found that more than one-quarter of the costs for young people are incurred in the education and juvenile-justice systems, which must deal with illnesses that, in many cases, could have been prevented.[7]

FIRST LINE OF DEFENSE

As parents, we must be the first line of defense for our children's mental health. We also have to make sure that their schools are safe places for them to be and to learn.

In a 2009 report titled *Preventing Mental, Emotional, and Behavioral Disorders among Young People: Progress and Possibilities*, the US Institute of Medicine and the National Research Council assembled voluminous evidence to show that mental illness is preventable in children. Programs that teach parents effective parent-child emotional communication skills are among the most useful that have been tried. There were also robust positive results from preventive interventions aimed at reducing substance abuse, conduct disorder, antisocial behavior, aggression, and child abuse, as well as programs aimed at helping children struggling with depression after a divorce, and others to reduce the rate of aggressive conduct in schools.[8]

The issue of drug use is a particularly important one for parents to grapple with. According to the University of Michigan's annual Monitoring the Future Survey, marijuana use by American adolescents—especially eighth- and tenth-graders—was up in 2009 for the third year in a row, reversing a decline tracked since 1992. Two other worrisome trends were reported in the survey. The age of first-time marijuana users is dropping, and fewer teenagers believe there is a serious health risk associated with the use of marijuana.[9] When Alex first started smoking pot, I didn't view it as his biggest problem behavior. Far bigger, I thought, was the fact that he hadn't done his homework in recent memory. Now we know too much to hold such a view. As Demian Rose told me, "The data are quite clear that heavy marijuana use increases the risk of developing chronic psychosis five to ten fold—even after young people stop using."[10]

A final note on school violence: in one study of 6,437 British twelve-year-olds, researchers found that a child's risk of psychotic symptoms was increased twofold if he'd been bullied between the ages of eight and ten years. If he was more severely and more often victimized by his peers, the child's risk of psychosis doubled or tripled.[11]

In the past, our culture has quietly condoned bullying as a rite of passage—by looking the other way. After a couple of decades filled with school shootings and other gruesome crimes committed by young people against their peers, this is no longer a popular stand. Still, playground bullying continues. It's moved online and has become more prevalent among girls. If your child is being regularly teased, pushed, tripped, verbally harassed, or ostracized at school or in the neighborhood; if he's being persecuted online through the misuse of social networking websites, you must be his or her first line of defense. Don't wait, act. The same goes if you witness another child being victimized in any of these ways or places.

GETTING THE RIGHT MENTAL HEALTH CARE

Treating a child for the first signs of mental distress is the essence of early intervention and secondary prevention—the type of prevention you do to avoid having an illness get worse. This does not necessarily mean introducing a psychiatric medication. The earlier the symptoms are noticed, the less invasive or onerous the treatment tends to be. However, if medication is what it takes to stop the advance of a disease process in a child, any concerned parent should give it serious consideration and weigh the risks and benefits carefully—just as we would for any serious illness, be it childhood leukemia, diabetes, or bipolar disorder. Most adult mental disorders begin in childhood or adolescence. Those that are treated before adulthood have the best outcomes—meaning the individual reaches a remission of symptoms. This is what we're after.

Stanford University's Kiki Chang in his *Frontline* interview offered an explanation of why sooner can be better in the treatment of childhood bipolar disorder. He refers to the "kindling theory," saying, "Certain stressful events or a stressful environment, together with these [bipolar] genes, are going to send you in a certain direction. . . . Eventually what happens is probably either before or after the first mood episode, you're not going to need as much of those stressors anymore, and the disorder is going to take on a life of its own. So your next episode is going to happen easier . . . and it will become harder to treat, too."

When asked if treatment necessarily means an antipsychotic medication, Chang answered: "If we can decrease the amount of stress that's going on in their family on a daily basis, maybe we can also decrease this progression. If we can improve their coping skills and their problem-solving skills within the family, maybe we can delay this progression."[12]

What Chang is describing in the last part of his answer is psychosocial education for parents, a form of outpatient care offered by trained mental health professionals. As noted previously, the reason these services are not readily available has to do with their cost, not their effectiveness. The evidence is also clear that the best treatment approach for many mental disorders consists of psychiatric medication, often short term, in combination with some form of psychotherapy.

USING FAMILY HISTORY AS A GUIDE FOR TREATMENT CHOICES

Decision making about treatment—when and how to treat the initial symptoms of a mental disorder—should always involve family history. Without it, mistakes can be made and unnecessary suffering added to the person's initial symptoms. This can occur, for example, in the case of a young female with a family history of bipolar disorder who develops symptoms of moderate or severe depression. A pediatrician treating her who is not familiar with the concomitant warning signs of pediatric bipolar disorder may quickly prescribe an antidepressant. However, given her genetic predisposition to bipolar disorder, an antidepressant might fuel a manic episode and send her on a negative cascade into more severe and frequent bouts of mania.

How can doctors tell the difference between unipolar and bipolar disorder? According to Husseini Manji, chief of the Mood and Anxiety Disorders Program at the National Institute of Mental Health (NIMH), "Until we learn more about how to distinguish the two, family history would be one way . . . from an academic standpoint, [a doctor should] *always* start with mood stabilizer to treat a child with depression and a family history of bipolar disorder."[13]

THE LONG REACH OF STIGMA

Even for those with access to adequate mental health care, stigma keeps people from seeking the help they need.[14] In my work as an advocate for families on mental health issues, I've discovered that no ethnic group deals particularly well with mental illness, especially when it hits home. Whether you're Irish, African American, Hispanic, Jewish, Asian, it seems everyone is "bad" with this issue because of the stigma that crosses all classes and cultures.[15] At a recent Families and Youth Roundtable conference, I heard University of Chicago psychologist Patrick Corrigan, who has spent decades investigating this problem, speak about why stigma toward the mentally ill remains so virulent in our culture. In his speech, Corrigan said that education and media campaigns don't have any real effect on reducing stigmatizing. About the only thing that does work, his research shows, is face-to-face, heartfelt contact between average people and consumers who are open about their mental illnesses. He suggested that those with mental disorders might consider adopting a strategy from the gay rights movement and selectively "come out" to those people at their workplaces and in the community who they feel would benefit by knowing that *the mentally ill are us.*[16]

It's jarring to me to find that in the twenty-first century there is still a loud minority of public opinion denying the *existence* of mental illness. The most extreme critics of today's mental health care system deride practitioners as pill pushers and have equally harsh words for those of us who take them or go to therapy.[17] I'm not surprised to find Scientologists among this group, although now they've disguised themselves as consumer advocates operating under names like the Citizens Commission on Human Rights International (CCHRI). On its website, CCHRI posts a photo of early-intervention pioneer Patrick McGorry with a headline attacking him for "going global" with a "pre-drugging agenda."[18]

A bit more surprising are the virulent antiscience messages spewing from libertarians, leftists, and intellectuals; including those who continue to identify with 1960s icons Michel Foucault and R. D. Laing, who were among the first to construe mental diagnoses as cultural constructs. It seems from their rhetoric that the central indictment that most of these critics make of psychiatry is that as a profession it is in greedy cahoots with "big pharma."[19]

To be fair, a sizeable number of former psychiatric patients who have suffered ineffective or coercive mental health care experiences in the past have become some of psychiatry's fiercest critics. While I understand the pain of mistreated former patients, many of whom now identify themselves as "survivors," I can't fathom how the necessary medications to advance mental health care will be developed without the leadership of drug and biotech companies. I have little patience for those who would have us believe that neurobiology is a sham and that all psychiatric medications are harmful. On the other hand, I am with advocates who call for transparency in doctor-pharmaceutical company relationships as well as strict government regulation of private-sector mental health products and services and consumer oversight of government-sponsored mental health care delivery. Lastly on this point, I urge consumers and parents to get involved with these issues and debates. However unsavory or ideological they become, we can't let our interests be subsumed by other agendas, not when our children's minds are at stake. What we must do instead is create and promote a proactive program for family mental wellness.

LEARNING RESILIENCY

Emotional resiliency is the ability to cope with stress and adversity and bounce back. Emotional self-regulation is the "how to" of emotional resiliency. Psychologist and author Daniel Goleman, who wrote the groundbreaking books *Emotional Intelligence* and *Social Intelligence: the New Science of Human Relationships*, observed that children who are well nurtured and whose parents model and help them learn how to calm down when they're upset seem to develop greater strength in the brain's circuits for handling distress.[20] Conversely, Goleman wrote that those children whose parents neglect them or fail to model such behaviors will be more likely to act on aggressive impulses or have trouble calming down when they're upset. As Goleman explains, distress kills learning. As any parent knows, it also makes life at home very unhappy for everyone in the family.[21]

In the same theoretical and practical vein as emotional resiliency, "positive psychology" is gaining traction both within the field of psychology and in the culture at large. Described by its practitioners as a scientific approach to maximizing the positive potential of the 50 percent of who we are that is shaped by our environment, the approach focuses "less on repairing past traumas or the broken things in their patients' psyches, and more on promoting individual and collective strengths."[22]

Teachers who've received training in techniques based on positive psychology and emotional resiliency help children focus not on weaknesses or failures but on their strengths and potentials.[23] In the classroom, this approach might translate into the difference between a student failing his math test and thinking "I can't do algebra," and then giving up. Or the same student failing the test and thinking, "Okay, I understand simple equations, but I'm missing some of the steps for longer formulas. I'll ask my teacher for extra help."

As old and simple as the ideas of positive psychology may sound, they are not so easy to carry out. When I started trying to consciously think more positively, I realized just how much negativity dominates my internal conversations on a daily basis. One simple exercise I found useful was to try to get through a morning without lapsing into any self-defeating mental or emotional potholes. When I'd catch myself falling into thinking "I can't do that," or "I can't talk to her; she doesn't like me," I'd make a note of it. Then I would try on a more positive, self-empowering thought, saying aloud to myself, for example: "You have no evidence that she doesn't like you. Make the call."

This mental reframing process should sound familiar. It borrows from cognitive behavioral therapy. A similar technique appears in twelve-step programs with the slogan "Act as if." In other words, if you don't believe that you can change your thoughts or behavior, try "faking it" until it comes "naturally." When reinforced with positive results, a behavior will become habit-forming. Acting in a positive manner brings about positive results in one's life—the notion may sound annoyingly trite and oversimplified, but that doesn't mean it isn't true.

These same principles of positive psychology have now been adapted for use in other fields. We now hear about "strength-based business management," "strength-based social work," and "strength-based recovery." For me, a strength-based recovery has meant viewing my compulsion to research things and my tendency to ruminate as strengths that led me to write this book. For Alex, recovery meant leading with his art. Sammy needed a place to feel needed and valued; he found it in Uganda. These are our continuing strength-based recoveries.

—◠◠◠—

THE NEW, NEW PARENTING

If you are from a chaotic family of origin where high emotional drama peppered with anger was used as a weapon of control, you've probably had to relearn how to express honest feelings responsibly. I certainly did—only to find another wrench in the works. The first time I heard about the pitfalls of "high-expressed emotion"—that is, the tendency of parents of troubled kids to get over-involved and overly emotional about everything they do—my reaction was . . . *Oh, shit, now what have I missed?*

The concept comes from an area of recovery research looking at the effects of how parents and other family members speak to and behave toward the child or adult who has a mental disorder. Studies show that the course of any mental illness is worsened by high-expressed emotion coming from parents and other family members. Among the most harmful examples of expressed emotion: criticism, hostility, and emotional over-involvement.

An atmosphere of high-expressed emotion multiplies the likelihood of relapse two or three times for a person who is currently stable on medication and/or therapy. High-expressed emotion sets up a conflict between family members. This conflict is unpleasant for everyone, but it also has negative neurobiological effects for those in recovery, according to David Miklowitz, author of *Bipolar Disorder: A Family-Focused Treatment Approach*. He explains, "Imaging studies show that fear centers are activated in the brain when depression-susceptible people hear a family member criticizing them."[24]

WHAT IS EXPRESSED EMOTION?

When parents use "high-expressed emotion," this concept refers to the loss of proper emotional boundaries between family members, which then manifests in the use of critical attitudes and overprotective behaviors toward an emotionally troubled or mentally ill child, adolescent, or other adult family member.

Critical attitudes	Over-involvement
Statements of dislike	Extreme overprotectiveness
Annoyance or resentment	Self-sacrifice
Accompanying negative voice tone	Exaggerated emotional responses

Expressed emotion is measured with ratings on a 0–5 scale, and it is considered high at 4 or above.[25]

Given the level of intense involvement I've had in my sons' recoveries, it's no wonder that I initially resisted this idea of expressed emotion and emotional over-involvement. My defensive reaction boiled down to a rationalization that, as parents of troubled kids, we have no choice but to "get our hands dirty"—my definition of over-involved. *If it works, so what? They're alive, aren't they?* Well, yes, thankfully, they are. But for real sustainable recovery to take place, we'd better find a way to be supportive without over-involvement and criticism. Otherwise we risk undermining our loved one's stability and recovery. After paying more attention to the fine points of "high-expressed emotion" and after learning some better ways of giving and getting emotional support, I've discovered that my hang-up with this concept had a lot to do with my unresolved guilt about the past, specifically my lingering view of myself as a "bad mother."

Even the act of learning about one's family history and the myriad of risk factors for mental illness can make a parent's guilt level increase. There's no sure or easy way to deal with feelings about mistakes we've made, but apologies can be very powerful. I've shared with my sons my chief regret: not getting treatment for my depression sooner in their childhoods. When I said those words aloud to them at one point when we were all together, they both looked at me, puzzled. Alex said, "I don't remember that." Sammy reassured me that he was fine, no matter. Still, I believe it was important for me to say, and for them to hear me say it. An expression of gratitude is also powerful medicine for its speaker and recipient. I'll never forget how happy I was when Alex thanked me for sending him to Wilderness Therapy—even if it took him ten years to get around to it.

The multifamily groups that have been developed to support young people in treatment for early psychosis teach parents how to tamp down their expressed emotion and be more supportive of the person in recovery. A great resource for learning the same techniques is the National Alliance on Mental Illness (NAMI) and the Mental Health Association (both listed in the Reader Resources section of this book), especially their Peer-to-Peer and family education programs, which are in every state and most cities of the United States. In many other countries, especially those with national healthcare systems, these same patient education programs and group therapy approaches have been integrated into primary healthcare. And while this methodology has been developed for work with the mentally ill, it has implications and applications to all families.

—⚏—

Science tells only part of the story of mental illness, even if it has become an increasingly large part. Within the scientific establishment, there are continuing fierce debates about whether it "pays" to invest the necessary research dollars and raise public hopes about preventing schizophrenia and other serious mental disorders—when the interventions being tried may not pan out. In response, I like this measured view from one scientist writing in *Schizophrenia Bulletin*. Answering the prematurity argument, he said,

> The history of medicine shows that there have been some spectacular applications of primary prevention based on incomplete knowledge. . . . The consumption of limes on long sea voyages was found to prevent scurvy without the benefit of an understanding of vitamin C. Conceivably, public health

approaches that have already been implemented in the developed and increasingly in the developing world, including control of infectious diseases, improvements in obstetric and neonatal care, and nutritional supplementation, may already be reaping benefits with regard to the prevention of psychiatric disorders of neurodevelopmental origin, including schizophrenia.[26]

By referencing obstetrical complications and nutritional deficits, this scientist raises risk factors that we as parents have some control over. Perhaps we resist the idea of prevention because we're uncomfortable dwelling in the gray areas where genes meet environment, or, as we've always thought of it, where nature meets nurture. But that is where the prevention of mental illness puts us. I call this place the "new, new parenting."

For a good example, I turn to the website of the Columbia University Department of Psychiatry, a wonderful resource where physicians take questions from parents who are dealing with mental health issues in their children. One mother wrote simply and poignantly of her family's dilemma: "My husband has SZ. My daughter has a speech delay and poor eye contact. Should she have an eval? Anything we can do to ward off the illness?"

The answer to this consumer's question came from Professor Cheryl Corcoran, MD, director of Columbia's Center of Prevention and Evaluation, who wrote: "Yes, she should get an evaluation for her speech delay and other symptoms. Her risk of schizophrenia is 15 percent based on her father, but with her [present] symptoms her risk is increased somewhat."

As to what else the parents could do to lessen their daughter's risk, Dr. Corcoran offered this great advice: "Focus on her strengths, protect her self-esteem, foster good coping and stress management, and have her stay away from drugs, especially marijuana."[27]

It's high time I answer the question I've raised again and again throughout these chapters: How can we determine who is the most vulnerable so that we can do everything possible to protect them from developing a mental illness? There are several things we can do, but it comes down to two basics strategies: we can learn the risk and protective factors for mental illness and, then, as Dr. Corcoran demonstrated on the Columbia website, apply them whenever possible to our daily lives.

There's nothing easy about new, new parenting. Recognizing and mitigating the risks for a psychological disorder for which we carry a genetic risk requires that we look closely at ourselves, our moods, and our behaviors. It necessitates being honest about the kind of environment we're providing for our children, everything from sound nutrition to how well we regulate our moods. Do we allow our anger to rule? What is the stress level in our homes and lives? How can we tamp it down?

These are questions requiring a fundamental shift in our orientation from *doing things* for our children to *being there* for them and us. And remember, imperfection is what we all must live with. An openness to learn better ways is our only sane course of action.

In my final chart, I've distilled what I've learned over the past decade and put it in a "top-ten list." Although the items on this list have been informed by what I've heard from the scientists and clinicians I've interviewed for this book—indeed, I've presented evidence for each in previous chapters—this distillation represents strictly my own point of view and my sense of priorities. I offer it for consideration by all parents, but especially for those of you who know or suspect there has been mental illness in your family's past.

THE TOP TEN THINGS A PARENT CAN DO TO SAFEGUARD A CHILD'S MENTAL HEALTH

1. Create a Family Mental Health History

Interview your living relatives and research the lives of deceased family members to create a family mental health history going back at least three generations. Record any recognized and treated mental disorders, but be sure to also include any suspected mental illness that went untreated. These might include habitual fighting and trouble with the law, addictions, unrelenting blues, extreme fastidiousness, and phobias. Be aware that if these disorders run in your family, you may have lost perspective and think that some of the symptoms are completely normal. The key is to identify extreme behaviors that interfere with a person's ability to function.

By all means, look closely into any tragic accidents that occurred to family members in the past, especially if alcohol or prescription drugs were involved. In the aggregate, you may see trends and patterns that would not be noticeable if you went only by individual diagnoses. Use your completed family mental health history to understand your risks and those of your children for mental illness. If the risks are high, monitor your children more closely. If a member of the family is being evaluated by a mental health professional, bring in your family mental health history and insist on it being part of the diagnostic process.

2. Plan Your Pregnancies

Whenever possible, begin a strict physical fitness and mental health regime three months before you start trying to conceive. If not before, get prenatal care immediately upon finding out you're pregnant. In addition to the things you already know (no drinking or smoking), consider your emotional health. If you're suffering from untreated depression or anxiety, talk to your mental health professional about the right course of treatment. Medication may pose fewer risks to your child than would severe depression.[28] But even without taking antidepressants, psychotherapy, diet, and exercise can help stabilize your moods and avert postpartum depression.[29]

3. Treat Yourself First

Your child may not yet show signs of a disorder, but perhaps you do. You may have put off getting diagnosed or treated for any of the typical reasons: no insurance coverage, stigma, lack of awareness that the symptoms are out of the ordinary. If you've been avoiding getting an evaluation, don't wait any longer; make an appointment with a mental health professional and seek treatment if it's indicated. Think of your actions as an act of prevention for your child's mental health.[30]

4. Talk Openly about Feelings and Thoughts

As soon as your child begins to recognize and name her own feelings and those of others, start an age-appropriate conversation about how our human emotions and minds work. Explain that feelings and thoughts exist on a broad spectrum (compare it to a rainbow). Within reason (excluding tantrums or aggression against others), make it clear to your child that unusual thoughts and strong feelings are not to be seen as right or wrong; more often, they represent individual differences. This "normalization" of divergent feelings and thoughts adds to your child's emotional intelligence—an important social and cognitive asset. It also makes it more likely that your child will confide any future psychological problems to you and be less inclined to stigmatize others.[31]

5. Monitor and Document Any Childhood Symptoms

If there's a history in your family of one or more mental illnesses, learn the symptoms of the most common childhood precursor for those illnesses (for example, ADHD for bipolar disorder; conduct disorder or self-harm for psychosis).[32] Remember, in mental health, disturbed behaviors are the clearest indicators of an underlying emotional or psychological problem. If you notice patterns of withdrawal, aggression, strange thinking, extreme fear/worry in a child, first monitor and document what you see in a daily log for one month or more. Then, if symptoms continue or worsen, bring this log to your pediatrician. If a doctor dismisses your concerns, insist on a consultation with a mental health professional. Don't give up.

6. Get Adequate Mental Health Care Wherever You Can

It is still very hard for many families to get access to the mental health care they need.[33] Psychotherapy, especially, is often under-covered by health insurers and harder to pay for out of pocket. If you have insufficient access to care through private insurance, go to your county public mental health clinic and stand in line. Though overworked and underpaid, these are often the most experienced mental health professionals you'll find anywhere. Another option is to sign up for any clinical trials offered by a respected academic institution. Good care can be obtained in these ways.

7. Have Zero Tolerance toward Bullying

Whether your child is the victim or the bully, do whatever it takes to stop it. This is not a "wait and see" option. Even if your child begs you not to make a fuss, understand that the potential psychological damage (including suicide) for him or her if the abuse continues is far worse than any temporary embarrassment.[34]

8. Stop a Teenager's Use of Marijuana

Kids begin using pot at a much younger age these days, as early as middle school.[35] If your family has a history of mental illness, cannabis use has a much stronger "dose-response" in terms of raising the risk of early psychosis in adolescence.[36] Again, do whatever it takes to stop your child from using it. Begin by talking about the science of cannabis. Anecdotally, I've heard it said that the genetically vulnerable child will (more often) experience paranoia instead of euphoria after using marijuana. Make room for your child to acknowledge this possibility, and the two of you may find it easier to get on the same side—that of your child's mental well-being.

9. Make Self-Esteem a Family Priority

Self-esteem has gotten a bad rap because it's been confused with having an outsized and incorrect sense of one's positive qualities and abilities. Self-esteem in a child comes from parents who model empathy, honor individuality, and reward real effort, not false achievement, in their children. True self-esteem is the basis of emotional resiliency, which gets severely tested at several points in childhood—especially during the tween years.[37]

10. Have Family Dinners as Often as You Can

Turn off the television and dust off your dinner table. Use shared dinnertimes as the central place and time for rebuilding your emotional intimacy as a family and for building communication. Share chores and responsibilities and have fun together. Keep the board games nearby for group play—after the dishes are done.

After I finally secured the right treatment for myself and my sons, I confronted another big personal challenge. It came when I was forced to see how I can still be complicit in passing on our family's tragic mantle of mental disturbance through my own negative habits of mind and behavior. Meditation has helped me, as it has many others, to manage this difficult but essential piece of personal mental and emotional housekeeping. This process of recognizing and letting go of my negative self-fulfilling prophecies and expectations is still a work in progress, as I suspect it will be for the remainder of my life.

I know that the principal wild card for me as the mother of two adult sons with our collective history of mental illness is stress. From my observations, Alex assiduously avoids potential stressful triggers; he refrains from cannabis, although he has no problem drinking beer and wine. He's made it through two multiyear romantic relationships and survived the breakups, always returning to his art. We've been through lost dogs, towed cars, him running out of money while backpacking in Italy, and getting laid off. *How much stress can he handle?* It's the big unknown. One thing I must acknowledge: Alex made his own treatment choices, and they were the absolutely right ones for him, including his decision to get off the antipsychotic medication when he did. The fact that it terrified me and I tried my hardest to talk him out of it notwithstanding—he knew best.

Sammy continues to pursue his biology undergraduate degree, with its concomitant and ever-increasing stress, and now talks about going to medical school. Watching and listening to them and trying to be supportive, it's very hard to extinguish my worry. But the only choice I have as a mother is to see that things with my sons are as they should be; in fact, they're fabulous—and then attend to my own sanity.

This is exactly what recovery looks like: one day at a time, some days better than others; at least without the crashing and burning I used to put myself through. I've learned that the best way you can prevent mental illness from starting or returning is to acknowledge what's really happening inside you and find out what's going on inside your children. Behavior is never random. There's always a connection between inside and outside.

As activists in the recovery movement, we can be hopeful that the finish line has been moved from the idea of "fixing" what's broken in some of us toward a different set of goals: early intervention at the first signs of psychological disturbance; making quality mental health care—including pharmacological and other forms of treatment—available to anyone who needs it; and, most of all, making a commitment to prevention. My vision is that everyone has access to the help they need, and that, collectively, we create the choices that reflect our higher aspirations to enable healthy minds for ourselves, our children, and our grandchildren.

ACKNOWLEDGMENTS

My gratitude begins with my sons, for allowing me to tell our story and for continuing to be the lights of my life. The three of us would not be here without the support of my mother Victoria, one special Aunt Lillian, Nana, and my brother, as well as the boys' dad and their paternal grandparents, Hank and Ellie. I wish to honor my family members who are gone: my sister Rita, my father Red, and grandparents Ellen and Michael Costello. To those who stayed behind in Galway and Roscommon, John and Bridget, Patrick, Margaret, and Julia Costello, John and Mary Mitchell: I've often felt you with us in spirit.

I thank those friends who are family to us: Martha Olson Jarocki and Gerry Jarocki, Jane Dundes, Judith Kirkman Scherer and Cliff Scherer, and Michele Voska. And to my sweetheart, Tom Cummiskey, who's there for me with love and humor, especially when the going gets tough.

For their encouragement and skill at critiquing early drafts, I express sincere appreciation to Sharon Guynup, Laura Fraser, Adair Lara, Rose Levinson, Charlotte Peterson, and Paul Pruett. At Mills College, where I rediscovered why I write, I thank the extraordinary English lit and writing professors Sarah Pollock, Kirsten Saxton, Elmaz Abinader, Thomas Strychacz, and Christian Marouby. My thanks go to the National Association of Science Writers for the fellowship that enabled my European research.

For helping me bring my story to the marketplace, I thank my agents at Inkwell Management: Charlie Olsen, Elisa Perini, and Michael Carlisle. At Prometheus Books, I salute my editor, Linda Greenspan Regan and her dedicated team.

Finally, I wish to acknowledge the Mental Health Association of San Francisco, an affiliate of Mental Health America, where I'm privileged to serve as a board member and a speaker in the SOLVE anti-stigma campaign. MHA-SF is a force to be reckoned with largely because of its dynamic executive director Eduardo Vega and board president Patricia Bennett. At San Francisco's Family Service Agency, where I am a consumer advocate and a producer of online training in strength-based recovery, I thank my colleagues Melissa Moore, Carol Alvarez-McKinley, Pat Miles, Bob Bennett, and Nicole Milan, along with the entire PREP, San Francisco clinic staff. All of you are working to achieve parity for those with mental illness and to lay the foundation for anyone to reach recovery. With you, I share the belief that this is the most important human rights struggle of our time.

READER RESOURCES

To keep abreast of online and in-person events for the release of *A Lethal Inheritance*, author Victoria Costello invites you to visit the official book website at http://www.lethalinheritance.com. You may also choose to visit http://www.MentalHealthMomBlog.com where Victoria writes a blog bringing together preventive mental health and recovery science news from all over the world.
To contact the author directly, e-mail victoria@victoriacostello.com

For more information about mental illness and how you can protect your family, contact these organizations:

The National Institute of Mental Health (NIMH) Public Inquiries: 301-443-4513, http://www.nimh.nih.gov/index.shtml

The National Institute of Drug Abuse (NIDA): 800-662-HELP, http://www.nida.nih.gov/nidahome.html
http://www.findtreatment.samhsa.gov (for referrals anywhere in the United States)

The National Mental Health Association: 800-969-NMHA [6642], http://www.NMHA.org

The National Alliance for Mental Illness: 1-800-950-NAMI [6264], http://www.nami.org

Depression and Bipolar Support Alliance (DBSA): 800-826-3632, http://www.dbsalliance.org. Child and Adolescent Bipolar Foundation: support@bpkids.org, http://ww.bpkids.org/

Families for Depression Awareness: http://www.familyaware.org/

The National Suicide Prevention Lifeline: 1-800-273-TALK [8255] (free, 24 hours), http://www.suicidepreventionlifeline.org/

International Early Psychosis Association, an international network for the study and treatment of early psychosis: http://www.iepa.org.au/Default.aspx

For a complete list of early psychosis clinics in the United States and worldwide, go to http://www.schizophrenia.com/earlypsychosis.htm#clinics

In San Francisco

PREP, San Francisco early psychosis clinic: http://www.prepwellness.org/index.html
MHA-SF and the SOLVE anti-stigma speakers program: http:www.mha-sf.org

Websites for Help with Family Mental Health History

The Mayo Clinic How to Begin . . . : http://www.mayoclinic.com/health/medical
-history/HQ01707
The US Surgeon General's online family health history-keeping tool:
https://familyhistory.hhs.gov/fhh-web/familyHistory/familyHistory.action

NOTES

Part 1. The Fourth Generation: Alex And Sammy

Chapter 1. Alex by the Dumpster

1. Kay Redfield Jamison, *An Unquiet Mind: A Memoir of Moods and Madness* (New York: Vintage Books, 1996), p. 190.

2. Dara Cannon, conversation with the author, Galway, Ireland, June 23, 2009.

3. Jonathan Savitz et al., "Amygdala Volume in Depressed Patients with Bipolar Disorder Assessed Using High Resolution 3T MRI: The Impact of Medication," *NeuroImage* 49, no. 4 (2010): 2966–76.

4. Dara Cannon, June 23, 2009.

5. About.com, http://biology.about.com/od/anatomy/a/aa032505a.htm (accessed March 23, 2011).

6. Fulvia Adriano et al., "Updated Meta-Analyses Reveal Thalamus Volume Reduction in Patients with First-Episode and Chronic Schizophrenia," *Schizophrenia Research* 123, no. 1 (2010): 1–14.

7. Mark Weiser, "Association between Cognitive and Behavioral Functioning, Non-Psychotic Psychiatric Diagnoses, and Drug Abuse in Adolescence, with Later Hospitalization for Schizophrenia," in *Risk and Protective Factors in Schizophrenia*, edited by Heinz Hafner (Germany: Steinkopff-Verlag Darmstadt, 2002), p. 163.

8. Barry J. Milne, "How Should We Construct Family History Scores? A Comparison of Alternative Approaches from the Dunedin Family History Project," *Psychological Medicine* 38 (2008): 1793–1802.

9. D. G. Cunningham Owens and Eve C. Johnstone, "Precursors and Prodromata of Schizophrenia: Findings from the Edinburgh High Risk Study and Their Literature Context," *Psychological Medicine* 36, no. 11 (2006): 1501–14.

10. Demian Rose et al., "Re-Envisioning Psychosis: A New Language for Clinical Practice," *Current Psychiatry* 9, no. 10 (2010): 20–28.

11. Jim van Os et al., "A Systematic Review and Meta-Analysis of the Psychosis Continuum: Evidence for a Psychosis Proneness, Persistence, Impairment Model of Psychotic Disorder," *Psychological Medicine* 39, no. 2 (2009): 179–95.

12. R. Tandon and Matcheri Keshavan, "Schizophrenia, 'Just the Facts': What We Know in 2008," *Schizophrenia Research* 102, no. 7 (2008): 1–18.

13. Avshalom Caspi et al., "Moderation of the Effect of Adolescent-Onset Cannabis Use on Adult Psychosis by a Functional Polymorphism in the Catechol-O-Methyltransferase Gene: Longitudinal Evidence of a Gene × Environment Interaction," *Biological Psychiatry* 57, no. 10 (2006): 1117–27.

14. William Woods et al., "The Case for Including Attenuated Psychotic Symptoms Syndrome in *DSM-5* as a Psychosis Risk Syndrome," *Schizophrenia Research* 123, nos. 2–3 (2010): 199–207.

15. E-How Family, http://www.ehow.com/facts_4925271_what-firstdegree-relative.html (accessed April 5, 2011).

16. Candice L. Odgers et al., "Predicting Prognosis for the Conduct Problem Boy: Can Family History Help?" *Journal of the American Academy of Child and Adolescent Psychiatry* 46, no. 10 (2007): 1240–49.

17. Rachel E. Gur, *If Your Adolescent Has Schizophrenia* (New York: Oxford University Press, 2006).

18. Boris Birmaher et al., "Lifetime Psychiatric Disorders in School-Aged Offspring of Parents with Bipolar Disorder, Pittsburgh Bipolar Offspring Study," *Archives of General Psychiatry* 66, no. 3 (2009).

19. Ronald C. Kessler and W. T. Chiu, "Prevalence, Severity, and Comorbidity of 12 Month *DSM-IV* Disorders in the National Comorbidity Survey Replication," *Archives of General Psychiatry* 62, no. 6 (2005): 617–27.

20. Joachim Puig-Antich et al., "A Controlled Family Study of Prepubertal Major Depressive Disorder," *Archives of General Psychiatry* 46, no. 5 (1989): 406–18.

21. Jack C. Westman and Victoria Costello, "Children's Mental Disorders," *CIG Childhood and Adolescent Psychology* (New York: Penguin, 2011).

22. Myrna Weissman, conversation with the author, September 21, 2009.

23. Evelyn Pringle, "Tracking the American Epidemic of Mental Illness—Part I," OpEdNews, June 10, 2010.

24. John Cloud, "When Sadness Is a Good Thing," *Time*, 2007.

25. Joanna Moncrieff, *The Myth of the Chemical Cure: A Critique of Psychiatric Drug Treatment*, rev. ed. (New York: Palgrave Macmillan, 2009).

26. Kessler, "Prevalence, Severity, and Comorbidity," 617–27.

27. Myrna Weissman and Priya Wickramaratne, "Brief Screening for Family Psychiatric History," *Archives of General Psychiatry* 57, no. 7 (2000): 675–81.

28. Tandon and Keshavan, "Schizophrenia, 'Just the Facts.'"

29. Joachim Klosterkötter, "The Phase Model of Schizophrenia," in Hafner, *Risk and Protective Factors in Schizophrenia*, pp. 193–206.

30. William R. McFarlane and William L. Cook, "Portland Identification and Early Referral: A Community-Based System for Identifying and Treating Youths at High Risk of Psychosis," *Psychiatric Services* 61, no. 5 (2010).

31. Patrick McGorry, "Evidence, Early Intervention and the Tipping Point," *Early Intervention in Psychiatry* 4, no. 1 (2010): 1–3.

Chapter 2. Early Signs and Risk Factors

1. Rudolph Steiner, *The Essentials of Education, Foundations of Waldorf Education* (Herndon, VA: Steiner Books, 1997).

2. Heinz Hafner and K. Maurer, "The Early Course of Schizophrenia," in *Risk and Protective Factors in Schizophrenia*, edited by Heinz Hafner (Germany: Steinkopff-Verlag Darmstadt, 2002).

3. Eve C. Johnstone and Klaus P. Ebmeier, "Predicting Schizophrenia: Findings from the Edinburgh High-Risk Study," *British Journal of Psychiatry* 186, no. 1 (2005): 18–25.

4. Terrie E. Moffitt, conversation with the author, King's College London, Institute of Psychiatry, June 16, 2009.

5. Joachim Klosterkötter, "The Phase Model of Schizophrenia," in Hafner, *Risk and Protective Factors in Schizophrenia*, p. 195.

6. Jeffrey A. Lieberman and Robert E. Drake, "Science and Recovery in Schizophrenia," *Psychiatric Services* 59, no. 5 (2008): 487–57.

7. Edward Shorter, *A History of Psychiatry* (New York: John Wiley & Sons, 1997).

8. Patrick A. McGuire, "New Hope for People with Schizophrenia—A Growing Number of Psychologists Say Recovery Is Possible with Psychosocial Rehabilitation," *Monitor on Psychology* 31, no. 2 (2000).

9. Rachel Loewy, conversation with the author, Langley Porter Hospital, San Francisco, December 17, 2010.

10. "California Program Stresses Early Detection, Treatment of Mental Illness," *PBS NewsHour*, February 3, 2011, available online at http://www.pbs.org/newshour/bb/health/jan-june11/mentalillness_02-09.html (accessed March 15, 2011).

11. Heinz Hafner, "Introduction," in Hafner, *Risk and Protective Factors in Schizophrenia*.

12. Rachel E. Gur, *If Your Adolescent Has Schizophrenia* (New York: Oxford University Press, 2006).

13. J. C. Westman and V. Costello, "Children's Mental Disorders," *CIG Child and Adolescent Psychology* (New York: Penguin, 2011).

14. F. Resch and P. Parzer, "Specificity of Basic Symptoms in Early Onset Schizophrenia," in *Risk and Protective Factors in Schizophrenia*, pp. 178–84.

15. Lucy Bowes et al., "Families Promote Emotional and Behavioural Resilience to Bullying: Evidence of an Environmental Effect," *Journal of Child Psychology & Psychiatry* 51, no. 7 (2010): 809–17.

16. Peter Jones, "Risk Factors for Schizophrenia in Childhood and Youth," in *Risk and Protective Factors in Schizophrenia*, pp. 142–62.

17. Louise Arseneault et al., "Childhood Trauma and Children's Emerging Psychotic Symptoms: A Genetically Sensitive Longitudinal Cohort Study," *American Journal of Psychiatry* 168, no. 1 (2011): 65–72.

18. Jim van Os et al., "The Environment and Schizophrenia," *Nature* 468, no. 11 (2010).

19. Jean Addington and Kristen S. Cadenhead, "North American Prodrome Longitudinal Study: A Collaborative Multisite Approach to Prodromal Schizophrenia Research," *Schizophrenia Bulletin* 33, no. 3 (2007): 665–72.

20. NIMH, http://www.nimh.nih.gov/health/topics/statistics/ncsr-study/index .shtml (accessed April 11, 2011).

21. Tomas Paus et al., "Why Do Many Psychiatric Disorders Emerge during Adolescence?" *Nature Reviews Neuroscience* 9, no. 12 (2008): 947–57.

22. "Identification and Evaluation of Children with Autism Spectrum Disorders," National Academy of Pediatrics, http://www.aap.org/pressroom/issuekitfiles/IDandEvaluationofChildrenwithASD.pdf (accessed April 6, 2011).

23. Boris Birmaher et al., "Lifetime Psychiatric Disorders in School-Aged Offspring of Parents with Bipolar Disorder, Pittsburgh Bipolar Offspring Study," *Archives of General Psychiatry* 66, no. 3 (2009).

24. Stephen J. Glatt and W. S. Stone, "Psychopathology, Personality Traits and Social Development of Young First Degree Relatives of Patients with SZ," *British Journal of Psychiatry* 189 (2006): 337–45; Matcheri Keshavan et al., "Psychopathology among Offspring of Parents with Schizophrenia: Relationship to Premorbid Impairments," *Schizophrenia Research* 103, nos. 1–3 (2008): 114–20.

25. David J. Nutt, "Rationale for, Barriers to, and Appropriate Medication for the Long-Term Treatment of Depression," *Journal of Clinical Psychiatry* 71, suppl. E1 (2010).

26. Demian Rose, conversation with the author.

27. "Nearly 1 in 10 U.S. Kids Have ADHD, Study Finds," *Morbidity and Mortality Weekly Report* 59, no. 44 (November 12, 2010): 1439–43, Centers for Disease Control, available online at http://www.cdc.gov/mmwr/preview/mmwrhtml/mm 5944a3.htm?s_cid=mm5944a3_w (accessed April 6, 2011).

28. "The Medicated Child," interview with Kiki Chang, *Frontline*, PBS, January 8, 2008, http://www.pbs.org/wgbh/pages/frontline/medicatedchild/interviews/chang.html (accessed April 17, 2008).

29. "Is Bipolar Disorder Overdiagnosed?" ScienceDaily, May 6, 2008, http://www.sciencedaily.com/releases/2008/05/080506074440.htm (accessed December 6, 2010).

30. Vinod Srihari and Nicholas J. K. Breitborde, "Early Intervention for Psychotic Disorders in a Community Mental Health Center," *Psychiatric Services* 60, no. 11 (2009): 3.

31. Glatt and Stone, "Psychopathology, Personality Traits and Social Development."

32. Marc Hébert et al., "Retinal Response to Light in Young Nonaffected Offspring at High Genetic Risk of Neuropsychiatric Brain Disorders," *Biological Psychiatry* 67, no. 3 (2010): 270–74.

33. Deborah Levy, conversation with the author.

34. Ibid.

35. Norman Sussman, "In Session with Kiki Chang, MD: Bipolar Disorder in Children and Adolescents," *Primary Psychiatry* 17 (2010): 23–26.

36. Ronald Kessler et al., "Lifetime Co-Occurence of *DSM-III-R* Alcohol Abuse and Dependence with Other Psychiatric Disorders in the National Comorbidity Survey," *Archives of General Psychiatry* 54, no. 4 (1997): 313–21.

37. Elaine Walker, "Prediction of Adult Onset SZ from Childhood Home Movies of the Patients," *American Journal of Psychiatry* 147 (1990): 1052–56.

38. Ian Kelleher et al., "Are Screening Instruments Valid for Psychotic-Like Experiences? A Validation Study of Screening Questions for Psychotic-Like Experiences Using In-Depth Clinical Interview," *Schizophrenia Bulletin* 37, no. 2 (2011): 362–69.

39. Guilherme M. Polanczyk et al., "Etiological and Clinical Features of Childhood Psychotic Symptoms," *Archives of General Psychiatry* 67, no. 4 (2010): 328–38.

40. Ibid., p. 330.

41. Ibid.

42. Ibid., p. 335.

43. Ibid., p. 334.

44. Ibid., p. 335.

45. Ibid.

46. Ibid.

47. Avshalom Caspi et al., "Children's Self-Reported Psychotic Symptoms and Adult Schizophreniform Disorder: A 15 Year Longitudinal Study," *Archives of General Psychiatry* 57, no. 11 (2000): 1053–58.

48. Polanczyk et al., "Etiological and Clinical Features," p. 334.

49. "Family History of Mental Illness," Emory University School of Medicine, http://genetics.emory.edu/pdf/Emory_Human_Genetics_Family_History_Mental_Illness.PDF (accessed April 8, 2011).

50. Lieberman and Drake, "Science and Recovery in Schizophrenia."

51. Stanley Zammit et al., "Investigating if Psychosis-Like Symptoms (PLIKS) Are Associated with Family History of Schizophrenia and Paternal Age in the ALSPAC Cohort," *Schizophrenia Research* 104, nos. 1–3 (2008): 279–86.

52. R. Tandon and Matcheri Keshavan, "Schizophrenia, 'Just the Facts': What We Know in 2008," *Schizophrenia Research* 102, no. 7 (2008).

53. Polanczyk and Moffitt, "Etiological and Clinical Features," p. 334.

54. H. Verdoux and Anne-Laure Sutter, "Obstetrical Complications, Maternal Psychopathology, and the Risk of Psychosis," in Hafner, *Risk and Protective Factors in Schizophrenia*, pp. 108–109.

55. Daniel Freeman and David Fowler, "Routes to Psychotic Symptoms: Trauma, Anxiety and Psychosis-Like Experiences," *Psychiatry Research* 169, no. 2 (2009): 107–12.

56. Elizabeth Cantor-Graae, "The Contribution of Social Factors to the Development of Schizophrenia: A Review of Recent Findings," *Canadian Journal of Psychiatry* 52, no. 5 (2007): 277–86.

57. Kristin Laurens et al., "Migrant Children: Psychotic-Like Experiences and Other Antecedents of Schizophrenia in Children Aged 9–12 Years: A Comparison of Ethnic and Migrant Groups in the United Kingdom," *Psychological Medicine* 38, no. 10 (2008): 1103–11.

58. Andrea Schreier et al., "Prospective Study of Peer Victimization in Childhood and Psychotic Symptoms in a Nonclinical Population at Age 12 Years," *Archives of General Psychiatry* 66, no. 5 (2009): 527–36.

59. Joachim Klosterkötter, "The Phase Model of Schizophrenia," in *Risk and Protective Factors in Schizophrenia*, p. 195.

60. Kristin Laurens et al., "Community Screening for Psychotic-Like Experiences and Other Putative Antecedents of Schizophrenia in Children Aged 9–12 Years," *Schizophrenia Research* 90, nos. 1–3 (2007): 130–46.

61. Salvi J. Horwood et al., "IQ and Non-Clinical Psychotic Symptoms in 12 Year Olds; Results from the AlSPAC Cohort," *British Journal of Psychiatry* 104, nos. 1–3 (2008): 279–86.

62. R. Upthegrove et al., "The Evolution of Depression and Suicidality in First Episode Psychosis," *Acta Psychiatrica Scandinavica* 122, no. 3 (2010): 211–18.

63. Tandon and Keshavan, "Schizophrenia, 'Just the Facts.'"

64. Mary C. Clarke et al., "Evidence for an Interaction between Familial Liability and Prenatal Exposure to Infection in the Causation of Schizophrenia," *American Journal of Psychiatry* 166 (2009): 1025–30.

65. David Dobbs, "The Science of Success," *Atlantic* 12 (2009), http://www .theatlantic.com/magazine/archive/2009/12/the-science-of-success/7761/ (accessed April 30, 2010).

Chapter 3. "Boys Will Be Boys" and Other Lies We Tell Ourselves at 3:00 a.m.

1. Judith S. Wallerstein, Julia M. Lewis, and Sandra Blakeslee, *The Unexpected Legacy of Divorce: A 25 Year Landmark Study* (New York: Hyperion, 2001).

2. Candice L. Odgers et al., "Predicting Prognosis for the Conduct-Problem Boy: Can Family History Help?" *American Academy of Child and Adolescent Psychiatry* 46, no. 10 (2007): 1240–49.

3. Julia Kim-Cohen et al., "Maternal Depression and Children's Antisocial Behavior," *Archives of General Psychiatry* 62 (2005):173–81.

4. Heinz Hafner and K. Maurer, "The Early Course of Schizophrenia," *Risk and Protective Factors in Schizophrenia*, edited by Heinz Hafner (Germany: Steinkopff-Verlag Darmstadt, 2002).

5. Fulvia Adriano et al., "Updated Meta-Analyses Reveal Thalamus Volume Reduction in Patients with First-Episode and Chronic Schizophrenia," *Schizophrenia Research* 123, no. (2010): 1–14.

6. Catherine Freer Wilderness Therapy Programs, http://www.cfreer.com/about/ (accessed April 6, 2011).

7. Fabian Trémeau et al., "Emotion Antecedents in Schizophrenia," *Psychiatry Research* 169, no. 1 (2009): 43–50.

8. Mark Weiser, "Association between Cognitive and Behavioral Functioning, Non-Psychotic Psychiatric Diagnoses, and Drug Abuse in Adolescence, with Later Hospitalization for Schizophrenia," in Hafner, *Risks and Protective Factors in Schizophrenia*, p. 163.

9. Terrie E. Moffitt and Avshalom Caspi, "Childhood Predictors Differentiate Life-Course Persistent and Adolescence-Limited Antisocial Pathways among Males and Females," *Archives of General Psychiatry* 62 (2005): 473–81.

10. Jack C. Westman and Victoria Costello, "Children's Mental Disorders," *CIG to Child and Adolescent Psychology* (New York: Penguin, 2011).

11. Ibid.

12. Ibid.

13. Odgers et al., "Predicting Prognosis for the Conduct-Problem Boy."

14. Terrie Moffitt, conversation with the author, April 4, 2011.

15. Odgers et al., "Predicting Prognosis for the Conduct-Problem Boy," p. 1247.

16. Joy Welham et al., "The Antecedents of Schizophrenia: A Review of Birth Cohort Studies," *Schizophrenia Bulletin* 35, no. 3 (2009): 603–23.

17. Ibid.; Peter Jones, "Risk Factors for Schizophrenia in Childhood and Youth," in Hafner, *Risk and Protective Factors in Schizophrenia*, p. 145.

18. Welham et al., "The Antecedents of Schizophrenia."

Chapter 4. Before the Storm: Pre-Onset Psychosis

1. Alison R. Yung and Patrick D. McGorry, "Is Pre-Psychotic Intervention Realistic in Schizophrenia and Related Disorders?" *Australian and New Zealand Journal of Psychiatry* 31, no. 6 (1997): 799–805.

2. Daniel Williams, "Drugs before Diagnosis?" *Time*, June 18, 2006.

3. Jean Addington et al., "North American Prodrome Longitudinal Study: A Collaborative Multisite Approach to Prodromal Schizophrenia Research," *Schizophrenia Bulletin* 33, no. 3 (2007): 665–72.

4. Tyrone D. Cannon et al., "Prediction of Psychosis in Youth at High Clinical Risk: A Multisite Longitudinal Study in North America," *Archives of General Psychiatry* 65, no. 1 (2008): 28–37.

5. Mark Weiser. "Association between Cognitive and Behavioral Functioning, Non-Psychotic Psychiatric Diagnoses, and Drug Abuse in Adolescence, with Later Hospitalization for Schizophrenia," in *Risk and Protective Factors in Schizophrenia*, edited by Heinz Hafner (Germany: Steinkopff-Verlag Darmstadt, 2002), pp. 162–84.

6. R. Upthegrove et al., "The Evolution of Depression and Suicidality in First Episode Psychosis," *Acta Psychiatrica Scandinavica* 122, no. 3 (2010): 211–18.

7. Jean Addington et al., "Validity of the Prodromal Risk Syndrome for First Psychosis: Findings from the North American Prodrome Longitudinal Study," *Schizophrenia Bulletin* 35, no. 5 (2009): 894–908.

8. Cannon et al., "Prediction of Psychosis in Youth."

9. Jean Addington et al., "A Randomized Controlled Trial of Cognitive Behavioral Therapy for Individuals at Clinical High Risk of Psychosis," *Schizophrenia Research* 125, no. 1 (2011): 54–61.

10. Williams, "Drugs before Diagnosis?"

11. Gary Greenberg, "Inside the Battle to Define Mental Illness," *Wired*, January 2011; Patrick D. McGorry, "Early Intervention in Psychotic Disorders: Beyond Debate to Solving Problems," *British Journal of Psychiatry* 187, no. 48 (2005): s108–s110.

12. Patrick D. McGorry and Alison R.Yung, "Randomized Controlled Trial of Interventions Designed to Reduce the Risk of Progression to First Episode Psychosis in a Clinical Sample with Subthreshold Symptoms," *Archives of General Psychiatry* 59, no. 10 (2002): 921–28.

13. Thomas H. McGlashan et al., "Randomized, Controlled Trial of Interventions Designed to Reduce the Risk of Progression to First Episode Psychosis in a Clinical Sample with Subthreshold Symptoms," *Archives of General Psychiatry* 163 (2006): 790–99.

14. Ibid.

15. Ibid.; Williams, "Drugs before Diagnosis?"

16. Kristen S. Cadenhead et al., "Treatment History in the Psychosis Prodrome: Characteristics of the North American Prodrome Longitudinal Study Cohort," *Early Intervention in Psychiatry* 24, no. 3 (2010): 220–26.

17. Marisa Elena Domino and Marvin Swartz, "Who Are the New Users of Antipsychotic Medications?" *Psychiatric Services* 59, no. 5 (2008): 507–14.

18. Steve Hasenberg, conversation with the author, March 14, 1998.

19. Mark Weiser, "Association between Cognitive and Behavioral Functioning, Non-Psychotic Psychiatric Diagnoses and Drug Use in Adolescence, with Later Hospitalization for Schizophrenia," in *Risk and Protective Factors in Schizophrenia*, pp. 163–74.

20. Steve Hasenberg, March 14, 1998.

21. Demian Rose, conversation with the author, December 3, 2010.

22. Ibid.

23. Williams, "Drugs before Diagnosis?"

24. Ibid.

25. Alison R. Yung and Hok Pan Yuen, "Declining Transition Rate in Ultra High Risk (Prodromal) Services: Dilution or Reduction of Risk?" *Schizophrenia Bulletin* 33, no. 3 (2007): 673–81.

26. Patrick D. McGorry, "Responding at the Earliest Opportunity to Emerging Mental Illness," http://www.patmcgorry.com.au/blog (accessed March 30, 2011).

27. D. G. Cunningham Owens and Patrick Miller, "Pathogenesis of Schizophrenia: A Psychopathological Perspective," *British Journal of Psychiatry* 186 (2005): 386–93.

28. Ibid.

29. William R. McFarlane et al., "Psychoeducational Multiple Family Groups: Four-Year Relapse Outcome in Schizophrenia," *Family Process* 34, no. 2 (1995): 127–44.

30. William R. McFarlane and William Cook. "Portland Identification and Early Referral: A Community-Based System for Identifying and Treating Youths at High Risk of Psychosis," *Psychiatric Services* 61, no. 5 (2010).

31. Demian Rose, December 3, 2010.

32. Patrick D. McGorry, "Evidence, Early Intervention and the Tipping Point," *Early Intervention in Psychiatry* 4, no. 1 (2010): 1–3.

33. Demian Rose, December 3, 2010.

34. Greenberg, "Inside the Battle to Define Mental Illness."

35. Scott W. Woods et al., "The Case for Including Attenuated Psychotic Symptoms Syndrome in *DSM-5* as a Psychosis Risk Syndrome," *Schizophrenia Research* 123, nos. 2–3 (2010): 199–207.

Chapter 5: Onset

1. Mark Weiser, "Association between Cognitive and Behavioral Functioning, Non-Psychotic Psychiatric Diagnoses, and Drug Abuse in Adolescence, with Later Hospitalization for Schizophrenia," in *Risk and Protective Factors in Schizophrenia*, edited by Heinz Hafner (Germany: Steinkopff-Verlag Darmstadt, 2002), p. 168.

2. Joachim Klosterkötter, "The Phase Model of Schizophrenia," in Hafner, *Risk and Protective Factors in Schizophrenia*, pp. 193–206.

3. PREP Early Psychosis Clinic Self-Assessment, available online at http://www.prepwellness.org/pg-b2.html (accessed April 11, 2011).

4. Klosterkötter, "The Phase Model of Schizophrenia," p. 196.

5. Jim van Os et al., "A Systematic Review and Meta-Analysis of the Psychosis Continuum: Evidence for a Psychosis Proneness, Persistence, Impairment Model of Psychotic Disorder," *Psychological Medicine* 39, no. 2 (2009): 179–95; Elaine Walker and Daniel Shapiro, "Neurodevelopment and Schizophrenia, Broadening the Focus," *Current Directions in Psychological Science* 19, no. 4 (2010): 204–208.

6. Thomas R. Insel. "Rethinking Schizophrenia," *Nature* 468, no. 11 (2010): 187–93.

7. Demian Rose et al., "Re-Envisioning Psychosis: A New Language for Clinical Practice," *Current Psychiatry* 9, no. 10 (2010): 20–28.

8. Ian Kelleher, "Psychotic Symptoms in the General Population—An Evolutionary Perspective," *British Journal of Psychiatry* 197 (2010): 167–69.

9. William Downes, *Language and Religion: A Journey into the Human Mind* (New York: Cambridge University Press, 2010), p. 24.

10. Joan Littlefield Cook and Greg Cook, *Child Development Principles and Perspectives* (New York: Pearson, 2005), p. 234.

Chapter 6. My Little Prince Comes Undone

1. Myrna Weissman, conversation with the author.

2. Robert O'Connor, *Undoing Depression* (New York: Berkley Books, 1997).

3. Robert J. Iledaya, *The Antidepressant Survival Guide: The Clinically Proven Program to Enhance the Benefits and Beat the Side Effects of Your Medication* (New York: Three Rivers Press, 2001).

4. "The Treatment for Adolescents with Depression Study (TADS) Long-Term Effectiveness and Safety Outcomes," TADS Team, *Archives of General Psychiatry* 64, no. 10 (2007): 1132–43.

5. Ibid.

6. Ibid.

7. Ibid.

8. J. C. Fournier et al., "Antidepressant Drug Effects and Depression Severity," *JAMA: Journal of the American Medical Association* 303, no. 1 (2010): 47–53.

9. Husseini Manji interview, Healthcommunities.com, http://www.mental-healthchannel.net/bipolar/evening-out-highs-and-lows-of-bipolar-disorder.shtml (accessed April 12, 2011).

10. James Strohecker, Nancy Shaw Strohecker, and David E. Bresler, *Natural Healing for Depression* (New York: Perigee Books, 1999).

11. Phillip B. Mitchell, "Is Antidepressant Prescribing Associated with Suicide Rates?" *Psychiatric Times* 21, no. 5 (2004): 53–59.

12. A. Cougnard et al., "Impact of Antidepressants on the Risk of Suicide in Patients with Depression in Real-Life Conditions: A Decision Analysis Model," *Psychological Medicine* 39, no. 8 (2009): 1307–15.

13. Z. Rihmer and H. Akiskal, "Do Antidepressants Threaten Depressives? Toward a Clinically Judicious Formulation of the Antidepressant–Suicidality FDA Advisory in Light of Declining National Suicide Statistics from Many Countries," *Journal of Affective Disorders* 94, nos. 1–3 (2006): 3–13.

14. Srijan Sen et al., "A Prospective Cohort Investigating Factors Associated with Depression during Medical Internship," *Archives of General Psychiatry* 67, no. 6 (2010): E2–9.

Part 2. Revisiting the Family Illness: Generations Two and Three

Chapter 7. The Depressed Mother

1. Carlos Blanco and Mayumi Okuda, "The Epidemiology of Chronic Major Depressive Disorder and Dysthymic Disorder: Results from the National Epidemiologic Survey on Alcohol and Related Conditions," *Journal of Clinical Psychiatry* 71, no. 12 (2010).

2. "Ask the Experts," Website Department of Psychiatry, Columbia University Medical Center, http://asp.cumc.columbia.edu/psych/asktheexperts/ask_the_experts_in_psychiatry (accessed April 11, 2011).

3. David J. Nutt, "Rationale for, Barriers to, and Appropriate Medication for the Long Term Treatment of Depression," *Journal of Clinical Psychiatry* 7, suppl. E1 (2010): e02.

4. Myrna Weissman, conversation with the author, New York City, September 21, 2009.

5. Constance Hammen et al., "Interpersonal Impairment and the Prediction of Depressive Symptoms in Adolescent Children of Depressed and Nondepressed Mothers," *Journal of the American Academy of Child and Adolescent Psychiatry* 42, no. 5 (2003): 571–77.

6. Ibid.

7. Bradley S. Peterson et al., "Cortical Thinning in Persons at Increased Familial Risk for Major Depression," *Proceedings of the National Academy of Sciences* 106, no. 15 (2009): 6273–78.

8. Ibid., p. 6275.

9. Ibid.

10. Andrew Solomon, *The Noonday Demon, An Atlas of Depression* (New York: Scribner, 2001), p. 19.

Chapter 8. My Sister Rita: Mental Illness and Self-Medication

1. Filip Geerardyn and Gertrudis Van De Vijver, *The Pre-Psychoanalytic Writings of Sigmund Freud* (London: Karnac Books, 2002), p. 73.

2. Edward Khantzian, "The Self-Medication Hypothesis of Addictive Disorders: Focus on Heroin and Cocaine Dependence," *American Journal of Psychiatry* 142, no. 11 (1985): 1259–64.

3. Ibid.

4. Richard Frances, reviewing *Understanding Addiction as Self Medication: Finding Hope behind the Pain*, by Edward Khantzian in *American Journal on Addictions* 18, issue 3 (May–June 2009): 255.

5. Rebecca Kuepper and Jim van Os, "Continued Cannabis Use and Risk of Incidence and Persistence of Psychotic Symptoms: 10 Year Follow-Up Cohort Study," *British Medical Journal* 342, no. d738.

6. Robert L. Dupont, *The Selfish Brain, Learning from Addiction* (Center City, MN: Hazelden, 1997), p. 15.

7. Ibid., p. 5.

8. Ibid., pp. 100–25.

9. Daniela Plume, "Self Medication Hypothesis," AddictionInfo, 2006, http://www.addictioninfo.org/articles/751/1/Self-Medication-Hypothesis-ADHD—Cocaine/Page1.html (accessed April 20, 2011).

10. Nancy Piotrowski, "Dual Diagnosis: Practical Considerations for Dealing with Both Problems," speaker's notes, summarized by Thomas T. Thomas, November 19, 1997, http://www.thomastthomas.com/Dual%20Diagnosis,%20Piotrowski,%20111997.PDF (accessed April 11, 2011).

11. George E. Woody and Charles P. O'Brien, "Depression and Anxiety in

Heroin Addicts: A Placebo-Controlled Study of Doxepin in Combination with Methadone," *American Journal of Psychiatry* 132, no. 4 (1975): 447–50.

12. Charles P. O'Brien and George E. Woody et al., "Substance Abuse Treatment Research Center Philadelphia VA Medical Center and the University of Pennsylvania," *British Journal of Addiction* 83, no. 11 (1988): 1261–70.

13. NIMH, http://www.nimh.nih.gov/statistics/SMI_AASR.shtml (accessed April 11, 2011).

14. Ronald Kessler et al., "Lifetime Co-Occurence of *DSM-III-R* Alcohol Abuse and Dependence with Other Psychiatric Disorders in the National Comorbidity Survey," *Archives of General Psychiatry* 54, no. 4 (1997): 313–21.

15. Ronald Kessler and W. Chiu, "Prevalence, Severity, and Comorbidity of 12 Month *DSM-IV* Disorders in the National Comorbidity Survey Replication," *Archives of General Psychiatry* 62, no. 6 (2005): 617–27.

16. Ibid.

17. Plume, "Self Medication Hypothesis," 2006.

18. S. E. Herman et al., "Longitudinal Effects of Integrated Treatment on Alcohol Use for Persons with Serious Mental Illness and Substance Use Disorders," *Journal of Behavioral Health Services and Research* 27, no. 3 (2000): 286–302.

Chapter 9. My Father Red: "The Heart-Ache and the Thousand Natural Shocks that Flesh Is Heir To"

*William Shakespeare, *Hamlet*, act 3, scene 1, "To be or not to be . . ."

1. George E. Vaillant, *The Natural History of Alcoholism, Revisited* (Cambridge, MA: Oxford University Press, 1995), p. 424.

2. Ibid., pp. 64–75.

3. Ibid., p. 285.

4. Myrna M. Weissman et al., "Families at High and Low Risk for Depression: A 3 Generation Study," *Archives of General Psychiatry* 62, no. 1 (2005): 29–36.

5. Robert L. Dupont, *The Selfish Brain, Learning from Addiction* (Center City, MN: Hazelden, 1997), p. 14.

6. Jonathan Yardley, "Shelve It under Navel Gazing," *Washington Post*, November 29, 2009, available online at http://www.washingtonpost.com/wp-dyn/content/article/2009/11/25 (accessed April 18, 2011).

7. Barry J. Milne and Avshalom Caspi, "Predictive Value of Family History on Severity of Illness," *Archives of General Psychiatry* 66, no. 7 (2009): 1–10.

8. Terrie Moffitt, conversation with the author, King's College London, Institute of Psychiatry, June 2009.

9. Ibid.

10. Dunedin Multidisciplinary Health and Development Research Unit, University of Otago, http://dunedinstudy.otago.ac.nz/ (accessed April 11, 2011).

11. Terrie Moffitt, conversation with the author, April 2, 2011.

Chapter 10. The First Generation, My Grandfather

1. Nancy Scheper-Hughes, *Saints, Scholars, and Schizophrenics, Mental Illness in Rural Ireland* (Berkeley: University of California Press, 2001).

2. Ibid., p. 24.

3. Ibid.

4. Ibid., p. 40.

5. J. Canavan, "The Role of the Family in Schizophrenia," *Trinity Student Medical Journal* (May 2000), available online at http://www.tcd.ie/tsmj/2000/Schiz.html (accessed April 13, 2011).

6. Dara Cannon, conversation with the author, June 24, 2009.

7. Scheper-Hughes, *Saints, Scholars, and Schizophrenics*, p. 143.

8. Ibid., p. 160.

9. Ibid., p. 157.

10. Ibid., pp. 193–94.

11. Ibid., p. 45.

12. B. Malzberg, "Mental Disease among Native and Foreign Born Whites in New York State," *Mental Hygiene* 48 (1964): 478–99.

13. Patrick Tracey, *Stalking Irish Madness* (New York: Bantam, 2008), p. 14.

14. Kenneth Kendler et al., "Evaluating the Spectrum Concept of Schizophrenia in the Roscommon Family Study," *American Journal of Psychiatry* 152, no. 5 (1995): 749–54; Kenneth Kendler et al., "The Roscommon Family Study: III. Schizophrenia-Related Personality Disorders in Relatives," *Archives of General Psychiatry* 50, no. 10 (1993): 781–88.

15. Richard E. Straub et al., "Genetic Variation in the 6p22.3 Gene DTNBP1, the Human Ortholog of the Mouse Dysbindin Gene, Is Associated with Schizophrenia," *American Journal of Human Genetics* 71, no. 2 (2002): 337–48.

16. Michael J. Owen, Nick Craddock, and Assen Jablensky, "The Genetic Deconstruction of Psychosis," *Schizophrenia Bulletin* 33, no. 4 (2007): 905–11.

17. Kristin R. Laurens et al., "Migrant Children: Psychotic-Like Experiences and Other Antecedents of Schizophrenia in Children Aged 9–12 Years: A Comparison of Ethnic and Migrant Groups in the United Kingdom," *Psychological Medicine* 38, no. 10 (2008): 1103–11.

18. Jim van Os et al., "Psychosis Proneness: A Systematic Review and Meta-Analysis of the Psychosis Continuum: Evidence for a Psychosis, Proneness, Persist-

ence, Impairment Model of Psychotic Disorder," *Psychological Medicine* 39 (2009) 179–95.

Chapter 11. Grandpa's Psychological Autopsy

1. New Advent Catholic Encyclopedia, http://www.newadvent.org/cathen/14326b.htm (accessed April 11, 2011).

2. Ibid.

3. Sigmund Freud, "Mourning and Melancholia," in *General Psychological Theory*, edited by P. Rieff (New York: Collier Books, 1962 [1917]).

4. Andrew Solomon, *The Noonday Demon, An Atlas of Depression* (New York: Scribner, 2001) pp. 64–67.

5. Genevieve Arsenault-Lapierre, Caroline Kim, and Gustavo Turecki, "Psychiatric Diagnoses in 3275 Suicides: A Meta-Analysis," *BMC Psychiatry* 4, no. 1 (2004): 37.

6. Thomas Joiner, *Why People Die by Suicide* (Cambridge, MA: Harvard University Press, 2005), pp. 46–62.

7. Ibid., p. 199.

8. "Myths and Facts," San Francisco Suicide Prevention, http://www.sfsuicide.org/prevention-strategies/myths-and-facts/ (accessed April 14, 2011).

9. R. V. Clarke and P. Mayhew, "Crime as Opportunity, A Note on Domestic Gas Suicide in Britain and the Netherlands," *British Journal of Criminology* 29, no. 1 (1989): 35–46.

10. Herbert Hendin, *Suicide in America* (New York: Norton, 1995).

11. Richard H. Seiden, "Where Are They Now? A Follow-Up Study of Suicide Attempters from the Golden Gate Bridge," *Suicide and Life-Threatening Behavior* 8, no. 4 (1978): 13.

12. Golden Gate Bridge Authority/Suicide Barrier, http://www.ggbsuicidebarrier.org/index.php (accessed March 23, 2011).

13. San Francisco Suicide Prevention, http://www.sfsuicide.org/ (accessed April 14, 2011).

14. Joiner, *Why People Die by Suicide*, p. 53.

15. "SUICIDE OR AN ACCIDENT?" *New York Times* obituary index, November 19, 1894.

16. John Lahr, "Demolition Man, Harold Pinter and the Homecoming," *New Yorker* magazine, December 24, 2007, available online at http://www.newyorker.com/reporting/2007/12/24/071224fa_fact_lahr?currentPage=all (accessed April 11, 2011).

Part 3. The Science and Practice of Recovery and Prevention

Chapter 12. *Thoughts of All Orders*

1. Patrick A. McGuire, "New Hope for People with Schizophrenia—A Growing Number of Psychologists Say Recovery Is Possible with Psychosocial Rehabilitation," *Monitor on Psychology* 31, no. 2 (February 2000).

2. Gardiner Harris, "Talk Doesn't Pay, So Psychiatry Turns Instead to Drug Therapy," *New York Times*, March 5, 2011, available online at http://www.nytimes.com/2011/03/06/health/policy/06doctors.html?_r=1&scp=1&sq=psychiatrist%20talk%20therapy&st=cse (accessed April 6, 2011).

3. McGuire, "New Hope."

4. Ibid.

5. Patricia Deegan & Associates, http://www.patdeegan.com/ (accessed April 6, 2011).

6. McGuire, "New Hope."

7. Ibid.

8. "How Many Americans Have a Mental Illness, but No Home?" *Psychiatric News* 45, no. 3 (February 2010): 7, available online at http://pn.psychiatryonline.org/content/45/3/7.2.full (accessed April 13, 2011).

9. California Department of Mental Health, Background on MHSA, http://www.dmh.ca.gov/prop_63/mhsa/default.asp (accessed April 13, 2011).

10. *Transformation of the Mental Health System through Client and Family Leadership*, introduction by MHSAOAC commissioner Eduardo Vega, MHSA Oversight Commission, March 2011.

11. R. Upthegrove et al., "The Evolution of Depression and Suicidality in First Episode Psychosis," *Acta Psychiatrica Scandinavica* 122, no. 3 (2010): 211–18.

12. Szabolcs Kéri, "Genes for Psychosis and Creativity: A Promoter Polymorphism of the Neuregulin 1 Gene Is Related to Creativity in People with High Intellectual Achievement," *Psychological Science* 20, no. 9 (2009): 1070–73.

13. Ibid.

14. Kiki Chang et al., "Creativity in Familial Bipolar Disorder," *Journal of Psychiatric Research* 39, no. 6 (2005): 623–31.

Chapter 13. *From Inkblots to Alleles*

1. Deborah Levy, conversation with the author, McLean Hospital, Belmont, Massachusetts, November 5, 2007.

2. Ibid.

3. "Prepulse Inhibition," *Wikipedia*, http://en.wikipedia.org/wiki/Prepulse _inhibition (accessed April 13, 2011).

4. Philip S. Holzman et al., "The Use of the Rorschach Technique for Assessing Formal Thought Disorder," *Scoring the Rorschach: Seven Validated Systems* (Mahwah, NJ: Lawrence Erlbaum Associates, 2005), pp. 55–95.

5. Maria Cheng, "Gene Therapy Improves Parkinson's Symptoms," Associated Press, March 16, 2011, http://www.msnbc.msn.com/id/42113755/ns/health -health_care/ (accessed April 13, 2011).

6. "Positive Results Announced in Trial of Gene Therapy for PD," Michael J. Fox Foundation for Parkinson's Research, June 22, 2010, http://www.michael jfox.org/newsEvents_parkinsonsInTheNews_article.cfm?ID=640 (accessed April 13, 2011).

7. Peter Jones, "Risk Factors for Schizophrenia in Childhood and Youth," *Risk and Protective Factors in Schizophrenia*, edited by Heinz Hafner (Germany: Steinkopff-Verlag Darmstadt, 2002), pp. 142–62.

8. Ibid.

9. Benedict Carey, "Report on Gene for Depression Is Now Faulted," *New York Times*, June 16, 2009.

10. Ibid.

11. Avshalom Caspi, "Influence of Life Stress on Depression: Moderation by a Polymorphism in the 5-HTT Gene," *Science* 301, no. 5653 (2003).

12. "Mental Illness Genetics among Science's Top 'Breakthroughs' for 2003," press release, NIMH, December 22, 2003.

13. Terrie Moffitt, conversation with the author, King's College London, Institute of Psychiatry, June 16, 2009.

14. Ibid.

15. Jim Van Os, Gunter Kenis, and Bart P. F. Rutten, "Gene-Environment-Wide Interaction Studies in Psychiatry," editorial, *American Journal of Psychiatry* 9, no. 166 (2009): 964–66.

16. Katja Karg et al., "The Serotonin Transporter Variant (5HTTLPR) Stress, and Depression Meta-Analysis Revisited," *Archives of General Psychiatry* (January 3, 2011).

17. D. G. Kilpatrick et al., "The Serotonin Transporter Genotype and Social Support and Moderation of Posttraumatic Stress Disorder and Depression in Hurricane-Exposed Adults," *American Journal of Psychiatry* 164, no. 11 (2007): 1693–99.

18. Karg et al., "The Serotonin Transporter Variant (5HTTLPR) Stress."

19. Avshalom Caspi et al., "Genetic Sensitivity to the Environment: The Case for the Serotonin Transporter Gene and Its Implications for Studying Complex Diseases and Traits," *American Journal of Psychiatry* 157, no. 5 (2010): 509–527.

20. Joan Kaufman et al., "Brain-Derived Neurotrophic Factor-5-HTTLPR Gene

Interactions and Environmental Modifiers of Depression in Children," *Biological Psychiatry* 59, no. 8 (2006): 673–80.

Chapter 14. Preventing Mental Illness

1. Joy Welham et al., "The Antecedents of Schizophrenia: A Review of Birth Cohort Studies," *Schizophrenia Bulletin* 35, no. 3 (2009): 603–23.

2. Andrea Schreier et al., "Prospective Study of Peer Victimization in Childhood and Psychotic Symptoms in a Nonclinical Population at Age 12 Years," *Archives of General Psychiatry* 66, no. 5 (2009): 527–36.

3. Rebecca Kuepper and Jim van Os, "Continued Cannabis Use and Risk of Incidence and Persistence of Psychotic Symptoms: 10 Year Follow-Up Cohort Study," *BMJ* 342, no. d738 (2011).

4. Candice L. Odgers et al., "Predicting Prognosis for the Conduct- Problem Boy: Can Family History Help?" *American Academy of Child and Adolescent Psychiatry* 46, no. 10 (2007): 1240–49.

5. Peter Jones, "Risk Factors for Schizophrenia in Childhood and Youth," *Risk and Protective Factors in Schizophrenia*, edited by Heinz Hafner (Germany: Steinkopff-Verlag Darmstadt, 2002), pp. 142–62.

6. Guillerme Polanczyk and Terrie E. Moffitt, "Etiological and Clinical Features of Childhood Psychotic Symptoms," *Archives of General Psychiatry* 67, no. 4 (2010): 328–38.

7. John Cloud, "Staying Sane May Be Easier Than You Think," *Time*, 2009.

8. Mary Ellen O'Connell et al., *Preventing Mental, Emotional, and Behavioral Disorders among Young People: Progress and Possibilities* (National Academies Press, 2009).

9. "Monitoring the Future Survey," National Institute on Drug Abuse (NIDA), 2009, http://www.nida.nih.gov/drugpages/mtf.html (accessed April 11, 2009).

10. Jennifer A. McLaren et al., "Assessing Evidence for a Causal Link between Cannabis and Psychosis: A Review of Cohort Studies," *International Journal of Drug Policy* 21, no. 1 (2010): 10–19.

11. Andrea Schreier et al., "Prospective Study of Peer Victimization."

12. "The Medicated Child," interview with Kiki Chang, *Frontline*, PBS, January 8, 2008, http://www.pbs.org/wgbh/pages/frontline/medicatedchild/interviews/chang.html.

13. Interview with Dr. Husseini Manji, Child & Adolescent Bipolar Foundation, http://www.bpkids.org/learn/library/interview-with-husseini-manji-md (accessed April 12, 2011).

14. Interview with Patrick Corrigan, "How Stigma Interferes with Mental

Healthcare," Medscape, December 9, 2004, http://www.medscape.com/viewarticle/494548 (accessed November 24, 2010).

15. Patrick Corrigan, "Patrick Corrigan Discusses the Stigma of Mental Illness," ScienceWatch.com, 2010.

16. Patrick Corrigan, speaking at Families and Youth Roundtable Conference, February 23, 2011, San Diego, California.

17. Evelyn Pringle, "Tracking the American Epidemic of Mental Illness—Part I," June 10, 2010.

18. From the Citizens Commission on Human Rights website, "CCHR Was Co-Founded in 1969 by the Church of Scientology and Professor of Psychiatry Emeritus," http://www.cchrint.org/about-us/about-us/co-founder-dr-thomas-szasz/, http://www.cchrint.org/about-us/ (accessed March 24, 2011), and http://www.cchrint.org/2010/06/16/australian-psychiatrist-patrick-mcgorry-wants-his-pre-drugging-agenda-to-go-global/ (accessed March 27, 2011).

19. Evelyn Pringle, "Tracking the American Epidemic."

20. Daniel Goleman, introduction, *Emotional Intelligence: 10th Anniversary Edition; Why It Can Matter More than IQ* (New York: Bantam, 2006).

21. Ibid.

22. "Mihaly Csikszentmihalyi," http://en.wikipedia.org/wiki/Mihaly_Csikszentmihalyi"; Martin Seligman, "Positive Psychology: An Introduction," *American Psychologist* 55, no. 1 (2000): 5.

23. Claudia Wallis, "The New Science of Happiness," *Time*, 2004; PDF available at http://www.authentichappiness.sas.upenn.edu/images/TimeMagazine/Time-Happiness.pdf (accessed February 7, 2011).

24. David Miklowitz, *The Bipolar Disorder Survival Guide: What You and Your Family Need to Know*, 2d ed. (New York: Guilford Press, 2010).

25. Ibid.

26. A. S. Brown and J. J. McGrath, "The Prevention of Schizophrenia," *Schizophrenia Bulletin* 37, no. 2 (2011): 257–61.

27. Department of Psychiatry, Columbia University Medical Center, http://asp.cumc.columbia.edu/psych/asktheexperts/ask_the_experts_in_psychiatry (accessed September 26, 2009).

28. Odgers et al., "Predicting Prognosis for the Conduct-Problem Boy."

29. Lisa A. Croen et al., "Antidepressant Use during Pregnancy and Childhood Autism Spectrum Disorders," *Archives of General Psychiatry*, published online July 4, 2011, doi:10.1001/archgenpsychiatry.2011.73.

30. Alice Park, "Antidepressant Use during Pregnancy Linked to Higher Risk of Autism," *Time*, July 5, 2011, http://healthland.time.com/2011/07/05/antidepressant-use-during-pregnancy-linked-to-higher-risk-of-autism/#ixzz1RHNZCD6q.

31. Constance Hammen et al., "Interpersonal Impairment and the Prediction of Depressive Symptoms in Adolescent Children of Depressed and Nondepressed Mothers," *Journal of the American Academy of Child and Adolescent Psychiatry* 42, no. 5 (2003): 571–77.

32. Demian Rose et al., "Re-Envisioning Psychosis: A New Language for Clinical Practice," *Current Psychiatry* 9, no. 10 (2010): 20–28.

33. Boris Birmaher et al., "Lifetime Psychiatric Disorders in School-Aged Offspring of Parents with Bipolar Disorder, Pittsburgh Bipolar Offspring Study," *Archives of General Psychiatry* 66, no. 3 (2009); Guilherme M. Polanczyk et al., "Etiological and Clinical Features of Childhood Psychotic Symptoms," *Archives of General Psychiatry* 67, no. 4 (2010): 328–38.

34. David J. Nutt, "Rationale for, Barriers to, and Appropriate Medication for the Long-Term Treatment of Depression," *Journal of Clinical Psychiatry* 71, suppl. E1 (2010).

35. Andrea Schreier et al., "Prospective Study of Peer Victimization."

36. Mark Weiser, "Association between Cognitive and Behavioral Functioning, Non-Psychotic Psychiatric Diagnoses, and Drug Abuse in Adolescence, with Later Hospitalization for Schizophrenia," in *Risk and Protective Factors in Schizophrenia*, p. 163.

37. Victoria Costello, "Spoiled, Risk Adverse, Cheaters, and Insecure to Boot: Why We Need to Stop (Over)Praising Our Kids," PsychologyToday.com, July 17, 2011, http://www.psychologytoday.com/blog/awakening-psyche/201107/spoiled-risk-adverse-cheaters-and-insecure-boot-why-we-need-stop-overpr.

INDEX

Aaron [pseud.] (former friend), 123–24

abandonment, feelings of, 66

abused children, resilience in, 211

accidents, unexplained, 54

addiction

  causes of, 130

  in family members, 54

addictive disorders, 55

ADHD (attention deficit hyperactivity disorder). *See* attention deficit hyperactivity disorder (ADHD)

adolescents and antidepressants, 104

adrenalin rush, 70

ADT (antidepressant therapy), 107

aggressive behavior, 71

Al-Anon (Adult Children of Alcoholics), 151

alcohol abuse, future predictors of, 145

Alcoholics Anonymous, 67, 151

alcoholism

  in Ireland, 158

  and other addictions in previous generations, 36

Alex [pseud.] oldest son

  at age 28 as a painter and sculptor, 187

  and alcohol consumption, 68

  and bachelor of fine arts degree, 188

  baptism, 23

  California GED, 24

  colic, 45

  and collision with fence, 24, 26

  at Concord Academy, 91

  and cutting his own hair, asymmetrically, 92

  disinterest in other people, 45

  dolphin painting, 91

  Fairfax High School, 95

  hallucinations, 29

  hospitalization of, 25

  insomnia, 93

  journal entries, 21–22, 68

  major changes and losses, 65

  marijuana, 65, 68

  and methamphetamine, 29

  Montessori preschool, 45

  as a newborn, 45

  on and off medication, 98–99

  paranoia and delusions, 29

  paranoid schizophrenia, 29

  quitting high school, 24

  remedial therapy, 46

  "Revelation" (poem), 23

  schizoid personality disorder, 93–94

  self portrait, 30

  shoeless state, 22, 93

  stealing, 65

  in *Suicide in B Flat* (play by Sam Shepard), 76–77

  "tagging" (graffiti), 65

  talking to Zack about suicide, 77

  throwing child off bike, 71

  visual learning disability, 46

allele, short, 111

Alzheimer, Alois, 204

Alzheimer's disease, 54, 123, 204

American Academy of Pediatrics, 50

American Psychological Association, 188

amygdala

  defined, 33

  described, 34

255

Ancestry.com website, 162
anorexia, 25
Antecedents of Schizophrenia, The
    (meta-study), 74
antidepressants
    benefits of, 126
    side effects and risks, 106
antidepressant suicide link, 105–106
antidepressant therapy (ADT), 107
anti-sociality, 38, 74
antisocial personality disorder (ASPD),
    72
anxiety and parental divorce, 66
anxiety disorders
    anorexia and bulimia, 40. See also
        anorexia
    and dual diagnosis, 136
    escalating and disabling fears, 40
    obsessive-compulsive disorder
        (OCD), 40
    phobias, 40
    separation anxiety disorder, 40
    social anxiety, 40
ASPD (antisocial personality disorder),
    72
asylum-era paradigm, 190
asylum era thinking, 48
attention deficit hyperactivity disorder
    (ADHD)
    and bipolar disorder in childhood, 49
    and DRD4 gene, 62
    and impaired PPI, 200
    most common mental disorder in
        children, 40
    and overmedication, 84
    symptoms of, 40
auditory hallucinations, 56
autism
    behavioral signs, 50
    screening for, 50

Autism Society of America, 50
Autism Speaks, 50
autonomic functions, 34

Bakermans-Kranenburg, Marian, 62
BDNF gene, 211
behavior, oppositional, 51
behavioral scientist, defined, 35
Bennett, Robert W., 48
biomarkers, 32–34
bipolar disorder (BP)
    "at risk" stage, 83
    brain changes caused by, 33
    and dual diagnosis, 136
    genetic and biological in nature, 47
    genetic predisposition, 217
    and genetic research, 195
    increased risk (genetic), 51
    pediatric, 49, 52
    prevalence of, 38
    and self-abuse, 173
    and smaller amygdala, 33
    summer camp for kids, 52–53
    versus unipolar, 217
Bipolar Disorder: A Family-Focused
    Treatment Approach (Miklowitz),
    221
body sensations, impaired, 47
boys
    externalizing, 74
    mental disorders affecting, 36, 50
brain
    cerebral cortex (gray matter), 34
    cortical thinning, 123
    critical periods for brain changes, 96
    deterioration of in people at high risk
        for depression, 122–23
    executive functions of, 34
    fear centers in, 221
    imaging studies, 32

plasticity of, 96
prefrontal cortex, 201
recalibration of, 189
right and left hemispheres, 34
scans, 33
structures and systems, 34
white matter of, 32
wiring of, 194
brain regions, communications
  between, 32
British Environmental Risk (E-Risk)
  Longitudinal Twin Study, 56–57
bullying, 215, 226
bupropion (Wellbutrin), 119

Camp Opehay, 53
cannabis. *See* marijuana
Cannon, Dara, 32–34, 157
carcinogenic toxins, 206
Carroll, Linda, 180–81
Caspi, Avshalom, 207–10
catechol-o-methyl transferase gene
  (COMT), 37
Catherine Freer Wilderness Therapy
  Program, 67
CBT (cognitive behavioral therapy), 79,
  84, 189
  CBT mantra, 86
CCHRI (Citizens Commission on
  Human Rights International), 218
cerebral cortex (gray matter), 34
Chang, Kiki, 52–55, 216
childhood-onset conduct disorder, 73
childhood symptoms, 226
Citizens Commission on Human Rights
  International (CCHRI), 218
cliff-edge behaviors, 97
Clinical Neuroimaging Laboratory, 32
clinical staging model, 84
clinical threshold, 54

clinical trials, 53
cocaine, 130
cognitive ability, 201
cognitive behavioral therapy (CBT), 79,
  84, 189. *See also* CBT (cognitive
  behavioral therapy), CBT mantra
cognitive decline, 36
cognitive skills, 97
communication skills, parent-child, 214
Community Housing Partnership, 192
comorbidity, 55
comorbid mental illness, 136
conduct disorder, 71–72
conspiracy of silence, 169
consumer (in US mental health care
  terminology), 31
control groups, 62
conversion, reduction of risk, 88
coping skills, 216
Corcoran, Cheryl, 223
core identity, 126
Corrigan, Patrick, 217
Costello, Bridgett Bourke, 161
Costello, Ellen (paternal grandmother),
  20, 165–66
Costello, John, 161
Costello, John Michael "Red" (father)
  adopted at age five by Michael
    Murphy, 146
  alcohol and smoking, 28
  death from lung cancer, 28
  Distinguished Flying Cross, 144,
    164
  passed out in basement, 143–44
  at Victoria's First Communion, 149
Costello, Michael John (paternal
  grandfather)
  bipolar disorder, 41
  cause of death as accidental
    drowning, 182

death certificate, 182–84
hit by train, 28, 162, 169, 172, 179–81, 183
naturalization certificate, 165
possible suicide, 28
Costello, Patrick, 161
Costello, Rita Laurie (sister), 129
attempted suicide, 139
bipolar disorder, 41
in a coma, 139
died 1992, 140
drug rehabilitation, 134
first near overdose, 130
hepatitis C, 139
heroin addiction, 28, 129
in Hollywood Hills, 138
marijuana, 129
and methadone, 134
possible suicide, 41
stealing, 129
three-day detox, 139
Costello, Thomas (brother of Michael), 165
Costello, Victoria
and alcohol consumption, 66, 117
at American University in Washington, DC, 131
divorce from Geoff (Alex and Sammy's father), 140
and drug use, 132
dual depression, 117
and imaginary world, 150
at Mills College, 126
onset of depression, 116
and pain upon father's death, 150
postpartum depression, 120
science journalist, 31
suicidal ideation, 123–24
trip to Ireland, 32
untreated depression, 43

Valium and alcohol, 123–24
County Kerry, Ireland (Ballybran), 157
creative impulse, 195
creativity and mental illness, links between, 193
creativity tests, 194

databases, national mental health, 31
decision-making process, 86
Deegan, Patricia, 188
delinquency, defined, 71
delusionary thinking, 57
denial, 72, 93, 102
depression
clinical or major, 40
dual, 117–19
and flat effect, 68
and fluctuations in blood sugar, 106
genetic risk for, 121
and genetic vulnerability for, 62
major, 103
mild or dysthymic disorder, 103
mild to moderate, 40
and multiple generations, 148
postpartum, 120
and prepsychotic state, 78
and schizophrenia, 78
and stimulants, 106
subtypes of, 106
types of, 40
developmental precursors to adult disorders, 57
Diagnostic and Statistical Manual of Mental Disorders, Fifth Edition (DSM-5), 83, 90
Diagnostic and Statistical Manual of Mental Disorders, Fourth Edition (DSM-IV), 82, 89–90
Didi Hirsch Community Mental Health Clinic, 98–99

discussion, interactive, 86
disease agent, exposure to, 59
divorce, and impact on children, 66
DNA, 35, 49, 206
Dobbs, David, 62
Dr. B. [pseud.], 116–19
Dr. C. [pseud.], 17, 25–31, 46–47, 82, 115
Dr. M. [pseud.], 93
dopamine, neurotransmitter, 37, 62
double-blind clinical trial, 80
double-blind studies, 62
DRD4 ADHD susceptibility gene, 62
Drevets, Wayne C., 33
dual diagnosis, 136
Duke University Medical School, 104
Dunedin Cohort study, 58–59, 73, 152, 154, 207
Dupont, Robert L., 135, 151
dysbindin gene, abnormality of, 160
dysthymia, 40
dysthymic disorder, 40

early intervention, cost benefit analysis of, 83
eccentric, origin of word, 187
economic pressures, 13
Edinburgh High Risk Study, 46–47, 59
educational problems, and psychiatric problems, 58
EEG (electroencephalograph), 199
Ellis Island Museum website, 163
Emory University, 55
Emotional Intelligence and Social Intelligence: the New Science of Human Relationships (Goleman), 219
emotional reactivity, increased, 47
emotional support, 211
emotions, regulation of, 34
endophenotypes, 197

environmental factors, 206
epilepsy, 206
evaluation for mental disorders, reasons for avoiding, 51
evolutionary selection, 194
expressed emotion, harmful examples of, 220
externalizing, 74
eye-tracking exam, 200

facts
    about mental illness, 42
    about suicides, 175
Fairfax High School, 21
false positives, 78, 83
Families and Youth Roundtable, 217
family
    dinners with, 227
    instability, 66
    secrets, 162
family-based programs, 52
family "genealogy project", 164
Family History Screen, (HS), 152
family legacy of mental illness, 183
family medical history, 27
family meeting at Freer program, 68–69
family mental health history, 224
family mental wellness, 218
family psychiatric history, 15
Family Service Agency, 48
    of San Francisco, 231
family studies, multigenerational, 55
fears, types of, 40
Fergus, Ann Costello (sister of Michael), 165
Fergus, James, 165
fictions
    about mental illness, 42
    about suicides, 175

financial incentives and the rush to medicate, 53
first-degree relatives, 37–38
5-HTT serotonin transponder, 111, 211
Foucault, Michel, 218
Fox, Michael J., 205
Frances, Allen, 89
Freud, Sigmund, 130, 171
Frontline (PBS series), 52

GABA, 205
GAD gene, 205
gene × environment (G × E effect), 61–62, 111
genealogy, 162
gene-environment interaction, 209, 211
gene therapy, 205
genetic loading, 133, 145, 153
genetic material, shared, 37–38
genetic mutations, 205
genetic predisposition
  for addiction, 136
  to bipolar disorder, 217
genetic risk for depression, 121
genetic testing and risk prediction, 33
genomes, anomalies of, 199
genomic scans, 197
genotypes, 111, 197, 211
Geoff [pseud.] (Alex and Sammy's father), 23, 69
Getty Museum, 92–93
Gibbs, Anne, 199
girls
  internalizing, 74
  mental disorders affecting, 50
Golden Gate Bridge Authority, 176
Goleman, Daniel, 218
  Emotional Intelligence and Social Intelligence: the New Science of Human Relationships, 219

hallucinations, 36, 82
Happy Valley School, 75
Harding, Courtenay M., 189
Harvard McLean Hospital, 54
Hasenberg, Steve, 27
heightened sensory perceptions, 36
Hendin, Herbert, 176
heritable, defined, 206
High-Density Schizophrenia Families, 160
"high-expressed emotion", 220
hippocampus, and memories, 34
Holzman, Philip S., 201
homeless mentally ill, 190
human behavior, continuum of aspects of, 97

informed consent, 27
inhibitions, reduced by alcohol, 174
inkblot test, 195, 201
internalizing, 74
interns' risk for depression, 111
interventions
  early, 42
  preventative, 214
  in suicide prevention, 177
Ireland's National University, 32
Irish diaspora, 161
Irish ethnicity, 156
Irish National Library, 161

James [pseud.] (brother)
  and memorabilia, 163
  snubbed on Easter, 147
Jamison, Kay Redfield, 32
Joel (minister), 23
Johns Hopkins School of Medicine, 32
Joiner, Thomas, 173, 179
  Why People Die by Suicide, 173
Jones, Peter, 206
journals, professional, 31

Kaplitt, Michael, 205
Kaufman, Joan, 211
Kéri, Szabolcs, 193
Kevin's suicide by train (Tom's
    brother), 179
Khantzian, Edward J., 130–31
kindling theory, 216
Klosterkötter, Joachim, 47
Kraepelin, Emil, 47–48, 63

Laing, R. D., 218
LaMacchia, Alesso (maternal grandfa-
    ther), 27
LaMacchia, Carmela Chiccitta "Nana"
    (maternal grandmother), 27, 145
LaMacchia, Lillian (aunt), 27, 75, 130
learning disorders, 54
Levy, Deborah, 197–201
Lewis, David Elliott, 192
life experiences, stressful, 210
Lilly, Eli, 80
limbic system, 34
lithium, 33
Loewy, Rachel, 48
loss of motivation, 36
lung cancer, 28

madness and creative genius, boundary
    between, 63
major mental disorder, chronic, 42
manic depressive. *See* bipolar disorder
    (BP)
Manji, Husseini, 106, 217
marijuana, 29, 36, 61, 67, 227
McFarlane, William, 88
McGill Group for Suicide Studies in
    Montreal, 172
McGlashan, Thomas, 80–83, 90
McGorry, Patrick, 79, 83–85, 90, 218
McGuire, Patrick, 188

McKeon, John, 180
medications "off-label" use, 81
meditation, 106, 228
melancholy, 171
memory, working, 200–201
mental disorders
    diverging by sex in adolescence, 50
    parent-child transmission, 51
mental health advocacy movement, 32
Mental Health Association of San Fran-
    cisco, 48, 191
    SOLVE program, 191
mental health budget cuts, 191
mental health history, 27
mental health insurance, lack of, 51
Mental Health Services Act (MHSA),
    190
mental illness, hidden, 136
mental reframing process, 219
meta-representation, 97
meta-study, 74
methamphetamine, 29
"miasma" theory, 12
Miklowitz, David, 220
    *Bipolar Disorder: A Family-Focused
        Treatment Approach*, 221
Millstein Division of United States His-
    tory, Local History, and Genealogy,
    167
Mr. B. [pseud.] (Irish story teller), 161
Moffitt, Terrie E., 11–13, 59, 74, 152,
    207–10
Moffitt-Caspi study, 211
molecular genetics researchers, 197
Monitor on Psychology (publication), 188
Montessori preschool, 45
mood, depressive, 55
Mood and Anxiety Disorders Program
    at the National Institute of Mental
    Health (NIMH), 217

Mood Disorders program at NIMH, 106
moodiness, 54
mood stabilizers, 217
MRI scanning, 32–33, 67
multifactorial disease model, 36
multiple sclerosis, 54

NAMI (National Alliance on Mental
    Illness), 31
Narcotics Anonymous, 151
National Alliance on Mental Illness
    (NAMI), 31
National Coalition for the Homeless, 190
National Comorbidity Survey (NCS),
    137
National Institute of Mental Health
    (NIMH), 80, 104, 137, 160, 197,
    222
  Mood and Anxiety Disorders
      Program, 33
National Institutes of Health, Bethesda,
    Maryland, 33
National Suicide Foundation, 176
National University of Ireland in
    Galway, 157
nature versus nurture, 16, 121, 123, 223
negative self-beliefs, 122
Nesse, Randolph M., 97
neuregulin 1 and creativity, links
    between, 194
neuregulin 1 gene, 193–94
neurobiological and genetic pathway
    for schizophrenia, 204
neurobiological problems, 40
neurodevelopmental process, initial
    signs, 47
neuroprotective actions, 42
neuroprotector, 49
neuroscience, 34, 63
neurotransmitter, 111

New York City Vital Records, 168
New York State Department of Health,
    Vital Records Section, 182
New York Times obituary index, 180
NIMH (National Institute of Mental
    Health), 80, 104, 137, 160, 197,
    222
Nixon, Richard, and war on drugs, 130
Noonday Demon, An Atlas of Depres-
    sion (Solomon), 126
"normalization" of divergent feelings
    and thoughts, 226
"normalizing", 86
North American Prodrome Longitudinal
    Study (NAPLS), 77

obsessive-compulsive disorder (OCD), 25
    and impaired PPI, 200
O'Connell, Mary Ellen
    Preventing Mental, Emotional, and
        Behavioral Disorders among
        Young People: Progress and
        Possibilities, 214
olanzapine (Zyprexa), 80–82, 94, 98
omega-3 fish oils, 84, 106
oppositional defiant disorder (ODD), 72
overlapping of symptoms in psychotic
    diseases, 36

panic attacks, 153
paranoia, 36
Parkinson's disease, 205
paternal age, and psychiatric problems, 58
"pathologizing", 86–87
Paxil, 119
Peer-to-Peer and family education pro-
    grams, 222
peer-to-peer information sharing, 31
personal failure, sense of, and suicide,
    174

pervasive developmental disorders (PDD)
  Asperger's syndrome, 40
  autism, 40
Peterson, Bradley, 122–23
phenotypes, 197
Philadelphia Veterans Administration
  (VA) Methadone Clinic, 136
physical maltreatment, and psychiatric
  problems, 58
physical self-abuse, habituation to, and
  suicide, 174
PIER Clinic (Portland Identification
  and Early Referral), 88
Piotrowski, Nancy, 136
placebo, 80, 104–106
positive emotional growth, 214
positive psychology, 219
postpartum depression, 120
precursor mental disorders, 77
Predictive Value of Family History on
  Severity of Illness, 152
predisposition, 53–54
  to specific disorders, 36
pre-onset psychosis, 75
PREP-PIER model, 89
pre-psychotic
  children, 58
  state, and depression, 78
  symptoms, 193
pre-pulse inhibition (PPI), 200
pre-schizophrenic
  children, 55
  markers of disintegration, 77
preventative mental health care, 53
Preventing Mental, Emotional, and
  Behavioral Disorders among
  Young People: Progress and Possi-
  bilities (O'Connell et al.), 214
Prevention and Recovery in Early
  Psychosis (PREP), 48, 85

primal therapy, 131
principle of anonymity, 151
problem-solving skills, 216
"prodrome" period, 78
Proposition 63 in California, 190
prospective versus retrospective, 58
Prozac, 105, 116
pseudonyms, use of, 16
psychiatric disorders, parents as carriers
  of, 54
psychiatric family history, 11
Psychiatry Department at Harvard's
  Cambridge Hospital, 130–31
psychoeducational treatment, 88
psychological autopsy, 171, 183
psychological issues, avoidance of by
  stealing, tagging, etc., 70
psychological vulnerabilities, 131
psychopharmacologic action of the
  drug of choice, 131
psychosis
  and childhood conduct disorders, 74
  clinical and suicidal behavior, 57
  and drop in an adolescent's cognitive
    abilities, 66
  early, 78
  early warning signs, 95
  first episode, 80
  in general populations, 36
  and higher risk in young people, 36
  inherited predisposition, 37
  negative (cognitive and behavioral)
    symptoms, 95
  positive (psychotic) symptoms, 95
  in teenagers, 77
psychosis and creativity, links between,
  193
psychosocial groups, family, 42
psychosocial interventions, 52–53
psychosocial rehabilitation, 189

psychosocial risk factors, 158
psychotherapy, 105
psychotic break, 50
psychotic symptoms
  low-level, 77
  in children, 56–57
puberty, 50

Quinn, George, 146
Quinn, Nora Murphy "Noni", 146

Racine (friend), 125
randomized and controlled (double-blind) study, 104
Reagan, Ronald, 138
real names, use of, 17
recovery
  complete, 42
  defining, 188
recovery movement, 228
rehabilitation, strength-based, 42
remissions, 42
Reno, Janet, 205
results of studies, quantifiable, replicable, 62
retinal eye defect, 54
risk, best predictor of, 35
Risk and Protective Factors in Schizophrenia, 206
risk factors
  genetic, 111
  for mental illness, 45
risperidone, 79
Rorschach, Hermann, 201
Rorschach test, 201. *See also* inkblot test
Roscommon County, Ireland, 157
Rose, Demian, 52, 83–97

St. Raymond's Cemetery, 166
Saints, Scholars, and Schizophrenics:

Mental Illness in Rural Ireland
  (Scheper-Hughes), 156
saliva tests, 211
Sammy [pseud.] (youngest son)
  career plans, 110
  and desire to join Marines, 107–109
  and Effexor, 102
  essay, 101
  "gap-year" volunteer projects/humanitarian project in Uganda, 109
  girlfriend, 110
  major depression, 102
  medical leave from college, 103
  perfectionism, 102
  social anxiety disorder, 102
  treatment resistant depression, 104
  and Zoloft, 110
Savitz, Jonathan, 33
Scheper-Hughes, Nancy, 156
  Saints, Scholars, and Schizophrenics:
    Mental Illness in Rural Ireland,
    156
schizoaffective disorder, 94, 160, 197
schizoid and schizotypal personality
  disorders, 197
schizoid personality disorder, 54, 81,
  160
schizophrenia
  and areas of the brain shrinking, 67
  "at risk" stage, 83
  and baby's low birth weight, 213
  and bullying, 49
  childhood risk factors, 59–63
  and chromosomal mutations, 199
  and depression, 78
  early signs, 76
  environmental (nongenetic) negative
    risk factors, 49
  first-degree relatives of patients, 197
  and flat effect (warning sign), 68

and the fragmentation of the affected
person's thinking, 203
genetic and biological in nature, 47
genetic anomalies that transmit, 197
genetic underpinnings of, 197
geographic comparisons, 13
in Ireland, 157
as a long-term neurodevelopmental
process, 96
mitigating factors, 49
"negative" symptoms of, 49–50
neurobiological and genetic
pathways, 204
and older father, 49
paranoid, 29
parent-child transmission, 51
and physical and behavioral traits,
197
"positive" symptoms of, 49–50
predictors in high-risk youth, 78
and prenatal infections, 61
prenatal risks, 213
prevalence of, 38, 51
rehabilitation, 189
and relapse, 192
risk and protective factors, 206
sociocultural and historical forces
that can raise risks, 160
spectrum, 51, 54
and urban environment, 49
Schizophrenia Bulletin, 222
schizophrenia spectrum of personality
disorders, 160, 197
schizophrenium spectrum, 94
schizotypal, 94
schizotypal/paranoid personality disorder, 160
school violence, 215
secondary prevention, 42
second-degree relatives, 37–38

secrecy and denial of mental illness, 39
Seiden, Richard H., 176
selective serotonin reuptake inhibitors
(SSRI antidepressant), 102, 110
self-empowering thoughts, 219
self-esteem, 227
self harm in children, 57
Selfish Brain, The (Dupont), 135
self-stigma, 99
sensory motor gating, 200
sensory perception, distorted, 199
serotonin, 111
gene, 209
signs of mental illness, early, 45
Snow, John, 12
social awkwardness, 74
social deficits, 47
social isolation
and suicide, 174
urban, 13
social networking websites, misuse of,
215
social-support networks, 13
social withdrawal, 36
Solomon, Andrew, 126
*Noonday Demon, An Atlas of Depres-
sion*, 26
SOLVE (Sharing Our Lives: Voices &
Experiences), 191
SSRI antidepressant (selective serotonin reuptake inhibitors), 102, 110
Stanford University's Pediatric Bipolar
Disorders Program, 52
startle response, 200
statistical prevalence, defined, 38
Steiner, Rudolph, 46
stigma, 38, 217
strange thoughts, 36
strength-based recoveries, 220
stress

coping with, 218
economic, 13
reduced tolerance to, 47
Structured Clinical Interview (SCID), 199
"Study of the Genetic Contributions to
    Schizophrenia", 198
suicidal
    ideation, 105, 123–24, 173
    thinking, 78
suicide
    attempts versus completed suicides, 174
    barrier on Golden Gate Bridge, 176
    notes, 176
    prevention, 176–77
    three key risk factors, 173
    warning signs, 177
suicides classified as "accidents", 41, 182
support group for parents of the men-
    tally ill, 30
survivor's guilt, 132
symptom management, 30
symptoms, remission of, 216

TADS, for Treatment for Adolescents
    with Depression, 105
talk therapy, 85
targeted therapies, 111
TDI (thought disorder index), 201
temporary waiver of rights, 27
Terry, Zackery "Zack", 76–77
thalmus
    in people with schizophrenia, 35
    and processing sensory information,
        34
theory of mind, 97–98
theory of self-medication, 130
third-degree relatives, 37–38
thought disorder index
    (TDI), 201
thought disorder symptoms, 54

thought-reframing drill, 88–89
thought slippage, 202
thought-speech dynamic, 54–55
tobacco use, and psychiatric problems,
    58
Tom (friend), 126, 179
top ten things a parent can do to safeguard
    a child's mental health, 224–29
Trafton, Erika, 191
trait markers, blood testing to identify,
    33
traumatic life events, 59
treatment approach, "needs based", 84
treatment response, 33
Twelve Step programs, 151

UCSF PREP early psychosis clinic, 190
ultra-high risk
    criteria, 84
    defined, 37
    proper diagnosis, 88
Unexpected Legacy of Divorce, The
    (Wallerstein et al.), 66
urban residence, and psychiatric
    problems, 58
US Institute of Medicine and the
    National Research Council, 214

Vaillant, George E., 145
Valium, 123–24
Vega, Eduardo, 191
vulnerability,
    degrees of, 54
    hypothesis, 61

Waldorf pedagogy, 46
Walker, Elaine, 55
Wallerstein, Judith S.
    Unexpected Legacy of Divorce, The,
        66

Weissman, Myrna, 41, 102, 118–20, 148
Wellbutrin (bupropion), 119
Why People Die by Suicide (Joiner), 173

yoga, 106

Zoloft, 110
Zyprexa (olanzapine), 80–82, 94, 98